[KEY CASES]
in FORENSIC &
CRIMINOLOGICAL
PSYCHOLOGY

[KEY CASES]

IN FORENSIC &

CRIMINOLOGICAL

PSYCHOLOGY

R. STEPHEN WALSH

Los Angeles | London | New Delhi
Singapore | Washington DC | Melbourne

Los Angeles | London | New Delhi
Singapore | Washington DC | Melbourne

SAGE Publications Ltd
1 Oliver's Yard
55 City Road
London EC1Y 1SP

SAGE Publications Inc.
2455 Teller Road
Thousand Oaks, California 91320

SAGE Publications India Pvt Ltd
B 1/I 1 Mohan Cooperative Industrial Area
Mathura Road
New Delhi 110 044

SAGE Publications Asia-Pacific Pte Ltd
3 Church Street
#10-04 Samsung Hub
Singapore 049483

Editor: Donna Goddard
Production editor: Rachel Burrows
Copyeditor: Sarah Bury
Proofreader: Brian McDowell
Indexer: Adam Pozner
Marketing manager: Camille Richmond
Cover design: Wendy Scott
Typeset by: KnowledgeWorks Global Ltd.
Printed in the UK

Library of Congress Control Number: 2020944247

British Library Cataloguing in Publication data

A catalogue record for this book is available from the British Library.

ISBN 978-1-5264-9485-6
ISBN 978-1-5264-9484-9 (pbk)

At SAGE we take sustainability seriously. Most of our products are printed in the UK using responsibly sourced papers and boards. When we print overseas we ensure sustainable papers are used as measured by the PREPS grading system. We undertake an annual audit to monitor our sustainability.

CONTENTS

ABOUT THE AUTHOR

R. Stephen Walsh is a Senior Lecturer in Psychology at MMU where he is part of the forensic team. He contributes to a wide range of courses at both undergraduate and postgraduate levels. Stephen's research has a particular focus on the role social identity plays in individual behaviour, and outcomes, and he has published widely in this area.

COPYRIGHT ACKNOWLEDGEMENT

The author and publishers wish to thank the American Psychological Association for permission to use copyright material from the DSM-5, as quoted in Chapter 11.

PART I
THEFT, FRAUD AND ECONOMIC CRIME

1
PSYCHOLOGY OF THEFT, BURGLARY, ROBBERY AND FRAUD: AN OVERVIEW

INTRODUCTION

Theft and economic crime, including fraud, are acquisitive crimes, meaning they centre on taking other people's belongings. More formally, acquisitive crimes are those that have as their central process the appropriation of money or goods. Interestingly, there are aspects to these crimes, for example enhancing one's power of reputation, that go beyond the obvious desire to acquire something of value (Canter & Youngs, 2009). Acquisitive crime ranges from filching the toiletries or the bible from your hotel room, to the armed robbery of cash in transit, to the multi-million-dollar Ponzi scheme perpetrated by Bernie Madoff. For as long as there have been human beings, there has been crime rooted in covetousness. Indeed, the crime of theft is 'probably concomitant with the possession of property' (Brown, 1930, p. 405). For as long as people have owned things there has been someone intent on stealing them. Part 1 of this book will explore these crimes in depth, using stand-out cases to illustrate the different themes in closer detail. In each case-chapter throughout the book you will find learning objectives to help guide your learning throughout the chapter, a synopsis of the case before we delve into the psychology behind it, reflective questions to help you to understand the details discussed, and further reading to take your learning beyond these pages.

KLEPTOMANIA

When thinking of the psychology of acquisitive crimes, in particular crimes of theft, the first thing that comes to many people's minds is kleptomania. The *Diagnostic and Statistical Manual of Mental Disorders* (DSM-5) (American Psychiatric Association, 2013) classifies kleptomania as an impulse control disorder that is marked by an inability to resist the impulse to steal. In many instances, the goods stolen by those with kleptomania have little monetary value and they are not needed for personal use.

Having an occasional impulse to steal is considered normal, as is thinking about the consequences that would follow if one were to steal. What marks those suffering from kleptomania apart is that they have these thoughts incessantly, and that they consistently lack the capacity to resist the urge to steal.

People afflicted with kleptomania will experience a build-up of tension before they steal, followed by an intense feeling of relief in the aftermath of stealing (American Psychiatric Association, 2013). Kleptomania is an ego dystonic disorder, meaning that the stealing behaviour is experienced by the kleptomaniac as repugnant, unacceptable, inconsistent with their self-concept and distressing (Gavin, 2014). The severity of kleptomania has been associated with disorders of compulsivity (Grant & Chamberlain, 2018). However, Kleptomania is a very uncommon disorder with a reported prevalence of 0.38% – occurring in fewer than four out of every 1,000 people (Odlaug & Grant, 2010). The vast majority of people who commit crimes associated with theft are not kleptomaniacs.

THEFT

'Thou shalt not steal.' Despite the admonishments of every world religion, and culture, against stealing and coveting, theft is extraordinarily common. Stealing always involves intent, and to steal is to violate, in some fundamental way, another's right of ownership. It is worth noting that this is different from saying that stealing is simply a violation of some particular set of property laws (Green, 2007). This distinction is important to note because, while it is very easy to conflate legal and psychological categories, it is not at all useful to do so.

Theft is taking property without the owner's consent, with the proviso that the person doing the taking knows that the property does not belong to them (Gavin, 2014). Taking someone else's dessert in error is a mistake, but it is not theft. However, most, probably all, of us have behaved in a way that results in something that might be legitimately called theft. A recent survey conducted by pen makers

Papermate, and reported by the BBC (2018), found that 100% of 1,000 office workers sampled admitted stealing a pen from a colleague.

There are cases in which a person is technically subject to the laws of theft even though many would hold the view that nothing has been stolen. This raises a question as to whether the fit between our understanding of theft from a descriptive perspective sits as well as it might with our view of theft from a moral, or normative, sense. The gap between law and norms with regard to widely accepted manifestations of theft (e.g. taking a towel home from a hotel break) is also useful because it facilitates a consideration of how groups, other than the ones that we ourselves belong to, regard theft. For example, few consider illegal downloading as theft, although that is precisely what it is. Thieving has been part of human behaviour for millennia and the roots of stealing behaviour are deeply embedded in the evolutionary past of our species. We even celebrate thievery in our culture. Almost everyone loves Robin Hood, and many regard the pirates of old with more than a little fondness.

The capacity to thieve is predicated on a functioning theory of mind. One must know that another perceives themselves as owners of a given object and that to take their property without consent is wrong (Green, 2007). A sense of morality is also necessary.

Theft is one of the most common crimes and it is found across all cultures (Gavin, 2014). The concept of theft seems to be in some way pre-legal. Small children understand what it is to steal (Green, 2007) as, it seems, do non-human primates, including rhesus monkeys (Flombaum & Santos, 2005). Because theft is omnipresent, it is highly unlikely that there is a specific psychology of theft.

As with all behaviour that is learned, knowledge about stealing is something that evolves and reacts to the environment (Gavin, 2014). In addition to conceiving them as acquisitive crimes, property thefts can be usefully understood as interpersonal transactions, even when the victim is not physically present. Our focus, in this section, is on one of the parties to this transaction, those perpetrating the thieving. With this focus, in considering individual crimes, it is useful to us that all thieves bring their store of 'professional' and life experiences to each 'transaction', to every offence that they commit.

BURGLARY

Burglary is one of the most common crimes and one that we find in the criminal histories of most offenders (Canter & Youngs, 2009). The Crime Survey for England and Wales (CSEW), covering the period to the year ending June 2018 (Office for National Statistics, 2018), indicated a rate of 27 burglaries per 1,000 population with 432,267 offences in total. In the United States, in their most recently published figures, the Bureau of Justice Statistics (BJS) reported 20.6 victimisations of burglaries per 1,000 households in 2017 (Bureau of Justice Statistics, 2018).

Burglary is categorised as a property crime and is a specific type of theft that requires unlawful entry onto premises in order to steal (Anderson & Kavanaugh, 2009). From a psychological point of view, there is much to consider with this crime. Detection rates for burglary are shockingly low. Hockey (2016) reports that for the years 2009–2012 roughly 87% of reported burglaries in England and Wales did not lead to a conviction, and he attributes this low detection rate to a range of factors: there is often no pre-existing relationship between perpetrator and victim, offences tend to be reported many hours after their commission, and there are generally no witnesses.

These facts, which feed into the low detection rates, render burglary a fascinating subject to those with an interest in crime because the 13% or so of burglaries that result in a conviction are a small subset of the total burglary committed. In extrapolating from this 13%, we are focusing on cases that are atypical and, in the process, learning much about unsuccessful criminals but little about those who 'get away with it'.

Canter and Youngs (2009) offer a useful take on burglary. From their perspective, burglary constitutes the crossing of a psychologically significant physical barrier in order to achieve material gain from the resources located on the other side of that boundary. They suggest that burglary differs in psychologically important ways from other acquisitive crimes, not least because burglary is an open-ended, exploratory and non-violent approach to illicit material gain. Compared to crimes involving fraud and threat, burglary can seem positively risky and adventurous, focusing as it often does on a battle of wits with security measures and staff. On the silver screen, there are few people not won over by the charm of movies like the *Thomas Crown Affair*, or George Clooney's character, Danny, in *Ocean's Eleven* (2001).

Building on the dramaturgical aspect, understanding burglary in terms of the stories that perpetrators weave about themselves opens up a path which facilitates a useful consideration of what burglary represents, psychologically, to the offender. This in turn facilitates a consideration of what the differences might be in the ways that individual offenders tackle their offences. It may well be that the stories that burglars tell themselves about their crimes is key to a psychological understanding of these crimes (Canter & Alison, 2000). This approach will be developed in a consideration of the Hatton Garden raid, presented in the next chapter.

ROBBERY

Robin Hood, Butch and Sundance, Bonnie and Clyde, Billy the Kid and Buster Douglas. From a cultural perspective, their crimes are perceived with admiration by many. Perhaps, in an abstract sense, robbery is seen as a way in which grievances with the powerful and wealthy can be redressed. However, the reality of this crime is decidedly less wholesome.

Robbery is distinct from burglary because violence is fundamental to the crime. Robbery, by definition, involves either the threat or use of violence. Robberies can be usefully classified based on whether they are commercial (e.g. from banks, post offices, shops, etc.) or personal (e.g. muggings, snatch thefts and/or street robbery) (Porter, 2010). In commercial robberies, the victim is often asked to surrender somebody else's money. This is a significant factor in the interaction between robber and victim as less force is likely to be needed when someone is being coerced into surrendering money or goods that are not their own.

In the United States, the Federal Bureau of Investigation (FBI) defines robbery as 'the taking or attempting to take anything of value from the care, custody, or control of a person or persons by force or threat of force or violence and/or by putting the victim in fear' (Federal Bureau of Investigation, 2014). In England and Wales, the Theft Act 1968, section 8(1), states that 'a person is guilty of robbery if he/she steals and immediately before or at the time of doing so, and in order to do so he/she uses force on any person or puts or seeks to put any person in fear of being and then subjected to force'. This legalese is somewhat verbose but the point is clear. As in the United States, threat, force and violence are also fundamental to the legal definition of robbery in the UK.

Robbery is a relatively low-volume crime in England and Wales with police recording 79,117 offences for the year ending June 2018. This amounts to a rate of four robberies per 1,000 in the population. The instances of recorded robbery in London are disproportionately high with 42% of all robberies taking place in the capital (Office for National Statistics, 2018). In the United States, the official rate is even lower. There were an estimated 319,356 robberies in the US during 2017, amounting to a rate of 0.98 per 1,000 in the population (Bureau of Justice Statistics, 2018). However, it is worth noting that the official police data from which these figures are compiled, appears to suffer from significant under-reporting (McCluskey, 2009).

As indicated at the outset, because of the nature of the crime, robbery is associated with a likelihood of physical injury and, in some cases, homicide. In the USA, data collected by the National Crime Victimization Survey (NCVS) in 2006 shows that about one-third of robbery victims were injured (McCluskey, 2009). Taking a more fine-grained look, research also shows that about half of those robbed by offenders armed with blunt objects or other weapons were hurt. Thirty-six per cent of victims of unarmed offenders and 31% of victims of criminals armed with knives were harmed during their victimisation. Victims of robbery where the perpetrator(s) were armed with blunt objects or weapons other than firearms were more likely to be attacked without prior threat (Perkins, 2003).

Consistent with the statistics presented above, robbers choose weapons to establish credible threats (McCluskey, 2009). Weapons and the use (or threat of) violence are all about the perpetrator establishing control. The victim–offender encounter is at the very heart of this. According to McCluskey (2009), this interaction is likely to be best understood in terms of a contest of coercive power. Injury, resistance and 'successful' completion of the robbery are all potential outcomes in the robbery transaction.

Paradoxically, using a gun to threaten a victim means that the actual use of force is less likely. On the other hand, unarmed robbers are unlikely to be perceived to have overwhelming coercive power and will need to demonstrate, through the actual use of violence, that they can force victims into compliance.

Wright, Brookman and Bennett (2006) found that it is sometimes the 'buzz' and excitement of robbery that provided the main motivation for UK offenders. One of the participants in the Wright et al. study reports that, in their view, the perfect robbery is one where the victim fights back – 'the point of street robbery is to get them to fight back, innit. I'd give him a couple of slaps and tell him to fight back, yeah. If he won't fight back, we just give him a kick and go' (Wright et al., 2006, p. 9).

The word 'we' is perhaps key in the previous sentence. It is noteworthy that robbery tends to be a group phenomenon, and across the whole spectrum of crimes that fall under the heading of robbery, group processes and patterns tend to be evident. Other important motivating factors in robbery include having money for both everyday items and drugs, status, fun and excitement, and generating reputation.

ECONOMIC CRIME

'Crime in the street and crime in the suite is an offence rather than an offender distinction' (Gottfredson & Hirschi, 1990, p. 200). Economic crime, also referred to as financial crime, and colloquially known as 'white-collar crime', is a term that covers illegal acts perpetrated in order to achieve financial or professional advantage. Sociologist Edwin Sutherland first conceived of 'white-collar crime' in 1939. Sutherland's interest was in 'respectable' people of high social status who committed crime and he used the concept to challenge conventional stereotypes in the 1930s and 1940s about criminals and criminality.

The word 'criminal' conjures up images of people who are a danger to society. Deviants. Dangerous. This is perhaps not the most useful way of approaching criminality. Consideration of economic crimes can aid our understanding of criminality, and challenge this 'deviant' view, by refocusing our attention on the situation. In many instances, understanding crime is best served by attending to the context of crime rather than harking back to long-distant childhoods and the complexities of human development (Weisburd, Waring, & Leeper Piquero, 2008). It is somewhat amusing to think that most 'white-collar' criminals see themselves as upstanding and respectable citizens.

The (shockingly) small number of senior banking executives whose convictions followed the 2008 financial crisis offer a good, recent example of one type of criminal who might be considered under the heading of 'economic crime'. The United Nations Office on Drugs and Crime gives a broad definition of the term 'economic and financial crime' as any non-violent crime that results in a financial loss (United Nations, 2005).

While the category is, at present, somewhat loosely defined, the term 'economic crimes' covers bribery, tax evasion, fraud, embezzlement and money laundering (Kryvoi, 2018).

Cybercrime is another area where there is currently a flourishing of economic crime. 'Cyber' refers to things digital, from Bluetooth to driverless cars, and an important focus of things cyber is the internet (Aiken, 2016). In the UK, cybercrime has been defined as 'entailing conduct proscribed by legislation and/or common law as developed in the courts, that involves the use of digital technologies in the commission of the offence, or is directed at computing and communications technologies themselves, or is incidental to the commission of other crimes. Computers may be incidental to the offences or indeed instrumental to criminal offences' (Ridley & Harrison, 2017, p. 8). Despite the relentless increase in cybercrime, and in common with crime generally, most cybercriminals remain unprosecuted.

Adding to the complexity of bringing cybercriminals to trial, there is often a cross border component to this category of offences which makes them difficult to prosecute.

One especially concerning aspect of cybercrime is banking confidentiality. According to Ridley and Harrison (2017), the banking industry has been withholding billions in losses caused by hackers stealing from their electronic systems. The reason given for this reticence on the part of bankers is that reporting these crimes would negatively impact the share prices of these publicly listed companies, thereby causing even further losses. In itself, this raises issues about full disclosure to investors of companies floated on stock markets.

Taken as a whole, economic crimes cause a plethora of woes to national economies and individuals, including damaged credibility for businesses and institutions, bankruptcy, job losses, pension losses and home evictions. These effects are often experienced especially sharply in the developing world where sustainable development can be curtailed because of limited government capacity and weak regulatory frameworks. In the first world, over recent decades, economic crimes, and the almost unimaginably large losses associated with high-level financial criminality, have undermined social security systems and put entire economies at risk.

Economic crimes generally span a significant period of time, and law enforcement and regulatory officials often only take action in the wake of financial disasters. Moreover, these financial disasters tend to be 'quintessentially organizational offences, requiring collective cooperation and mutual reinforcement – what might be called cultures of non-compliance' (Snider, 2008, pp. 47–48). Social and organisational psychology should therefore be part of any attempt to understand these crimes.

Of particular interest from a social psychological point of view are the machinations which facilitate, for example, 'aggressive tax planning', the over-valuing of assets, the hiding of debts, and the reporting of inflated profits. There is considerable esteem associated with such criminal chicanery. Bankers and executives can benefit from massive bonuses because of criminal behaviour. It is worth pausing for a moment to contrast this treatment with the opprobrium heaped on 'welfare cheats' and 'blue-collar' criminals who can lose liberty, housing and income as a consequence of crimes that come with a fraction of the cost to society.

A brief example will illustrate the enormous impact of economic crime. In 2018, David Drumm, a former chief executive of the collapsed Anglo-Irish Bank, was convicted of €7.2 billion fraud and false accounting at the height of the financial crisis in 2008. The bank had used a circular transaction between Anglo and Irish Life & Permanent as a vehicle to make the bank's deposits look larger than they were as the institution headed for collapse. When the bank eventually did collapse, Irish taxpayers picked up the Anglo debt. The bill was €34.7 billion. In attempting to deal with this and other bank debt, the Irish government lost control of their finances and the Anglo collapse contributed to the imposition of a European Union/International Monetary Fund bailout and consequential long-term austerity for the Irish people. 'White-collar' crime is not victimless.

In Chapter 4, we will use the collapse of another bank, Barings, and interrogate the role of rogue trader Nick Leeson to further explore the issue of economic crime. It might be interesting to reflect on how you perceive crime. For example, is a burglar or a robber 'worse' than a fraudulent banker? What is your perception of 'criminal'?

FRAUD

The term 'fraud' is a generic one that comprises several distinct categories of crimes which themselves fall under the broad rubric of economic crime. Fraud can be understood as an unlawful, purposeful act intended to deceive, manipulate or provide false statements to harm others (Ostas, 2018). The key motivator for fraud is financial reward. Fraud is the cause of more losses than robbery, theft and burglary combined (Dodd, 2000). There are a multitude of ways that fraud can be described. For example, it can be based on the target, such as credit card fraud, welfare fraud, insurance fraud, etc., or another (although not the only) useful way to think of fraud is in terms of whether it is perpetrated against individuals or corporations.

The central task of investigative psychology is to identify distinct offending styles in order that inferences can be made about offender characteristics. In the case of fraud, this task has some particular complexities (Canter & Youngs, 2009). It is noteworthy that for a significant proportion of fraudsters, fraud is not regarded as a particularly serious crime, and by some, fraud is not regarded as a crime at all. Canter and Youngs (2009), for example, report that a significant proportion of people would, and do, commit fraud when they have the opportunity to do so. Insurance fraud is especially common (Skiba, 2017).

The understanding of fraud as something 'clever' rather than something criminal is a function of social group memberships and identity related factors. Indeed, it has been reported that many fraud investigators are of the opinion that fraudsters, of both large and small sums, do not understand themselves as criminals (Dodd, 2000). I expect this view of the fraudster will be consistent with the real-life experiences of many. Advice, for example, to make an annual claim on one's house insurance in order to cover the premium is not clever. It is fraud. At a more extreme level, Skiba (2017) reports a federal investigation conducted in the USA which revealed that, over a three-year period, a particular medical centre performed unnecessary cardiac catheterisation surgeries on more than 700 patients.

These surgeries included life-threatening open heart and cardiac bypass procedures. The procedures were unnecessary, and their purpose was to increase billable amounts. This was not clever. It was fraud.

Fraud Diamond Theory (FDT) (Wolfe & Hermanson, 2004) is a useful conceptual framework, which is employed to think about the factors that must combine in order for fraud to be successful. The framework builds on the pioneering fraud triangle, introduced by Cressey (1953). Cressey's original triangle included three elements: motivation/incentive, opportunity and rationalisation. One of the big strengths of this model was that it combined factors pertaining to individuals with factors pertaining to the environment. In order for a fraud to succeed, a person must be motivated, have the opportunity and be able to rationalise their actions. What the fraud diamond adds, which was missing from Cressey's original model, is an acknowledgement that the person committing the fraud must also have the capacity to do so. The fraudster must have certain personal traits and abilities, including knowledge, self-belief, the capacity to deceive and an immunity to stress. This was certainly so with Bernie Madoff, one of the most 'successful' fraudsters ever, whose case will be discussed in Chapter 5.

CONCLUSION

Economic crime is a broad and varied category with many different types of characters committing these crimes. Chapters 2–5 will delve into these different crimes in more detail, giving you an insight into a key case in each area and the characters and the psychology behind them.

2

THE HATTON GARDEN BURGLARY

LEARNING OBJECTIVES

By the end of this chapter you should be able to:

- Describe the main points of the Hatton Garden case, including some background of the main protagonists
- Detail the meaning of 'burglary'
- Discuss psychological factors associated with burglary, and how they are distinct from the legal factors associated with burglary

SYNOPSIS OF THE CASE

During April 2015 a gang of thieves, with at least five of them over retirement age, entered the Hatton Garden Safe Deposit building by force and with stealth in order to steal as much as £200 million worth of goods. As with all learned behaviour, current theorising indicates that perpetrators' environments influence their 'know-how' with regard to stealing. This chapter will look at the detail of this high-profile case, examine the individuals who were part of it and use the example of 'Basil', who was not apprehended for the crime until March 2018, to illustrate a major limitation in the current psychological knowledge of burglary – we know little or nothing of those who are not caught and convicted.

DESCRIPTION OF THE CASE

Over Easter weekend 2015, a gang of burglars broke into a secure vault in 88–90 Hatton Garden, central London. The raid was the biggest burglary in UK history. There is no exact figure available for how much the burglars made off with, but estimates in excess of £14 million were common in the press. Some estimates ranged as high as £40 million. The burglary was perpetrated by pensioners, whose ailments included diabetes, a heart condition, continence problems, hip problems and obesity. One of them even made their way to the crime scene on public transport using a bus pass. You could not make it up. Philip Sinclair, the lawyer who represented one of the gang, described the burglary as well planned and well executed, and said that he could appreciate the group's audacity because 'no one was hurt in it, no one was even scared' (Greenwood, 2016, n.p.). It is no surprise that they made a movie about this case.

Seven men were initially convicted of the crime. Brian Reader (aged 76), Terry Perkins (67), who has since died in prison, Danny Jones (58) and Kenny Collins (75) formed the core of the gang. Carl Wood, Billy Lincoln and Hughie Doyle played more peripheral roles. The burglar known as 'Basil', who was later identified as Michael Seed (58), an alarm specialist, was convicted in March 2019 for his role in the crime.

Individual Backgrounds

Brian Reader

Brian Reader, more than likely the 'mastermind' behind the Hatton Garden job, was born into poverty in a London tenement in 1939. His father, Henry, a known dealer in stolen goods, abandoned the family when Brian was seven years old. After the Second World War, Brian's family moved from the city centre to the suburbs of south London where the young Reader began to engage in petty crime. In 1963, the Great Train Robbery was committed. This crime brought a level of perceived glamour to thievery and inspired some young men of Reader's generation to treat the robbery of banks and security vans as their chosen profession. Brian Reader was one such young man.

On the night of 11 September 1971, Lloyds Bank on Baker Street, central London, was burgled by a gang who had tunnelled underneath an adjacent building, working at weekends to avoid their equipment being heard. When the gang gained access to the Lloyds vault, they stole the contents of 268 deposit boxes, worth more than £3 million (probably more than £20 million in today's money). At the time, the Lloyds heist was the biggest British burglary on record, and it was very similar in many respects to the Hatton Garden raid that took place a couple of miles away, 40 years later. The Lloyds gang had a cheeky side, daubing a sign on the wall of the Lloyd's bank vault which read 'Let Sherlock Holmes solve this one'. Brian Reader was believed by many to have played a role in this theft, a claim he denied. The parallels, however, between the Lloyds burglary in 1971 and the Hatton Garden burglary in 2015 are thought-provoking. Career book-ends, perhaps?

In the summer of 1980, a well-known crook, 'Skinny' Gervaise, turned super-grass following his capture by Scotland Yard's Flying Squad for the part he played in a £4 million silver bullion robbery committed in London during March of that year. Gervaise claimed that Brian Reader was part of a nationwide burglary gang who had raided scores of safes and vaults across the UK. Arrested and bailed while awaiting trial for these crimes, Reader went 'on the run', leaving the UK for Europe and then slipping back into England again a couple of years later when things had quietened down.

A couple of years later, in 1983, a group of armed robbers stole £25 million worth of gold bullion from the Brink's-Mat security warehouse near Heathrow airport and Brian Reader was again involved. If you are wearing gold jewellery fabricated in the last 35 years you may well be closer to this crime than you imagine. Police believe that a gang of six raiders was responsible. However, only two thieves, Mick McAvoy and Brian Robinson, were ever convicted of this crime. Both received 25-year sentences. Following the Brink's-Mat raid, the thieves needed to melt down the Brink's-Mat gold in order to turn it into cash. This is where we know that Brian Reader came in. It is estimated that by the beginning of 1985, Brian Reader had handled at least £4 million of the Brink's-Mat bullion. In May 1986, Reader was convicted of handling stolen Brink's-Mat gold and VAT fraud, and sentenced to nine years' imprisonment.

Terry Perkins

Also in 1983, a raid took place at the Security Express depot in Shoreditch, London, close to the City's financial district, over the Easter weekend of 1983, when armed robbers got away with £5,961,097. Terry Perkins, who readers might be familiar with as the Hatton Garden thief who needed to inject himself with insulin during the burglary because of his diabetes, was one of the armed robbers. Perkins, from North London, was 35 years old at the time. Perkins was sentenced to 22 years for his part in the crime.

While in prison, Terry Perkins hooked up with Brian Reader. The pair had a lot in common, both having been involved in the biggest crimes ever to have been perpetrated in the UK. It is fair to say that when it came to 'one last job', 30 or so years later, Reader and Perkins were very well known to each other.

Danny Jones

The first recruit to join Reader and Perkins for that 'one last job' at Hatton Garden was 60-year-old Danny Jones. Jones and Perkins had known each other for many years. They both drank in The Castle pub in Islington, North London. Jones was a professional criminal with convictions for robbery, handling stolen goods and burglary. Jones read widely on the topic of crime. Detectives found a *Forensics for Dummies* book during a search of his Enfield home. Jones was one of the Hatton

Garden raiders whose relatively slim frame allowed him to enter the vault once the vault wall had been breached.

Kenny Collins

Kenny Collins was 67 years of age at the time of the burglary and another professional criminal known to Reader, Perkins and Jones. Brian Reader, in particular, had a long acquaintance with Collins and wanted him to be a member of the gang. Collins, known as a break-in expert, was morbidly obese and suffered from hip problems, which forced him to use a walking stick. A list of Collins' previous convictions included fraud, jewellery theft and handling stolen goods.

Together, these four were described by prosecuting Counsel Philip Evans QC as the ringleaders and organisers of the conspiracy.

William Lincoln, Carl Wood and Hughie Doyle

In more peripheral roles were William Lincoln, aged 60, Carl Wood, 59, and Hughie Doyle, 49. Lincoln had acquired the moniker 'Billy the Fish' as a result of his practice of supplying family and friends with seafood purchased at the Billingsgate fish market. His role in the raid was to control the stolen goods and arrange for them to be taken to Jones and Collins. Lincoln suffered from sleep apnoea, bladder problems and osteoarthritis. At the time of his arrest, Lincoln was in receipt of disability and employment support allowances. Carl Wood was also on disability benefits at the time of the raid. Wood did not benefit financially from the crime because, although present at the scene, he had got cold feet and walked away before the gang had gained access to the vault. Last, but not least, Hughie Doyle, an Irish plumber living in London, had a close relationship with Kenny Collins and allowed the gang use of his premises in Enfield, London.

'Basil'

Michael Seed, a 58-year-old electronics and alarm specialist was identified as 'Basil'. He was the last of the gang to be arrested and convicted, some three years after the burglary. Seed, who lived in Islington, North London, was a man who paid no income tax, claimed no benefits and avoided using a bank account. He was arrested with a large number of items stolen from Hatton Garden in his possession.

Planning

Prosecutors suggest that the build-up to the Hatton Garden raid began in 2012. Two years later, preparation had become significantly more specific, with the burglars researching what sort of drill would be best suited to breaching the thick concrete wall surrounding the vault. In January 2015, planning was stepped up, including surveillance of 88–90 Hatton Garden, with Collins and Jones making frequent trips to the site in February and March of 2015.

The burglars settled on Easter weekend as the optimum moment to conduct their crime as the building's security guards were on leave from the evening of 2 April to the morning of Tuesday, 7 April for the Bank Holiday.

Execution of the Burglary

At 8pm on the evening of 2 April, the crime commenced. Brian Reader had arrived on public transport, using a bus pass. The rest of the gang came in a white van driven by John Collins. On arrival, Jones and Wood got out of the van, sauntered up and down the street and checked out the building. Lionel Wiffen, a jeweller whose business was located in 88–90 Hatton Garden next to the vault, was still inside. At 9.22 pm Lionel finished up for the evening, locked up, and exited the building.

Shortly afterwards, 'Basil', a tall man whose features are impossible to discern clearly on any existing security video, entered the building through the main doors. He had to have used both a key and a four-digit key-code to gain access. 'Basil' then opened a fire door and allowed the rest of the gang to enter. Meanwhile, John Collins went across the road to 25 Hatton Garden, let himself into this building, and set himself up as 'lookout'.

Inside 88–90 Hatton Garden, the burglars took the building's lift to the second floor and disabled it. The sensor for the lift doors was left hanging in order to keep the doors open. With the lift out of action, the gang were able to jump down the relatively short drop from the ground floor to the basement via the lift shaft in order to access the area immediately adjacent to the vault.

Shortly after midnight, the police believe, the burglars opened the outer gate into the vault. At this stage, the alarm system sent a text message to an alarm monitoring company. The monitoring company in turn made contact with Alok Bavishi, a member of the family who owned the vault, and told him that the alarm was signalling. Bavishi was also told, incorrectly, that the police were at the scene. Bavishi then contacted security guard Kevin Stockwell, who made his way to Hatton Garden where he checked that the main door and fire exit were secure. On completion of this check, Stockwell again contacted the building's owner, Bavishi, and informed him (wrongly) that the alarm was a false one. Amazingly, it seems that 'lookout' Collins never noticed the security guard making his checks because he had fallen asleep at his post.

Between about 1.15 am and 7.50 am on Friday, 3 April the gang used a diamond tipped Hilti DD350 drill to cut through the thick concrete vault wall in order to make a 'crawl-able' breach that the raiders could use to access the vault. They then tried, and failed, to use a hydraulic ram, placed inside the hole that they had just drilled, to knock over a cabinet located inside the vault. The cabinet was bolted to the wall from floor to ceiling. At 7.50 am on the Friday morning the gang walked away empty-handed from Hatton Garden. Brian Reader would not return to the vault. It is speculated that Reader was physically exhausted from a night of operating the heavy-duty Hilti drill. It has also been speculated that he believed that the raid could not be completed.

At about eight o'clock the next evening, Saturday 4 April, the jeweller Lionel Wiffen, the last occupant of 88–90 Hatton Garden to exit the building before the holiday weekend, returned with his wife to make arrangements for an electrician who was due to carry out some work for them on Easter Sunday. When they arrived, the Wiffens found the fire escape door of 88–90 Hatton Garden open. They then checked the internal door to the vault, and it was locked (presumably by Basil as he left). The Wiffens were in the building for about an hour, leaving again at about 9pm on the Saturday evening.

Shortly after 10pm on the same Saturday evening, the burglars returned to 88–90 Hatton Garden for another go. 'Basil' once again entered through the street-level door and allowed Jones, Collins and Wood to enter through the fire escape. At this point, Wood decided that he too wanted out. It seems that he was afraid that the raiders would be caught. Re-entering an already burgled building is a high-risk undertaking.

In the absence of Reader and Wood, the rest of the gang proceeded with the raid on the security vault in 88–90 Hatton Garden for a second night. The gang had with them a new hydraulic ram, bought in D&M tools, Twickenham, which they were able to use to good effect. The burglars were able to knock over the large cabinet that had thwarted them on the first night and 'Basil' and Daniel Jones then crawled through the opening into the vault. Once inside, 73 of 999 safety deposit boxes in the vault were jimmied open and their contents stolen. The contents filled two wheelie bins and several bags. Between 5.45 and 6.45 that Easter Sunday morning, the burglars left 88–90 Hatton Garden with their loot. Collins, Jones and Perkins left through the fire escape. 'Basil' exited through the ground-floor doors of the building. The biggest burglary in English history was over.

LINKS TO THEORY AND RESEARCH

The first issue that a consideration of the Hatton Garden raid demands us to address is precisely what the term 'burglary' means. On the face of things, it seems somewhat odd to classify breaking into a secure vault and stealing multi-million pounds worth of jewellery and cash in the same category as fellows who might climb through your kitchen/shed/workshop window and pinch your property while you have nipped out to the shops for a pint of milk. But that is the law. This point illustrates the difference between legal and psychological understandings of crime.

What Does Burglary Mean Psychologically?

Burglary is a crime that is found within the criminal history of most offenders and is common to the early offending of many rapists, violent offenders and drug offenders. Therefore, as a group, burglars tend to be rather heterogeneous (Canter & Youngs, 2009).

One important issue to note with the legal and police methods used to classify types of burglary is that legal and police classifications may not align well with psychological understandings of offences. Gavin (2019), for example, cites the finding of Yokota and Canter (2004) that police reporting of burglary distinguishes between shop and office burglaries. This approach misses the fact that there are distinct themes within the expertise and specialisation of burglars, and that these themes do not necessarily correspond to the categorisation in police reporting. For example, both shops and offices are unlikely to be occupied at night time and from a psychological point of view these types of premises have more in common than dividing them.

The Interpersonal Dimension of Burglary

It may be that we are making a category error when presenting burglary as a property crime rather than as an interpersonal crime. Merry and Harsent (2000, p. 33) argue that 'the burglar's behaviour is an expression of his/her attitudes towards others'. One useful way of classifying a crime is by having regard to where a given crime falls on an instrumental–expressive continuum. Instrumental crimes, for example tax evasion, are understood as being simply for the purpose of material gain. In contrast, expressive crimes articulate a need that is not material. Sexual crimes, for example, are instances of expressive crimes (Blackburn, 1993). Burglary falls somewhere towards the centre of this continuum (Merry & Harsent, 2000).

Classification of Burglary

On the legalities, an important point to highlight is that the legal definition of burglary does not require goods to be stolen. According to the 1968 Theft Act, any entry onto a property without appropriate consent or a legitimate reason is burglary (Goodwin, 2008). Had the Hatton Garden raiders not gained entry to the security vault and been able to take goods from the safe deposit boxes on their second attempt, they would still have been guilty of burglary. Indeed, this is reflected in the sentence handed down to Brian Reader and Carl Wood, who were not at the scene of the crime at the point in time when the goods were stolen.

It is also noteworthy that the word 'burglary' covers both domestic and non-domestic break-ins (i.e. break-ins to businesses, sheds and outbuildings that are not part of an inhabited property; Canter & Youngs, 2009). Interestingly, while the vast majority of research pertaining to burglary is oriented towards domestic burglaries, it seems that there is little difference between the motivations for commercial and residential burglary (Wiersma, 2007).

Motivation

Bennett and Wright (1984) conducted an interview study with more than 300 burglars in which they found three main things. First, the decision to burgle is usually a sequential one. Burglars generally made their decision to burgle away from the crime scene because they had an imminent need for money. Second, burglars were found to be interested in cues signifying occupancy, accessibility, security and surveilability. Third, burglars had a systematic and rational approach to selecting their targets. These findings support the idea that the decision to burgle is like all other everyday decisions that people make – a function of previous experience. Gavin (2014) notes that, as with all learned behaviour, stealing is something that evolves and reacts to the environment.

With a focus on commercial burglaries, Wiersma (2007) reports that about half of his sample were motivated to commit commercial burglary for money, 39% said that they had burgled commercial premises for the excitement and thrill of it, and 36% said that they had burgled because they had just 'drifted into it'. Money, excitement, happenstance. All of these factors would seem to play a role in the Hatton Garden raiders, with Hughie Doyle in particular being a person who 'just drifted into it' through his association with Kenny Collins.

Wiersma (2007) also points out that most of those who participated in his study were 'professionals' who had committed offences beyond burglary. About one-third of those who took part in his study had carried out a robbery and almost all were responsible for more than one commercial burglary. Again, these findings fit well with our knowledge of the Hatton Garden gang, whose previous offences include armed robbery, handling stolen goods and fraud.

Intelligence, Transportation and Timing

Where things become very interesting, to my mind, is where Wiersma (2007) considers how prospective burglars glean intelligence on their target, how they travel to and from the scene of their crime, and how they time their burglary.

Wiersma reports that 84% of his participants gained intelligence through observation. This finding aligns well with our knowledge of the Hatton Garden raid. We know that Collins and Jones made frequent trips to the area in early 2015. Wiersma also says that in 56% of cases involving his participants, an employee of the burgled company was a source of information. We do not know that the Hatton Garden raiders had an 'inside' person. However, it has yet to be explained how 'Basil' managed to access either the door keys or the four-digit pin code which allowed him access to the building.

With regard to transport, Wiersma sets out how, in most burglaries, the means of transport is generally a car or a van, probably stolen or hired in order to reduce suspicion and complicate registration number tracing. ANPR (automatic number plate recognition) was a significant factor in the apprehension of the Hatton Garden gang. In the weeks immediately after the raid, Scotland Yard detectives, utilising the Metropolitan Police's number plate recognition system, noticed that a white, top-of-the-range Mercedes had been in and out of Hatton Garden on many occasions, including the two nights of the raid. When they looked more closely, they found that the car was registered to Kenny Collins, who was well known to the authorities for his long record as a professional criminal. Images of the car with three occupants wearing high-visibility jackets on the second night of the raid, which was consistent with the clothing visible on CCTV images from 88–90

Hatton Garden, made detectives even more suspicious. This monumental slip up on the part of the thieves led to a surveillance operation, which in turn ultimately involved police lip-readers discovering, to their amazement, that a group of pensioners drinking in The Castle pub on Pentonville Road were the perpetrators of the biggest burglary in British history. Indeed, this fairly obvious mistake, of using one of their own cars in connection with the burglary, in common with the burglars buying a second hydraulic ram in nearby Twickenham when the first one failed, suggests that the gang's 'professionalism' was tainted with incompetence. The source of this incompetence was an almost complete lack of awareness of the capacity of contemporary technology to trace and track the movement of individuals. They were, for example, also seemingly unaware that their movements could be tracked via their mobile phones.

The timing of the Hatton Garden burglary was carefully chosen for Easter weekend 2015. It is perhaps significant that one of the ringleaders, Terry Perkins, had previously been involved in a major heist over an Easter weekend at the Security Express Depot in 1983. Nee and Taylor (2000) report that burglars' selection of targets is highly habit-driven and based on prior successful learning. It may well be that the timing of the Hatton Garden raid constitutes more than coincidence.

KEY THEORISTS: CANTER AND YOUNGS (2009)

Degrees of Focus

According to Canter and Youngs (2009), much of the work on the classification of burglars has focused on competence and effectiveness, that is, skill. Canter and Youngs point out that this focus on skill/professionalism is problematic because the skill expressed by the burglar is a function of the demands of a 'job' rather than any capacities that the burglar might have. Canter and Youngs propose instead that 'degree of focus' is an overarching psychological concept that unites all the myriad psychological processes manifest on the part of the burglar when he or she is focused on completing a successful and effective burglary.

Crime as a Social Transaction

In tandem with the concentration on task focus, Canter and Youngs (2009) propose that understanding crime as a social transaction allows us to put ourselves in the shoes of the burglar and attempt to identify the interpersonally directed actions of the burglary that are significant to the offender. There is a communicative aspect to burglary that this concept allows us to tap into. In the Hatton Garden raid, it seems reasonable to suggest that an awareness of the victims produced an alertness to the risk of the victims returning, which in turn highlighted the advantages of breaking in over an extended Bank Holiday weekend.

CONCLUSION

According to Canter and Youngs (2009), one of the things that distinguishes burglary from other crimes is the open-ended approach that burglars are adopting to material gain. Theirs is a risky strategy that incorporates exploratory and perhaps even adventurous aspects. Where fraud demands manipulation and subterfuge, and robbery relies on threat, burglary is an enquiring approach. Coming to terms with, and thinking about, what burglary means psychologically to the burglar facilitates a focus on what the differences may be in the ways that burglars tackle their crimes. In itself, this can allow criminal profilers to pinpoint behavioural differences between burglars that ultimately contribute to their apprehension.

REFLECTIVE QUESTIONS

1. Maruna (1999) presents the verifiable truth that the vast majority of offenders stop offending. There is a point in the lives of most criminals where, for some reason, they desist from crime. Why was this not the case with the Hatton Garden gang?
2. In his book about the raid (listed below), Clarkson (2016) suggests that this crime is a classic example of men seeking a purposeful group identity. Does Clarkson's suggestion add to our understanding of this crime?
3. There has been some glorification of this burglary, for example the movie *King of Thieves* starring Michael Caine. What, if anything, do such portrayals reveal about our attitudes as a society to burglary?

FURTHER READING

www.independent.co.uk/news/uk/crime/hatton-garden-ringleader-brian-reader-also-masterminded-lloyds-baker-street-heist-45-years-ago-a6814956.html

www.express.co.uk/news/uk/634714/Hatton-Garden-heist-gang

Clarkson, W. (2016). *Sexy Beasts: The True Story of the 'Diamond Geezers' and the Record-Breaking $100 Million Hatton Garden Heist*. New York: Hachette Books.

3

THE SECURITAS RAID

LEARNING OBJECTIVES

By the end of this chapter you should be able to:

- Define armed robbery, kidnap and tiger kidnap
- Discuss why people at risk do not adhere to security training

SYNOPSIS OF THE CASE

On the evening of 21 February 2006, an armed gang stole, literally, a lorry load of money from the Medway House Securitas cash depot in Tonbridge, Kent. The raid began with the kidnap of Securitas Medway manager Colin Dixon and, shortly afterwards, the tiger kidnapping of his family. Having forced Dixon to allow the gang access to the Medway facility, raiders took the Securitas staff inside hostage and stole as much of the cash being processed there as they could carry. The raid ended in the early hours of 22 February when the robbers drove away from the Securitas depot with their haul. The gang had to satisfy themselves with robbing only a portion of the cash present in the Medway depot. This is because the £53 million they took was enough to fill the entire 1,000 cubic feet capacity of the rented, 7.5 tonne Renault truck used in the heist. Still, even allowing for the fortune they had to leave behind, the raiders had managed to pull off the largest peacetime robbery of cash in the history of the world.

DESCRIPTION OF THE CASE

Kidnap and Tiger Kidnapping

The Securitas heist began with the kidnapping of Colin Dixon, which was followed shortly afterwards by the tiger kidnapping of the Dixon family. The label of 'tiger kidnap' is a relatively new one and refers to cases where a criminal gang takes a hostage in order to force a family member, or other closely connected person, to facilitate robbery or some other gain-focused crime.

In 2006, the Dixon family lived in Herne Bay, about an hour away from Colin Dixon's job in Tonbridge, Kent, where he worked as a Securitas cash centre manager. On 21 February Colin left work at about 5.30 in the evening to commute home in his Nissan Almera. Some 45 minutes later, as Colin crested a hill on the A240 near The Three Squirrels pub, he was signalled to stop by men in police uniforms who were driving a Vauxhall car with police markings and blue flashing lights. Colin pulled over in his Nissan, complied with an instruction to switch the engine off, and got out of the vehicle as he was told. As the manager of a cash depot, Colin's training was clear. He should not have got out of his car. Colin was quickly handcuffed and put into the back seat of the Vauxhall. It rapidly became clear that the uniformed men were not police. They were kidnappers. The kidnappers told Colin that if he refrained from doing anything silly, he would not get hurt. They also pulled a 9mm pistol and told him that they were not 'fucking about'. It was clear that the risk of extreme violence was real. Colin was then driven to a farmyard in rural Kent where he was put in the back of a van, with his eyes taped and his legs bound.

Meanwhile, in Herne Bay, Colin Dixon was late for his usual dinnertime of 6.30 pm. Colin's wife, Lynn, was starting to worry as Colin normally phoned when he was about 20 minutes away. Lynn tried to contact Colin on his mobile, but he didn't answer. At about half past seven, Lynn took their child upstairs for a bath and bed. With the child asleep and having come back downstairs, Lynn was watching TV when two policemen came to the door and informed Lynn that Colin had been involved in a road traffic accident. Lynn roused her child from bed so that the officers could take her to the hospital with them in their police car. On sitting in the back of the car with her child, Lynn noticed that Magic FM was playing on the radio. Like her husband a short time earlier, Lynn quickly realised that the 'officers' were not police and that the vehicle she was in was not a police car. Also, again like her husband, Lynn and her child were transferred from the 'police' car into the back of a commercial vehicle.

With the Dixon family now in their custody, the gang quizzed Colin about the people working at the cash depot that evening, the location of alarms and panic buttons and the CCTV system at Medway House.

Robbery

The gang that entered Medway House comprised seven men. They were armed with a 9 mm pistol, a pump action shotgun, an AK47, and a machine pistol.

Accompanied by their hostages, the group travelled in convoy between the farmyard where the Dixons had been held and the Medway House cash depot. The convoy was made up of three vehicles: a white rented 7.5 tonne Renault truck in which Mrs Dixon and her child were held, the Vauxhall 'police' car that had been used to kidnap Colin Dixon, and a Volvo car. Colin Dixon travelled in one of the cars. At 1.22 am on 22 March 2006, Colin Dixon, accompanied by a 'policeman', entered the pedestrian gate to Medway House using Colin's key fob and rang the doorbell. There was no good reason for the cash centre manager to be returning to work at this late hour. If correct procedures had been followed, Colin Dixon would have been asked for an explanation. Instead, he was simply buzzed in by the man in the Medway control room, Gary Barclay. Gary then allowed Colin Dixon and the 'policeman' into the air lock. At this point, while Dixon and the 'policeman' were in the man trap, the reason for their presence at this late hour should definitely have been asked. If the 'policeman' had not been allowed to pass through the air lock, the robbery could not have proceeded. Instead, Gary Barclay allowed both men through the air lock and into the control room. Security was now fatally breached. Dixon told Barclay to do whatever the 'policeman' said because the raiders had Dixon's wife and child captive. Barclay was handcuffed. The depot vehicle gate was opened and the Vauxhall, Volvo and Renault truck drove in.

In attire reminiscent of the movie *Oceans 11*, the robbers emerged from their vehicles wearing black boiler suits, black gloves and boots, and black balaclavas or masks. Again, like *Oceans 11*, the raiders took staff in the building hostage and used black cable ties to bind captives' hands.

Taken by surprise as they were, none of the staff tried to raise the alarm and none tried to resist. However, despite their compliance, their captors roughly handled staff, to the extent that all were in pain because of their bindings. All were deeply worried about what might happen next. Lynn Dixon and her child were in fear for their lives. As the robbers gained control of the premises, Lynn and child were corralled with the other hostages.

At this point, the gang forced Colin Dixon to give them access to the cash centre vault where there was in excess of £200 million in cash. A fundamental principle of cash centre security is dual control – a principle whereby any single member of staff cannot, on their own, access the most secure area of the building. Two key-holders are needed. In a breach of procedure, Colin Dixon had previously overridden this protocol and given himself access to both keys to the vault as well as both entry combinations. Inside, the money was bound into colour-coded money bricks: fives in green wrapping, tens in blue wrapping, twenties in red and fifties in yellow.

Using a power lifter, pallet truck and shopping trollies, the gang loaded cash into the Renault lorry. They took significantly less than half the contents of the vault and less than 30 minutes to fill the truck.

As the raid came to its conclusion, many of the hostages began to think that their time was up. The gang forced the Dixons and Medway staff into the cages used for transporting cash, which were then locked shut. Captives were ordered not to 'be silly' and were reminded that the gang knew where they lived. The raiders removed cups that they had drunk from on their way out, presumably because they were aware that the empty cups could provide police with DNA evidence.

One astonishing aspect of this robbery was that it happened under the noses of the police without any alarm being raised. Medway House was purposely chosen as an appropriate location for a cash centre because of its close proximity to three 24-hour police stations. The nearest station was a mere 300 yards from the cash centre. At 2.33 am on 22 March 2006, the Securitas robbers drove their rented lorry away from Medway House with its load of £53 million cash. Their time from entry to exit was 75 minutes.

Apprehension and Conviction

One intriguing aspect of the Securitas robbery is the way in which it swung from the extraordinarily adept to the extraordinarily clumsy. Notwithstanding the security lapses, and plain good luck, which fell their way, many in the criminal world admire the crooks at the heart of the Medway House raid for the manner in which they executed their heist. Gaining access to a cash centre, robbing it and getting away afterwards is no mean feat.

However, within 36 hours of the heist, investigators were making significant arrests. The first to be arrested were two hairdressers who had helped disguise the robbers. Within five days, three of the seven who had entered Medway House were in custody and within a couple of months six of the seven were in custody.

Informants and the fact that the heist 'mastermind', Lee Murray, had accidentally recorded himself plotting the raid on his mobile phone helped police considerably in their investigations. The phone had fallen into police hands because of an unrelated car crash that Murray had been involved in.

Tip-offs from informers led police to, among other things, cash stashed at a lock-up in Southborough (£8.6 million) and £9.7 million hidden at a garage in Welling. Officers acting on 'information received' searched a van parked at a hotel in Ashford. Inside they found a blue ballistic vest and balaclava matching those used by the robbers, a Skorpion machine pistol matching the one used in the raid, significant DNA evidence and £1.3 million in cash stuffed into suit cases with a dispatch note from Medway House showing that the money had been processed just 15 minutes before the robbery.

Rental Truck

A perplexing aspect of this robbery is that the business partner of one of the gang members used his personal credit card to rent the truck driven by the gang. Why would the gang have allowed such an apparently obvious path to connect them with the robbery?

John Fowler, a motor dealer, was the man who rented the truck. Fowler, who was acquitted of taking part in the crime, said he rented it because he was asked to do so. The gang also used Fowler's farm as a base and some of the cash stolen from Medway House was found on his premises.

One who 'Talked and Walked'

While most of the gang who committed the Securitas heist were masked, those who undertook the kidnapping were disguised as police. These 'policemen' instead relied on disguises in the form of prosthetic noses and chins, make-up, latex, false beards and wigs. These disguises were created by Michelle Hogg, an employee of the hair salon 'Hair Hecktik', which was owned by the friend of a gang member.

Chelle, as her friends called her, whose father was a policeman, had undertaken a course in theatrical make-up, including prosthetics, at the London College of Fashion. Chelle had taken two weeks' holiday from work before the robbery to make the disguises that would be used in the Securitas raid. Following a tip-off, police were knocking on Chelle's door within 24 hours of the robbery, and she was charged with conspiracy to commit robbery and conspiracy to kidnap. Halfway through her trial, Chelle had all charges against her dropped in return for turning Queen's evidence against others in the crime. Chelle had 'talked and walked'.

Aftermath

The Securitas gang were prosecuted in four trials. The first three trials were in the UK, and the third was in Morocco. The first trial, at the Old Bailey, resulted in the conviction of five men: Lea Rusha, a 35-year-old roofer, Stuart Royle, a 49-year-old car salesman, Jetmir Bucpapa, a 26-year-old who was unemployed, and Roger Coutts, a 30-year-old garage owner. All were given indeterminate sentences in January 2008 and told that they should serve a minimum of 15 years. Emir Hysenaj, an 'inside man' who had provided information to the gang, was given a 20-year sentence, and could be eligible for parole after 10 years. Michelle Hogg, the hairdresser who provided disguises to the gang, was cleared of all charges in return for turning Queen's evidence. She is currently under the witness protection scheme. John Fowler, the car dealer and businessman whose farm was used as a base and who rented the Renault lorry used in the robbery, was acquitted.

The second Securitas trial commenced in October 2008. In the dock were Paul Allen, the highest security remand prisoner in England at the time, and Michael Demetris, Michelle Hogg's boss at Hair Hecktik. Demetris was found not guilty of conspiracy to kidnap and rob. The jury could not decide on Paul Allen and a retrial was ordered. The third Securitas trial began in September 2009. Allen entered a guilty plea to all charges: conspiracy to kidnap, to commit robbery and possession of a firearm. Allen had pleaded not guilty to all of these offences in his first trial. The plea was entered on the basis that Allen was not an active robber or kidnapper during the raid, but was part of the planning and preparation. A defence point was that Allen had not handled the firearm; he had simply been in possession of it.

Lee Murray: The Fourth Trial

The last person prosecuted for the Securitas raid was the man who 'masterminded' the robbery, ringleader Lee Murray, a drug dealer and professional mixed martial arts fighter from London. This fourth trial took place in Morocco because Murray, entitled to claim Moroccan citizenship through his father, had fled there in the wake of the raid. This was a crucial move on Lee Murray's part, because under Moroccan law citizens cannot be extradited for trial abroad. However, unfortunately for Murray, this did not protect him from prosecution – it merely prevented his extradition. In 2010, a court in Rabat sentenced Murray to 10 years' imprisonment for his part in the Securitas heist. Murray appealed, hoping to get out sooner. The court of appeal instead increased his sentence to 25 years. Murray, 33 years of age at the time, will be in his late fifties before he is released from the Moroccan prison system.

LINKS TO THEORY AND RESEARCH

This case can be usefully considered in two parts: first, the kidnap and tiger kidnap of Colin Dixon and his family, and second, the armed robbery itself.

Hostages, Abduction, Kidnap and Tiger Kidnap

Kidnap is a crime that looms large both in popular culture and in the collective imagination, e.g. the Lindbergh case (1932) in the United States, John Paul Getty III (1973) in Rome, journalist John Cantlie (kidnapped in 2012, and believed to remain captive) in Iraq. Yet academic research around the psychology of kidnap is surprisingly sparse. A search of the psychINFO database (07/06/19) using the keyword 'kidnap' threw up a mere 29 journal articles published between 1977 and 2018.

When I think of the word 'kidnap', an archetype, drawn from Irish mythology, springs immediately to mind: 'Niall of the nine hostages'. The details of the ancient Niall's hostage taking are superfluous to the present discussion, but what the archetype does reveal is a common conflation of hostage taking, kidnap and abduction. Before proceeding further, it is necessary to define these terms.

The meaning of hostage is relatively straightforward: one is a hostage if held against one's will and in a situation such that release is dependent upon meeting the demand of one's captors. Hostages are ultimately there to make sure that their captors' bargaining hand is strengthened (Faure, 2003).

According to Warburton (2007), under English law, kidnap requires two key elements: first, there must be an infringement of the personal liberty of the victim; second, kidnap must include the taking away of one person by another without consent and without lawful excuse, and it must include either force or fraud.

Tiger kidnapping is a particular type of kidnap where a hostage is taken in order to force another, usually a family member or other closely connected person, to facilitate a robbery or some other crime, whose ultimate goal is profit (Noor-Mohamed, 2014).

Abduction is a term that is often treated as if it were synonymous with kidnap (e.g. Synnott, Canter, Youngs & Ioannou, 2016). Noor-Mohamed (2014) argues that abduction should be reserved for those cases where there is no political or economic motive and where those held against their will are not seen as having an exchange or trade value. Be that as it may, the term 'abduction' is often treated as being identical to kidnap and readers should be aware of this.

In western countries, including the UK and the USA, kidnapping is a rare crime. In the period between 1979 and 2001, 7,362 people were convicted of kidnap in England and Wales (Liu, Francis, & Soothill, 2008). This is a very small number given the population of these countries. Most kidnappers are in their mid-20s and, in contrast to popular understandings, most kidnappings are not for ransom, but rather for sexual and violent purposes (Hollin, 2013).

The Securitas raid involved kidnapping (Colin Dixon), tiger kidnapping (Mrs Dixon and her child), and hostages (the Dixons and all the staff held in the Medway facility). It is known that kidnapping can result in serious physical and psychological injuries (e.g. Zannoni, 2003), so it is important that future research is conducted into issues around the implications of kidnapping, particularly the implications with regard to post-traumatic stress disorder (PTSD) and the mental health of former hostages.

Profiling

Synnott et al. (2016) conducted the first academic investigation into the offence of tiger kidnapping. Their study highlights the complexity of tiger kidnapping. For example, the study found similarities and differences between tiger kidnappings conducted on either side of the Irish border. In Northern Ireland, offences were committed by former paramilitaries whereas this was not the case in the Republic of Ireland. However, they found that Irish tiger kidnappers were not inclined to cross the border, regardless of which side of it they were on. This highlights the importance of internal mental maps, carried in the minds of offenders. What matters is not how close locations are, but rather how close offenders perceive them to be. As this line of research evolves, it is likely to prove useful in terms of geographic profiling, with particular regard to the role that environmental learning plays in offenders' spatial movements.

Armed Robbery

Robbery is defined as a crime in which the threat of force, or the use of force, is employed in the commission of theft. The definition applies regardless of the amount of money or property stolen (Hollin, 2013).

Armed robbery, that is robbery involving the use of a weapon, is a low-volume crime in the UK. The Office for National Statistics (ONS) (2019a) reported that 77,103 robbery offences were recorded in England and Wales during the year to March 2018. Firearms were used in approximately 2.2% of these robberies. In addition to being low volume, the crime of robbery tends to be low yield. Reilly, Rickman and Witt (2012) reported that the average armed robbery had a value of £20,331, with one third of robberies yielding nothing at all. Split between a couple of gang members, the proceeds of armed robbery are rarely the stuff of Hollywood lifestyles. It is also interesting that armed robberies are, more often than not, robberies of personal property (Hollin, 2013).

Conklin (1972) has classified those who perpetrate robbery into three types, in a manner that remains useful today. Conklin described the 'professional robber' who plans carefully, generally targets commercial businesses, and makes their living from the proceeds of robbery. Conklin also describes the 'opportunist robber' who acts spontaneously, often stealing from vulnerable targets, and the 'addict robber' who steals in order to feed their alcohol or drug habit.

In their consideration of robbery, Canter and Young (2009) report that it is unusual for robbers to carry out extensive planning, to target locations that are especially rich in cash or valuables, or to wear a disguise. Most robbers are not therefore 'professional'. By these standards, the Securitas raid was a highly atypical robbery. The level of sophistication in terms of disguise and planning might seem more akin to Hollywood than real life. What is emphatically typical about the Securitas raid, from a psychological point of view, is the willingness on the part of the perpetrators to interact directly with others.

Canter and Youngs (2009) argue that what marks robbery apart from other forms of property crime, such as burglary or shoplifting, and from other forms of violent crimes is 'the preparedness to interact directly with the victim and, importantly, in this interaction overtly pursue a criminal goal' (Canter & Youngs, 2009, p. 269). The psychological distinctiveness of robbery lies in the willingness of perpetrators to confront other people and to take directly from these people. Robbery requires the confidence to take, and maintain, control of an interpersonal interaction and it demands that the robber impose his or her will directly upon victims.

Why Didn't Staff Adhere to Their Training?

One fascinating aspect of the Securitas raid pertains to staff training. If all staff had behaved entirely in line with the way they were trained, it is unlikely that the raid could have succeeded. Why did they not do so? Questions that arise include the following: Why did cash centre manager Colin Dixon stop for 'the police' (i.e. kidnappers disguised as policemen), when his training had taught him not to pull over for police but rather to follow them to the nearest police station? Why did Colin Dixon not adhere to the fundamental principle of dual control, as he had been trained to, whereby two key-holders are needed to access the most secure area of the cash centre? Why did Gary Barclay not satisfy himself that there was a sound explanation for Colin Dixon's arrival at the cash centre late in the evening, with a 'policeman', before allowing both access to the control room and thus fatally breach security?

When people are practised at a given task, their minds transfer responsibility for the performance of that task to the non-conscious part of the mind (e.g. Damasio, 2010, p. 275). The example of driving is often used to illustrate this point. An inexperienced driver will note every gear shift, indication, traffic light and bus lane as they navigate their way from A to B. In contrast, the person who has been driving for 30 years will, on occasion, somehow arrive home from work in their car with little recollection of the journey that they have just completed. The explanation for this lack of conscious awareness lies in automatic processing. Cognitive processes have long been understood as situated on a spectrum that ranges from the automatic to the controlled (e.g. Allport, 1954). Those processes that are the most automatic – the most overlearned or 'hardwired' – are the most efficient. In contrast, those more controlled cognitive processes, which allow flexibility and are most sensitive to the specifics of a situation, also demand the most time and effort (e.g. Rand, Tomlin, Bear, Ludvig, & Cohen, 2017).

Kahneman (2011, p. 35) argues that when it comes to thinking, laziness 'is built deep into our nature'. Moreover, people see what they expect to see. To illustrate this point, Kahneman deploys what he calls the 'Moses illusion' (Kahneman, 2011, p. 73): 'How many animals of each kind did Moses take into the Ark?' Most people answer incorrectly. Moses did not take any animals into the Ark. Noah did. The explanation for the Moses illusion lies in norm theory. The mention of animals and the Ark primes us to think of a biblical context, and Moses is not out of place in that context. The chances are that you did not expect Moses, but his presence is not surprising, and so you accepted it.

My suggestion is that exactly the same process was present when Colin Dixon was pulled over by 'the police' as he drove home on the evening that he was kidnapped. The same process was also at play when Gary Barclay buzzed Colin Dixon and 'the policeman' into Medway House on 21 February 2006. In both cases, the men were confronted with something that they didn't expect, but neither of the situations was surprising, and the apparently obvious were therefore accepted.

With regard to Colin Dixon and his failure to adhere to the dual control procedure in order to access the most secure area of the cash centre, this failure might be usefully understood as a procedural violation. Exactly the same form of error occurred in the Chernobyl nuclear disaster when the operators failed to adhere to plant procedures and switched off successive safety systems. The Chernobyl operators' failure to follow procedure ultimately triggered the catastrophic explosion in the core of the nuclear reactor (Reason, 2000). At least in Colin Dixon's case nobody died.

James Reason, a psychologist of human error, has been the referent for the investigation and prevention of industrial accidents since he introduced the Swiss Cheese Model (SCM) in 1990 (Reason, 1990; see also Larouzée and Guarnieri, 2015). Reason (2000) argues that we can understand human errors in two ways: in terms of people and in terms of systems.

The person approach understands errors as arising because of abstract mental processes: laziness, carelessness, recklessness, and so on. With a person approach, errors are understood as moral issues – bad things happen to bad people.

A system approach is much more useful. Systems approaches recognise that people make mistakes and that when things go wrong the important issue is not who is at fault, but rather how things went wrong and why the defences failed. Applying this line of thinking to Colin Dixon and his failure to adhere to the dual control procedure for entering the most secure part of the Medway cash centre, a systems approach suggests that errors are to be expected. Things will go wrong (Reason, 2000). Defence in depth is important in countering this type of error. The doctrine of defence in depth comes from the world of nuclear safety and is based on three concepts: barriers, or physical protection systems; defensive lines, i.e. structural resources and organisational security; and levels of protection, i.e. the arrangement of barriers and defensive lines according to a standard objective (Larouzée & Guarnieri, 2015).

CONCLUSION

It is noteworthy that there is typically little difference in moral culpability between those failures followed by few or no consequences and those resulting in catastrophic consequences. Errors are by definition unintentional and what best insulates organisations against human error is the culture of an organisation. An open, transparent and accountable reporting culture is the best bulwark against human error (Ameratunga, Klonin, Vaughan, Merry, & Cusack, 2019).

REFLECTIVE QUESTIONS

1. Is Conklin's (1972) classification of types of robbery useful today?
2. What training did Securitas cash centre staff not adhere to?
3. Why did cash centre staff not follow their training?

FURTHER READING

Reason, J. (2000). Human error: Models and management. *British Medical Journal*, *320*(7237), 768–770. doi:10.1136/bmj.320.7237.768

Sounes, H. (2010). *Heist: The True Story of the World's Biggest Cash Robbery*. London: Simon & Schuster.

4

NICK LEESON AND BARINGS BANK

LEARNING OBJECTIVES

By the end of this chapter you should be able to:

- Outline the case of Nick Leeson and describe the collapse of Barings Bank
- Detail the main points of the fraud triangle
- Discuss the fraud triangle with reference to Nick Leeson and his trading activities at Barings Securities
- Set out a psychoanalytical understanding of the collapse of Barings Bank

SYNOPSIS OF THE CASE

In the 1990s Nick Leeson was a Singapore-based rogue trader whose initial unauthorised trades made a significant profit for his employer, Barings, Britain's oldest bank at that time. When Leeson's unauthorised trades started to go sour, he chased his losses to the extent that, by 1995, they amounted to $1.4 billion. About to be found out, Leeson left a note saying 'I'm sorry' and ran. Arrested shortly afterwards, his actions resulted in the collapse of Barings Bank and a significant prison sentence. The details of this case are used to consider the effect of individualistic understandings versus a systems-level understanding. The 'Fraud Diamond' is also considered.

DESCRIPTION OF THE CASE

Background: Barings Bank

Famous as the Queen's bank, Baring Brothers and Co. was the world's first merchant bank. Barings Bank was founded by Francis Baring in London in 1762. The bank's early clients included the British government, for whom it provided finance during the Napoleonic wars, the Imperial Russian government, and the US government. Barings Bank was renowned for its role in facilitating the purchase of Louisiana by the United States, from the French, in 1803, the largest land purchase ever, and a deal which is arguably one of the most significant trades in history. Barings continued as the dominant player in banking during the nineteenth century. However, towards the end of the nineteenth century, Barings got itself into significant financial difficulties as a result of over exposure to investments in faraway Argentina. A portent of things to come perhaps. In 1890 the Bank of England stepped in and, supported by powerful figures in British banking, provided a bailout fund of £17 million – a serious amount of money at the time.

Following the bailout, Barings never properly regained its previous dominance in the banking market. Rather, the bank, still dominated by members of the Baring family and others of aristocratic background, emerged from its financial crisis as a conservative, discreet and rather dour institution. Over the course of the next century, Oxbridge graduates and Old Etonians populated Barings management. Conservative aristocracy prevailed.

Background: Barings Securities

The election of a Tory government in 1979 changed the world of British banking forever. Following their election, the Conservatives instigated their 'Big Bang' deregulation of financial markets. Financial institutions were now allowed to take part in a wide range of business activities, in a wider range of markets, than ever before.

Deregulation led to something of a frenzy in the City of London's banking sector as established banks snapped up brokerage houses and brokerage house employees. This was the era of the yuppie and 'greed is good' (a quote from the 1987 movie *Wall Street* starring Michael Douglas – well worth a look if you have not yet seen it).

Barings, as part of this brave new Thatcherite banking world (Reaganite if you are in the USA) decided to buy a small brokerage firm that specialised in Far Eastern markets, from Henderson Crosthwaite. The newly acquired entity was initially branded as Baring Far Eastern Securities and was led by the man who had headed up the Henderson Crosthwaite group, Christopher Heath.

Heath was not a man from the traditional, conservative, Barings mould. Instead, Heath was a high-rolling, passionate gambler with a penchant for earning and spending money. Cars, yachts and racehorses were among his spending pleasures. Heath had a policy of employing likeminded 'hungry' individuals cut from the same cloth as himself.

From the outset, Baring Securities, as Barings Far Eastern Securities had quickly become known, eschewed managerial control by its parent organisation, Baring Brothers Bank. As such, Baring Brothers did not have conventional management controls over its rapidly expanding subsidiary. Barings Securities commenced with 15 employees in 1984 and by 1991 it had 19 offices populated with some 1,100 staff, and was contributing over half of the Baring Group's profit. Heath became the UK's most highly paid businessman in 1986, and in 1991 the brokerage house won the Queen's Award for Export for the second time.

However, all was not well in the world of Barings. The Barings Brothers bankers considered their brokerage arm to be something of an irritant, while Heath, the head of Baring Securities, complained to staff about having to fund the extravagant employee bonuses of a 'pisspot, third-rate bank' (Fay, 1996, p. 61).

A hostile 'us' and 'them' dynamic, combined with significant class and cultural differences, is thus clearly evident between Barings Brothers Bank and its brokerage subsidiary from the outset.

Background: Nick Leeson

Nick Leeson is an ordinary lad from Wigan. His father was a plasterer and Nick was raised in a council house. At school, Nick did not shine particularly brightly. It is perhaps worth noting that he failed maths at O-level, but it is fair to say that his younger days were unexceptional. In the early 1980s Nick got a job as a clerk with Coutts Bank and he followed this up with jobs in a couple of other banks before moving to Barings Securities for a back-room job in the settlement of futures and options in 1989.

As a young man, outside work, Nick might be described as a little on the wild side. However, at work, Nick Leeson's diligence impressed his bosses. As a book keeper, Nick was very good at accounting for derivatives – securities whose prices are a function of (or derived from) one or more underlying assets. But Nick wanted to be more than a book keeper and a back-office man. He wanted to be a trader. This role shift to trader was impossible in London, where his application to become a trader was rejected because of unpaid debts and county court judgements against him. However, Nick's hard work and diligence was rewarded with a promotion in March 1992 when he became back-office manager for the Barings Securities office in Singapore. In investment banking, the back office is the place where trades conducted in the front office are settled. Settlement is about processing the documents associated with trades and it included the recording of contract prices.

After moving to Singapore, Nick Leeson resurrected his trading ambitions. He passed the Institute of Banking and Finances Future Trading Test. Perhaps ominously, in order to gain his licence as a trader, Nick did not disclose the background information that had previously prevented him from obtaining a trader's licence in the UK.

The collapse of Barings Bank

When Nick Leeson began trading in 1992 the Singapore Money Exchange market (SIMEX) where he worked he was a relative newcomer in the world of financial markets. As a newcomer, and in order to attract business, SIMEX's rules and charges were laxer than those of other markets in the Middle East, and deregulation was regarded as key to the market's future.

Leeson had become a trader because he had concealed information that would have prevented him from gaining a licence had it been disclosed. He was also managing both front and back offices – a position which, according to an internal auditor's report that precedes the bank's collapse, exposed Barings to enormous risk. Leeson was effectively acting as his own control system. In retrospect, this clearly looks like a car crash waiting to happen.

From the outset in Singapore, Leeson was regarded both by other traders and by his employers with awe and respect. Here was a 'wonder kid' with the Midas touch. Leeson appeared to have the capacity to generate incredible amounts of profit, and ensure enormous bonus payments for those around him. Arbitrage, the exploiting of price anomalies between markets, was a central plank of this Midas touch. However, all was not as it appeared. Within a couple of days of Barings gaining membership of SIMEX, Leeson opened Account 88888,[1] apparently as an error account. This account was lacking direct oversight.

Error accounts are commonly used by traders to net minor errors that accrue during a day's trading. At the end of each day, the net position is supposed to be closed and reported as it impacts the day's profit. This procedure was never applied to Account 88888, indicating that the purpose of the account was never to serve solely as an error account.

During the course of 1993, Account 88888 was primarily used to generate profit in the ordinary trading accounts of either Barings' clients or proprietary traders. This activity had the effect of making Leeson appear to be a 'star' and enhancing his reputation by generating the impression that there were significant profits when there were, in fact, only losses. Leeson's unauthorised trading resulted in cumulative losses of about $36 million, which, until October 1993, were always recouped. After this date, losses increased gradually until they completely exploded in the last two months immediately prior to the collapse of Barings Bank. But I am getting ahead of myself.

---

[1] Leeson used the number 8 because, in Singapore, the number 8 is considered lucky. '8' means 'to prosper'. Interestingly, the number 5, which equates to the number of digits in the 88888 Account number is understood to mean 'never'. Thus, the Account 88888 can be interpreted as meaning 'never prosper'.

The very, very, short version of what Leeson was doing was following a strategy of doubling: as prices fell, Leeson continuously doubled his position, betting that the market would bounce back. Leeson was gambling on three markets: the Nikkei stock index, futures on 10-year Japanese government bonds, and Euroyen futures. Leeson's gambles never paid off but, insanely, the more money he lost, the more money it looked as if Leeson was making because he was making his losses appear as profit by hiding them in Account 88888 and then presenting a matched double entry for profit elsewhere in his returns.

It does need to be noted that Leeson's activities did not take place in an environment that was wholly benign towards him. Two managers in particular were like Cassandras in calling out the rogue trader. Tony Hawes, Treasurer of Barings Investment Bank, and Ian Hopkins, Head of Treasury and Risk, both continually questioned Leeson about his activities, and continuously warned other senior managers about weaknesses in the bank's controls. But, at best, the warnings that issued from Hawes and Hopkins were ignored.

A robust group of senior managers within Barings Securities, including Simon James, Geoff Broadhurst and Ron Baker, actively defended Nick Leeson. These Barings Securities managers were very different in style and substance from the conservative and aristocratic types that formed the core of Barings Bank's senior management team. On one occasion, Broadhurst went as far as telling Hopkins to 'Fuck off!' when Hopkins was trying to gather further information about Leeson's activities. Separately, Tony Hawes compiled 20 blunt questions addressing Leeson's trading. This list of queries reached Ron Baker, who went berserk, noting 'bastard' and 'fucking idiot' next to some of Hawes' queries before vociferously complaining about both Hawes and his queries to senior management.

In January 1995 things were forced to a head. There was a devastating earthquake in Kobe, a place at the heart of Japan's industrial production. This dealt a final and fatal hammer blow to Leeson's fraud. Leeson had been betting that the Japanese economy would bounce back. Instead, following the earthquake, the downward movement of the market gained momentum such that even Barings' considerable resources could not cover Leeson's losses. By 27 February 1995, the accumulated losses of Account 88888 amounted to approximately £830 million.

Leeson, knowing that the game was up, faxed his resignation into Barings Securities and ran, finally being arrested in Germany and extradited back to Singapore. In Singapore, Leeson was tried and sentenced to six and a half years in prison. The 233-year-old Baring Investment Bank was left bankrupt in his wake.

LINKS TO THEORY AND RESEARCH

In the past, fraud and economic crimes fell under the rubric of 'white-collar crime', a term that is now thought outdated (Gavin, 2019). Outdated or no, white-collar crime is a useful concept because, whether we like it or not, acquisitive crimes of a non-violent nature, committed by a person who does not perform manual labour, are treated differently by both society and courts from those crimes that are committed by people who come from what used to be called 'blue-collar' back-grounds. White-collar crimes include fraud, embezzlement, money laundering, tax evasion, bribery and insider trading. Just one of these categories, fraud, has been declared by the Department of Justice in the United States to be the number two crime facing that country (Skiba, 2017). Fraud is often seen as a low punishment but high reward offence and, importantly from our perspective, fraud is understud-ied from an academic point of view (Skiba, 2017).

One important issue that needs to be considered is whether fraud, of the type perpetrated by Nick Leeson, can be best understood in terms of individual psy-chology, social psychology, or some sort of interaction between both. At present, the literature is not clear on this. Brown and Steenbeek (2001, p. 83), for example, report that Leeson's 'activities were the main cause of the eventual collapse of Barings bank'. They are clearly situating the blame entirely on the individual. Brown (2005), in contrast, argues that a discourse positioning Nick Leeson as wholly responsible for the downfall of Barings serves to protect the regulatory bodies and others in positions of authority. On the other hand, there is undoubtedly an important argument that systems omissions and failures played a major role in creating the space in which Nick Leeson was able to trade without explicit author-ity and thus bring about the collapse of Barings Bank (e.g. Drummond, 2003). The following section will present research that is useful in addressing the question of whether Nick Leeson was a bad apple, or merely an apple in a bad barrel.

The Fraud Diamond

Fraud Diamond Theory (FDT) (Wolfe & Hermanson, 2004) provides a useful con-ceptual framework for thinking about the factors that come together in fraud (see Figure 4.1). The fraud diamond framework builds on an earlier idea, originally introduced as the fraud triangle (Cressey, 1953). The initial fraud triangle had three elements: motivation/incentive, opportunity and rationalisation. A strength

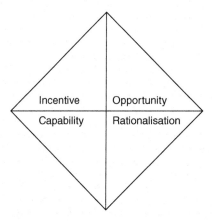

Figure 4.1

of the fraud triangle model was that it considered both individual and environmental factors. In order for a fraud to occur, a putative fraudster must be motivated, have the opportunity to commit fraud and be able to rationalise their actions.

Looking first to motivation, Schuchter and Levi (2013) report that fraud is not all about money, rather fraud is about what money can represent to a person. It seems that what motivated Leeson was not the money itself but rather a burning drive to become a successful and powerful trader (Greener, 2006). According to Frunza (2016), Leeson talked about the competition between individuals, firms and even markets in the world of investment banking. He identified profit as the metric of importance. As Leeson said:

> it is not about how ethical you are or how compliant you are or how safe your business is, the measurement is still how much money you are making. … I often described it as a modern-day amphitheatre where the gladiators go into battle and the best, the strongest, the most successful survive and the rest of the people don't. … I wasn't particularly risk averse and I was particularly quite stubborn and undisciplined in terms of the trading that I was doing and that from a psychological perspective is not the type of person you want exhibiting that risk for you. (Frunza, 2016, p. xxiv)

Amen to that.

The second facet of the fraud triangle is opportunity. Opportunity was a key factor for Nick Leeson. We will look a little more at the systems side of things in the later stages of this chapter, but allowing Leeson to manage simultaneously both the front and back offices of the Barings Securities Singapore Office provided an opportunity to perpetrate fraud. It is an opportunity that should not have been allowed. Letting Nick Leeson simultaneously work in both offices broke one of Barings' basic rules and it made the fraud possible (Stein, 2000). Another opportunity was afforded by the culture within Barings. Traders were encouraged to work, at the same time, for both themselves and clients. There is no doubt that it was this culture that provided traders with substantial opportunities to commit fraud (Stein, 2000).

The third facet of the fraud triangle is the ability to rationalise. This aspect focuses on how the fraudster justifies what they are doing to themselves. An example from the wider literature might be an insurance claimant who adds a little to their claim because they have paid their premium for years, never claimed anything, and feel that their insurance company owes them (Skiba, 2017). Nick Leeson saw himself as someone who was pushing boundaries: 'When you are in a risk taking environment and the deterrent and the control are not strong and in place, I think there is the tendency to push those boundaries all the time and that's certainly what I did from an individual perspective' (Frunza, 2016, p. xxv).

What the fraud diamond added to the original (fraud triangle) framework is an acknowledgement that the person committing the fraud must also have the capacity to do so. The fraudster must have the personal traits and abilities to enable the fraud, including knowledge, self-belief, the capacity to deceive and an immunity to stress. This last point is one that really makes me wonder about the personal resources possessed by some of those who commit fraud. An astonishing level of immunity to stress was certainly the case with Nick Leeson. Indeed, for many, myself included, this is one aspect of the Barings collapse that is eye-popping. How did Nick Leeson do it? How did he get out of bed in the morning and go through his daily routine while at the same time coping with the stress of these millions upon millions of pounds that he was deceiving his employers about? It is not the case that Leeson was entirely free of stress. Stein (2000), for example, reports that, nearing the collapse of Barings, Leeson literally threw up before a meeting with bank CEO Peter Norris in February 1995. However, Leeson could cope with the stress. In the case of the meeting with Norris, Leeson still managed to meet the bank's CEO and engage with him in a sufficiently coherent manner that he did not give the game away. Indeed, Norris even reminded Leeson at the meeting to be at a Barings dinner the same evening. Leeson was well on his way to a billion dollars in fraudulent losses and here he was chatting about dinner. It is extraordinary.

A Psychoanalytic Understanding

Stein (2000) applied a psychoanalytic perspective to a consideration of the collapse of Barings Bank. In particular, Stein produced three hypotheses:

1. Annihilation anxiety associated with the (then) recent changes in the banking sector led senior management to find a 'saviour' for the bank.
2. Senior management sought a 'saviour' who was the shadow (i.e. the opposite) to themselves, especially with regard to risk taking.
3. Unconscious guilt in the chosen 'saviour' (Leeson) led to his generating evidence that should have resulted in his being stopped.

Hypothesis 1: Annihilation Anxiety

Before diving into the detail of Stein's (2000) analysis, it is important to note that the unconscious processes suggested by Stein were, by definition, outside the conscious awareness of those senior managers who were driven by them. In his first hypothesis, Stein (2000) suggests that because the senior executives running Barings perceived the changes wrought by Tory deregulation of the banking market at the time as being so threatening to the very survival of their bank, they had to find someone to save it. When this 'saviour' was found, executives then unconsciously abdicated their response to this saviour. This explains why first Heath, and then Leeson, at Barings Securities were given such free reign to undertake what senior management unconsciously perceived as necessary in order to save the bank.

A by-product of this annihilation anxiety was that other members of the senior management group needed to do very little. Why would they, they had a saviour on board? This unconscious perception of the presence of a saviour also accounts for the manner in which people were left to 'get on with it' and could break basic rules, such as the segregation of front- and back-office activites.

Hypothesis 2: Saviour as Shadow

This is a particularly interesting hypothesis. It has been outlined that the senior management of Barings Bank were of the very dour, upper-crust type, steeped in conservative banking, and, if not outright aristocrats, then as close to them as it is possible to be. The senior management of Barings Securities were a different kettle of fish. Nick Leeson was an ordinary man from an 'ordinary' town with an ordinary background and an 'ordinary' education, but he had a reputation for being somewhat on the wild side outside work. Leeson's defenders in Barings Securities were similarly unaristocratic and certainly not dour: for example, Geoff Broadhurst who told Hopkins to 'fuck off!' when Hopkins was trying to collect information about Leeson, and Ron Baker a boisterous Australian who arranged off-site meetings known as 'rock tours' (Stein, 2000).

The evidence certainly seems to support the idea that Barings Bank executives possessed an unconscious fear that their own conservatism would lead to their demise, and that they therefore went out of their way to create an entity in Barings Securities that was the shadow, or opposite, of their bank. The idea is that this shadow would do the things that the Bank could and would not, in order to be the type of organization that it could and would not be. The management of Barings Securities can fairly be described as risk takers.

Hypothesis 3: Unconscious Guilt

Stein (2000) suggests that Nick Leeson was trying, unconsciously, to draw attention to his guilt through his wider behaviour. One evening in Singapore, a drunken Leeson had 'mooned' some women in a bar. Mooning is considered a serious offence in Singapore, and Stein believes that Leeson was unconsciously attempting to draw attention to the trouble he was in on the markets. While on bail for mooning, Leeson had phoned Ron Baker, his head of derivatives trading, and said that he'd done wrong, let himself down, got into trouble, and needed help (Stein, 2000).

I generally find psychoanalytic analyses unconvincing, and I am not at all sure about the value of hypotheses pertaining to unconscious processes. However, Stein's (2000) paper is an exceedingly good piece of research and provides us with some excellent food for thought. It is most definitely worth a read, and his points are worthy of serious consideration.

Consideration of Systems

The systems that were around Nick Leeson in his role as a trader at Barings Securities are of particular importance, especially when trying to understand the psychology of what happened and in considering the apportioning of blame. Leeson tends to be regarded as the man who singlehandedly brought down England's oldest bank (e.g. Brown & Steenbeek, 2001). Brown and Steenbeek (2001) were interested in Nick Leeson because he followed a doubling strategy and doubling strategies are dangerous from a systemic point of view.

Doubling strategies are when a gambler, or an investor, increases their stakes by a multiple of two each time a bet, or a trade, or an investment results in a loss. Every time there is a payoff, the gambler, or the trader, resets and begins again. Investment banks need to have systems that track and take out traders who are following doubling strategies. We know that doubling strategies, be they in gambling or investment banking, are deceptive because while they look as if they offer a high probability of earning low-but-steady returns, in reality they offer a positive probability of experiencing catastrophic losses. Moreover, these losses can occur in a very short time period. In Nick Leeson's case, 75% of his losses happened in the last month (Marthinsen, 2018).

An added issue arising from the likely and rapid accumulation of losses when a strategy of doubling is followed is the issue of risk. We know that managers will take additional risks in order to escape a situation perceived as threatening (Shapira, 2002) and we know that people will undertake more risk in order to avoid a loss than they will undertake to secure a gain (Tversky & Kahneman, 1986). Taken together in the act of doubling, these psychological considerations present a heady mix. The solution is for institutions to have, and implement, systems that track and eliminate these traders at the earliest possible stage. If Leeson had been found out and stopped one month earlier, by the end of January 1995, the total amount lost would have been about one quarter of the final figure and Barings would probably have survived.

Given the known fallibilities of human decision making, is it appropriate to wholly blame individuals when systems fail to operate as they should? Who benefits when we do construct individuals as the sole source of problems in the context of economic crime and banking fraud?

CONCLUSION

From a social psychological perspective, in considering Nick Leeson's culpability with regard to the collapse of Barings, it is worth taking account of the discourse around the bank's demise. A good place to start is by looking at who benefits from the discourse. Reason (2000, p. 768) reports that 'seeking as far as possible to uncouple a person's unsafe acts from any institutional responsibility is clearly in the interests of managers. It is also legally more convenient, at least in Britain.' Much of the discourse about Nick Leeson positions him as having sole responsibility, which certainly serves to protect the status quo.

There are some rather interesting tensions in the literature. Contemporary reports (e.g. Stonham, 1996) suggest that the types of trades executed by Leeson evidence his incompetence as a trader, for example Leeson's failure to use a risk management system or run a pricing model. Yet the Board of Banking Supervision, in their report on the Barings' collapse, presents a picture of Leeson as a clever and insightful fraudster who relied on complex tactics (Brown, 2005). This is important because if Leeson were not an exceedingly accomplished operator, how could he possibly have duped Barings and those bodies who were responsible for its regulation? Perhaps we will leave that question hanging.

Finally, it is important to remember that all of the elements of the fraud triangle, and by extension the fraud diamond, are dependent upon the perception of the fraudster themselves (Schuchter & Levi, 2013). If people don't think that they have the incentive, opportunity, rationalisation and capacity, fraud will not happen.

REFLECTIVE QUESTIONS

1. Is there anything to Stein's suggestion that Leeson was unconsciously attempting to draw attention to the trouble he was in on the markets at the time of the 'mooning' incident?
2. Is the best explanation for the collapse to be found in individual psychology?
3. Does responsibility for the collapse of Barings lie solely with Nick Leeson?

FURTHER READING

Brown, A. D. (2005). Making sense of the collapse of Barings Bank. *Human Relations*, *58*(12), 1579–1604. doi:10.1177/0018726705061433

Drummond, H. (2003). Did Nick Leeson have an accomplice? The role of information technology in the collapse of Barings Bank. *Journal of Information Technology*, *18*(2), 93–101. doi:10.1080/0268396032000101153

Stein, M. (2000). The risk taker as shadow: A psychoanalytic view of the collapse of Barings Bank*. *Journal of Management Studies*, *37*(8), 1215–1230. doi:10.1111/1467-6486.00222

5

BERNIE MADOFF

LEARNING OBJECTIVES

By the end of this chapter you should be able to:

- Outline the case of Bernie Madoff and the collapse of his Ponzi scheme
- Detail the three aspects of the dark triad
- Discuss the dark triad with reference to Bernie Madoff
- Debate the importance of social capital to fraudsters

SYNOPSIS OF THE CASE

In 2009 Bernie Madoff was convicted of masterminding the largest Ponzi (or pyramid) scheme in history: $65 billion dollars was lost in the scheme. At first, the motivation to defraud seems simple – greed. However, greed is not illegal. Many large businesses make huge profits and individuals can acquire enormous amounts of wealth and goods without breaking the law. In this chapter the history of Ponzi schemes will be introduced, and illustrated with reference to the case of Bernie Madoff, the highest profile Ponzi scheme of recent years. Linking the material presented to theory and practice, the chapter will consider the dark triad of personality traits and the importance of social capital in cases of fraud.

DESCRIPTION OF THE CASE

Few people outside of Wall Street had heard of Bernie Madoff before he confessed to his epic fraud in 2008. In the decade since, he has become the personification of greed – and a household name. (cnbc.com)

The last chapter looked at the fraud perpetrated by Nick Leeson in Barings Securities. This chapter looks at another epic fraud, the Madoff Ponzi scheme. Both frauds were committed in financial markets but there is a vitally important difference between the two. Leeson arranged a fraud from within an organisation that he was part of. Madoff, on the other hand, arranged and built an entire organisation around a fraud.

Bernie Madoff, former NASDAQ Chairman and founder of the Wall Street firm Bernard L. Madoff Investment Securities LLC, is an affable and charming man. He is the kind of guy who can make you feel that you are the most important person in a room. He has a calm, confident, polished manner. 'Steady, sage-like, kindly, and predictable – like a much-beloved uncle' (Berkowitz, 2012, p. 198). Madoff radiates confidence into others by putting people at their ease. Bernie has that golden manner that allows him to make people feel as if they are both clever and in control. An inspirer of trust.

Bernie was born in 1938 to first-generation, East European Jewish immigrants in the United States. He grew up in the mainly Jewish neighbourhood of Laurelton, Queens, New York. Both Bernie's parents were involved in the finance business but without much success. Bernie's mother, Sylvia Madoff, registered as a stock broker-dealer in the 1960s. Sylvia's company was called Gibraltar Securities and it listed the Madoffs' home address in Queens as its office. The Securities and Exchange Commission forced the closure of the Gibraltar Securities business because of a failure to submit financial documents. The Madoff family home had a tax lien[1] against it between 1956 and 1965, and there were rumours that Gibraltar Securities was a front for dodgy dealings associated with Sylvia's husband and Bernie's father, Ralph. Perhaps this was prescient of things to come.

In his high school and college years, Bernie did not look as if he was much interested in finance. He attended Far Rockaway High School where he met and dated Ruth Alpern. Bernie was a member of the high school swim team and worked part time as a lifeguard at the Silver Point Beach Club in Atlantic Beach, Long Island. On finishing high school, Bernie went to the University of Alabama in Tuscaloosa, Alabama – some believe the only university that he could get into at the time – but within a year he had returned to Hofstra University in New York, from which he graduated with a BA in political science. While attending Hofstra, Bernie married his high school sweetheart Ruth Alpern in 1959. His studies at Hofstra were followed by a brief sojourn, of less than a year, at Brooklyn Law School. Bernie had made it through university and emerged with a BA, but academia does not seem to have been his strongest suit. So, in 1960, with a now legendary $5,000 that he had reputedly saved from his work as a lifeguard and a job installing sprinklers, combined with a $50,000 loan from his in-laws, Bernie and wife Ruth launched Bernard L. Madoff Investment Securities LLC.

---

[1] A lien is the right to hold the property belonging to another person until a debt owed by that person is paid.

With the establishment of Bernard L. Madoff Investment Securities LLC, Bernie looked to the outside world as if he had found his niche. The firm managed money for friends, relatives and others. Religious, ethnic and family connections were all exploited. Word of mouth and contacts made through Bernie's father-in-law, a retired accountant, pulled together to establish a lucrative client base for Madoff Securities. The early 1960s were heady times to be working in finance. Stock-trading middlemen could accrue enormous profits. Bernie was one such stock-trading middleman and in the first couple of years of Madoff Securities he was on a roll.

Then, out of the blue, in 1962, everything went wrong. Wall Street was hit by the biggest crash since 1929. The value of the type of lucrative, over-the-counter stocks that Bernie had bought for his clients had instantly vanished. However, Bernie didn't let his conservative and trusting clients know that their investments had failed and their stocks had plummeted. Perhaps Bernie Madoff just could not face failure.

Instead, Bernie borrowed enough money to cover the losses accrued in his client accounts. His clients never knew that Madoff had lost their savings. Instead, they thought that they had been guided through the worst stock market crisis in more than 30 years by a gifted savant without losing a penny! Whether it was intentional or not, the reputational enhancement enjoyed by the young Bernie Madoff and his investment firm during this period was significant. Here was an investment sage with the knack of navigating a dangerous marketplace to his clients' advantage, a trader who could be trusted as having a steady hand, even in the most precarious of times.

Over the coming years and decades, Madoff Securities continued to expand and the personal wealth, standing and power of Bernie and Ruth Madoff, and their wider family, mushroomed. Bernie and Ruth's first son, Mark, was born in 1964 and their second son, Andrew, was born in 1966. As adults, both sons would join the family business. Bernie's brother Peter joined the firm in 1969 as chief compliance officer. Peter's daughter, Bernie's niece, Shana Madoff, joined Madoff Securities in 1995 where she worked as the firm's in-house counsel and compliance officer. Madoff Securities became, for a time, one of the biggest players on the NASDAQ (National Association of Securities Dealers Automated Quotations) exchange and the firm was also one of the biggest players on Wall Street. Madoff Securities was a business that generated enormous amounts of wealth, prestige and power for the Madoff family.

The Fraud

On 10 December 2008, Madoff Securities senior executives Mark and Andrew Madoff informed the authorities that their father had just owned up to running a Ponzi scheme (also known as a pyramid scheme) and that he had defrauded clients of more than €50 billion. The next day, federal agents confronted Madoff to ask whether there was any substance to the allegations that had been made by his sons.

At this stage, the authorities had no evidence beyond both sons' report of their father's confession. Bernie Madoff told FBI agents that there was no innocent explanation for his admission of running the Ponzi scheme. The fraud was over.

Had my great-grandparents encountered the form of fraud perpetrated by Bernie Madoff, they would most probably have recognised it and referred to it as a 'Peter to Paul scheme'. The scam is, at its heart, an exceedingly simple one known colloquially as 'robbing Peter to pay Paul'. Money is stolen from new investors in order to pay profits to earlier ones. Dividends are comprised of money that new investors have been conned into contributing. The con relies on the promise of a return. An example of the unsustainable geometric progression of a classic pyramid scheme is shown in Figure 5.1.

The Peter to Paul swindle became widely known as a Ponzi scheme in the 1920s when a Boston-based Italian immigrant, Charles Ponzi, perpetrated a spectacular scam based on claims about arbitrage profits netted from an international trade in postage stamps.

In 1920 the Spanish peseta had fallen in value against the dollar. Spanish international postage coupons had a fixed exchange rate against the US postage stamps and a fall in the exchange rate of the peseta against the dollar had created a gap. A postage reply coupon bought in Spain could be redeemed in the US for a 10% profit. Buying enormous amounts of postal reply coupons would create the potential for enormous profit. Ponzi sold this simple idea to thousands of people. Of

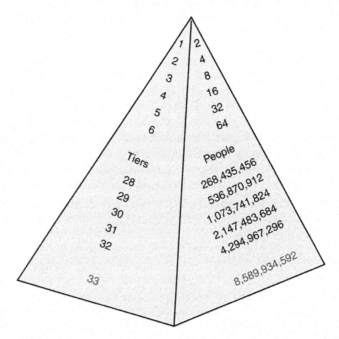

Figure 5.1   Pyramid scam population growth

Source: White, 2013

course, he did not actually buy the postage coupons. The fraud generated a staggering amount of money but lasted less than 10 months.

In their archetypal form, Ponzi schemes rely on investors falling for a promise that is too good to be true. They are outlandish schemes where slick operators turn people's desire for profit against them and thus ensnare victims.

Madoff's scam did not differ in form from any other Ponzi scheme. Madoff used the money from newer investors to pay off older clients and to generate the impression that Madoff Securities were deftly navigating a treacherous market. Where Madoff's Ponzi scheme does stand out is in terms of subtlety and investment return. The returns offered to investors were small enough not to attract the attention of the regulatory authorities, or most other participants in the marketplace. Most of Madoff clients received returns that appeared to be in line with promises of unspectacular but steady income. There was little appearance of easy money or a quick buck, although one important indicator of fraud was frequently overlooked. Fraud investigator Harry Markopolos claims that he knew Madoff was a fraud within five minutes of looking at the return stream and could prove it within 20 minutes: 'His performance line went up at a 45 degree angle; that only exists in geometry class' (Manning, Stokes, Visser, Rowland, & Tarba, 2018, p. 1452). Nor did Bernie Madoff ever go for the hard sell. Quite the opposite.

Because of Madoff's apparent reticence to accept new business, there was some status associated with Bernie accepting your money. Individual clients included Stephen Spielberg, John Malkovitch, Larry King and the estate of John Denver. However, not everyone was convinced. Goldman Sachs and Credit Suisse were notable institutional sceptics which would not deal with Madoff. For years, Harry Markopolos, an independent fraud investigator and former securities industry insider, suspected that Madoff was operating a Ponzi scheme. Markopolos contacted the US Securities and Exchange Commission (SEC), with documentation supporting his suspicions on three different occasions, but his warnings were not heard. Similarly, the journalist Erin Arvedlund raised serious doubts about Madoff in 2001. She was not listened to either. Madoff himself believed that he had been found out in 2003/04 and again in 2006. Yet still the fraud was allowed to rumble along.

Events Come to a Head

All Ponzi schemes eventually collapse under their own weight. The case of Madoff Securities has shown us that this might not happen for a long time – but it will eventually come to pass. Madoff claims that the fraud began in the 1990s. Investigators suggest that it might have started a decade or so earlier. A third option, which I find plausible, is that Madoff Securities were operating fraudulently from the very foundation of the firm. The reason that events came to a head when they did is that there was a global liquidity squeeze. Investors wanted to reduce their exposure to risk as the global economy weakened, and investors were pulling out of hedge funds.

Consequences

The Madoff Ponzi scheme wiped out $65 billion in the paper wealth associated with investor accounts. Victims comprised financial institutions ranging from the Royal Bank of Scotland (RBS) to the Korea Teachers' Pension fund. Many 'ordinary' individuals and charitable organisations had their wealth, pensions and savings wiped out. Some of those who lost everything, for example those who had others invest savings on their behalf, did not even know that they were involved with Madoff Securities. Suicides followed the collapse. These included Madoff's oldest son Mark, who committed suicide on the second anniversary of his father's arrest. Madoff's Ponzi scheme entailed an 'immense human and financial toll' (Henriques, 2018, p. 748). The 80-year-old Madoff is serving a 150-year sentence in a medium security federal prison. He will die in jail.

LINKS TO THEORY AND RESEARCH

Fraud comes in a range of flavours. Bernie Madoff's fraud is of a different variety from Nick Leeson's fraud at Barings, which was instructive because it illustrated the usefulness of the fraud triangle (Wolfe & Hermanson, 2004). Madoff's fraud is instructive for three reasons. First, Madoff's case reveals that most contemporary understandings of Ponzi schemes is either out of date or misleading (Henriques, 2018). Second, Madoff embodies the dark triad of personality traits (Jonason & Webster, 2012), and these need to be taken into account when seeking to understand individuals who engage in undesirable or counterproductive behaviours in the workplace (Jonason, Wee, & Li, 2015). Fraud certainly fits the criteria of undesirable and counterproductive behaviour. Third, investment fraud, as it manifests in a Ponzi scheme, requires human contact, social networks and the exploitation of social capital. A consideration of social capital is therefore necessary in understanding white-collar crime (Manning, 2018). This aspect is perhaps especially important in the Madoff case.

Contemporary Understanding of Ponzi Schemes

According to Henriques (2018), there are at least six points where common perceptions regarding Ponzi schemes are inaccurate. It is commonly believed that:

- Those who run Ponzi schemes are larger than life characters
- Ponzi schemes are localised, free-standing entities that are limited geographically by the schemer's immediate circle of trust
- Ponzi schemes are fast burning because the returns paid to early investors quickly outpace the income derived from new investors
- Ponzi schemes make extravagant promises of overnight wealth
- 'You can't cheat an honest man' – victims are complicit in illegal behaviours because of greed
- Ponzi schemes are complex

There is no doubt but that Bernie Madoff could turn on the charm (e.g. Berkowitz, 2012). However, it would be a big stretch to describe him as larger than life. Journalist Mark Seal (2009, n.p.) reports supermodel Carmen Dell'Orefice, who lost her life savings in the Madoff Ponzi scheme, describing Madoff as follows: 'Bernie was quiet, not a storyteller, not a conversationalist … I often thought he was perhaps bored. He was just Bernie, pleasant and polite.'

It is interesting to contrast this perception of Madoff as bland and dull with perceptions of 'the original' Charles Ponzi, who was certainly a larger-than-life character. Ponzi was so much larger than life that somehow two detectives assigned to investigate the original Ponzi scheme were signed up to it (Henriques, 2018)! Indeed, if you look up Charles Ponzi's mugshot online, you are likely to be met with a face that successfully casts its charm over the hundred odd years since it was taken. The larger-than-life aspect is evident in his grin that charms. This cannot be said of the smirking frown that you will find glowering from Bernie Madoff's mugshot if you look it up online.

The Madoff case shows that Ponzi schemes are not necessarily localised, free-standing entities. Madoff's fraudulent Ponzi scheme was hidden within a large and successful,trading business that had a global reach (Henriques, 2018). This hiding of a Ponzi scheme within Madoff's bona fide business also impacted the speed at which the scheme, of necessity, collapsed under its own weight. This is because at the time of the fraud, the legitimate brokerage side of the Madoff business was operating in an environment where the stock index was rising. Between 1993 and 2013 the S&P 500 stock index swung from a 36.5% loss to a 32% gain (Henriques, 2018).

In the old days, Ponzi schemes were relatively easy for the financially literate to spot because fraudsters made extravagant promises of overnight wealth. It was widely accepted that 'You can't cheat an honest man' and that victims were complicit in illegal behaviours because of greed. There was perhaps some truth to these notions. Ponzi's predecessor, William '520 percent' Miller, fleeced investors to the tune of more than $1 million in 1899. Ponzi himself offered a 'plan' in which investors received 50% interest in 90 days. Ponzi subsequently revised this offer so that investors were promised 50% interest in 45 days (Darby, 1998). The 'you can't cheat an honest man' outlook is not valid in the case of Madoff, and indeed in the case of the many other, relatively low-yielding Ponzi schemes that continually pop up in contemporary financial markets. Blaming investors for being insufficiently sceptical and overly trusting is not feasible in our contemporary economy, an economy that relies heavily on trust (Henriques, 2018).[2]

The Dark Triad of Personality Traits

The dark triad of personality traits are psychopathy, narcissism and Machiavellianism (Paulhus & Williams, 2002) (see Figure 5.2). These traits have been linked

---

[2] Without trust there would be no Amazon, PayPal, credit cards, and probably no economy.

Figure 5.2   The dark triad of personality traits

Source: https://commons.wikimedia.org/wiki/File:The_Dark_Triad_Image.png

to fraudulent behaviour and they are embodied in the person of Bernie Madoff (Jonason & Webster, 2012).

Psychopathy, although not listed in the current *Diagnostic and Statistical Manual* (DSM) (American Psychiatric Association, 2013), is a personality disorder characterised by a willingness to exploit and manipulate other people, which is accompanied by a guiltless lack of empathy associated with having done so (Hare, 2006). Psychopaths are charming and socially skilled. Holmes (2010) cites the capacity of serial killer Ted Bundy to disarm his victims as a function of the charm and social skills associated with psychopathy. Psychopaths typically live a parasitic lifestyle, have a grandiose sense of self-worth and lie pathologically (Holmes, 2010). These characteristics certainly resonate with the published analyses of Madoff's characteristics. Madoff certainly feels no guilt and is lacking in empathy. He is reported by Somaiya (2010, n.p.), who was quoting one of his neighbours in prison, as saying 'Fuck my victims. I carried them for 20 years and now I am doing 150 years'. Madoff is also reported as having stated that his victims were simply 'rich and greedy and wanted more' (ibid.).

Narcissism is a personality trait that is both clinical and sub-clinical in its manifestation (Furnham, Richards, & Paulhus, 2013). Narcissistic individuals are highly self-centred and grandiose, with an overriding concern for themselves that is only matched by their disdain for the welfare of others. Narcissistic people believe that they can only relate to people with high status like themselves, and they tend to ignore 'ordinary' people (Holmes, 2010). It is hard to refrain from speculating that this trait sits remarkably easily with what we know about Madoff's 'honouring' of high-status people when he allowed them to become his clients, that is, when he conned them.

The final trait included in the dark triad is Machiavellianism. Machiavellian personalities manipulate and deceive in the pursuit of self-interest. Those who employ Machiavellian interpersonal strategies (aka high Machs) are identified by four criteria: a lack of interpersonal affect, a lack of concern for conventional morality, a low ideological commitment and a lack of gross psychopathology. Machiavellianism is like psychopathic behaviour, but it is more context-dependent and lacks the pathological lying and anxiety that are often linked with psychopaths. Machiavellianism is arguably a component of social intelligence (Russell & Swartout, 2016). Again, these characteristics are all present in Madoff's character.

Social Capital

'The regulators get calls all the time', Madoff says. 'They didn't investigate because I had the reputation at the time for being the gold standard. I had all the credibility. Nobody could believe at that time that I would do something like that' (Gelles & Tett, 2011, n.p.). Madoff is correct. Reputation was a key ingredient in his fraud. The reason that reputation is key is that reputation is a fundamental component of social capital.

The term 'social capital' refers to the 'networks, norms of reciprocity, and trust among members of a neighbourhood or community that develop through social interaction and mutual cooperation' (Haslam, Jetten, Cruwys, Dingle, & Haslam, 2018, p. 7). Discussions of social capital tend to present it as a benign thing, it is seen as something that catalyses human output into optimal performance, improves productivity and health, and so on. Human beings are understood as being wired for motivation through social group acceptance, group attributions of value, and perceptions of esteem from the social group (Lieberman, 2013). Social capital is linked to innovation and entrepreneurship (Putnam, 2001). In the round, the consensus seems to be that social capital is a good thing.

However, almost every good thing has a dark side,[3] and there is a dark side to the innovation, entrepreneurship and social capital that were central to Madoff's Ponzi fraud (Manning et al., 2018). Brenkert (2009) argues that it is implicit in the concept of the entrepreneur that one must break the rules in order to take advantage of the opportunities that one identifies or that one can create. However, the darkness tied up with rule-breaking is often overlooked on the basis that 'common sense'[4] accepts as a given that entrepreneurship and innovation are good. Dark innovation destroys value rather than creating it.

Bernie Madoff and his family were regarded as pillars of their community. The Madoff name was associated with traditional values, conservatism and low-risk investment strategies (Manning, 2018). Madoff's Jewish identity was an important aspect of this public reputation and social capital, which Madoff used to his advantage (Berkowitz, 2012). In particular, Madoff purposefully targeted his own ethnic group in order to perpetrate his fraud. The reason for this is simple: high levels of

---

[3] The dark sides of things are often the most interesting and revealing. My personal favourite is Nadler's work on how helping behaviour can be used to keep others down (Nadler, 2002).

[4] 'Common sense' is a pet hate of mine. It hurt to type it.

trust and shared culture and values facilitate white-collar crime (Manning et al., 2018). Madoff purposely targeted his own community from the beginning because the ties that bind – trust, friendship, respect – can be exploited. The Madoff fraud was based on affinity in the sense that, because of their shared group memberships, Madoff's clients were less sceptical than they might have been. This downside of affinity needs to be highlighted, and it needs to be guarded against.

CONCLUSION

The Madoff case is an excellent example of a focal point where the social meets the psychological. Madoff is a man who embodies the dark triad of personality traits. He followed a cheating strategy and engaged in dark innovation that made him fabulously wealthy before a final, dramatic implosion in which lives and wealth were destroyed. This is the stuff of Greek tragedy. It is important that we understand it, for there are lessons to be learned and conclusions to be drawn.

The most important things to be learned from the case of Bernie Madoff are as follows. Those with money to invest, and indeed those managing the money of others, need to robustly ensure that exceptional performance is indeed exceptional performance and not actually something else. Where doubts are raised, they should always be seriously considered, no matter how eminent the person. Finally, a more healthily sceptical attitude to entrepreneurship, innovation and wealth creation would benefit us all. Contrary to *Wall Street*'s Gordon Gekko, greed might not be good.

Thinking about profiling for a moment, there is a consensus that white-collar criminals do not have a homogeneous profile. There are, however, some traits that Madoff possessed that are noteworthy. For example, Madoff was adept at exploiting interrelationship weaknesses. He was very effective at manipulating those he planned to scam to bond with him, although this was rarely reciprocated. He was deeply embedded in his community. In terms of his abilities more generally, he was rather 'normal'. 'In most respects, he was just another con man' (Manning, 2018, p. 330).

REFLECTIVE QUESTIONS

1. Where do you think the line between innovation based on pushing regulatory boundaries and fraud lies?
2. In relation to the above question, where should the line be drawn?
3. Might there be anything to Madoff's assertion that his victims were complicit in their own defrauding?

FURTHER READING

Berkowitz, M. (2012). The Madoff paradox: American Jewish sage, savior, and thief. *Journal of American Studies*, *46*(1), 189–202. doi:10.1017/s0021875811001423

Henriques, D. B. (2011). *The Wizard of Lies: Bernie Madoff and the Death of Trust*. Basingstoke: Macmillan.

PART II
TERRORISM

6

TERRORISM: AN OVERVIEW

DEFINING TERRORISM

It is important to acknowledge from the very outset that terrorism is a contentious term and that the concept of terrorism is a complex one. What can be stated with certainty is that the signature attribute of terrorism is communicative violence (Innes & Levi, 2017).

It is also important to be clear from the start about what terrorism is not. Terrorism is not generally understood as something that is perpetrated by states. This is not to say that states are not responsible for crimes. Quite the opposite. 'With a few honourable exceptions, criminology has ignored a simple truth about crime – that serious crime is predominantly committed by states and their officials' (Green & Ward, 2017, p. 438). States do commit many heinous crimes, for example genocide, war crimes, torture, police violence and corruption. These state crimes can, and often do, portray terror as an essential component of a fight against perceived threats to their perceived social order. However, such crimes as these, which violate human rights and are driven by state agencies, are best defined as state crimes, not terrorism.

A terrorist is one who commits an act of terrorism. This is probably the only uncontentious thing we can say when discussing the term 'terrorism'. Whether or not we perceive a given act as terrorism is generally a function of morality rather than fact (Hamden, 2019). Terrorism is a label that, in contemporary discourse, we apply in order to convey a disparaging sense of moral outrage (Taylor, 2018). It is striking that individuals perceived by others to have carried out acts of terrorism may not always perceive themselves, or be perceived by their communities, as terrorists (Hudson, 2018). Social and cultural contexts have an effect on who we consider to be a terrorist, who we consider to be a freedom fighter, what we consider to be justifiable acts of war and what we consider to be terrorism. The importance of context can be illustrated with reference to two independent and relatively young states.

The first of these is the United States of America. During the period of colonial expansion in the United States, the lives of very many indigenous people were ended by colonists in a way that was violent, political, planned, communicative, and beyond the remit of the state. Such behaviour seems to sit easily with the basic criteria used to define terrorism. Indeed, going beyond individual and anonymous 'settlers', it could be argued that George Washington himself was a terrorist, based on the manner in which he embraced political violence and encouraged a civilian population to make war on their legitimate government (Gage, 2011). However, few would regard America as a state founded on terrorism.

The second example is Israel. Menachem Begin was the leader of the Irgun, an underground force which fought for Israeli independence. In one particularly bloody attack, the Irgun planted bombs intended to blow up the King David Hotel in Palestine. The hotel was considered to be an important target because it was a site of British Colonial prestige in Israel and the Irgun were focused on puncturing that prestige. Over 90 people, many of them civilians, were killed in the King David Hotel attack (Law, 2016). Menachem Begin went on to become the sixth prime minister of Israel and he was awarded a Nobel Peace Prize in 1978.

Like many terrorist organisations, the Irgun spawned an offshoot, LEHI, an acronym which in Hebrew stands for Fighters for the Freedom of Israel. This organisation was headed by another future Israeli Prime Minister, Yitzhak Shamir. Shamir unashamedly took on the mantle of terrorism. In 1943 he stated that 'terrorism is for us a part of the political battle being conducted under the present circumstances, and it has a great part to play: speaking in a clear voice to the whole world, as well as to our wretched brethren outside this land, it proclaims our war against the occupier' (Law, 2016, p. 190).

History regards Washington, Begin and Shamir with esteem. It is tempting to wonder what history might make of them had their causes not emerged victoriously from their respective conflicts. These examples also serve to emphasise and illustrate Hamden's (2019) point that the concepts of legitimacy and lawfulness mean that terrorism is always in the eye of the beholder. When 'our' side kill people, terms such as 'patriotism', 'collateral damage' and 'freedom' tend to be used. When 'they' kill people, terms such as 'extremism' and 'murder' apply.

In 2001, United Nations Security Council Resolution 1373 deemed all acts of terror to be criminal acts. Much like aspirations for universal harmony, almost everyone agrees with this. The problem lies in what we understand terrorism to be and, as of 2019, no consensus has been reached that clarifies either the term 'terrorism' or those acts considered to be terrorist (Hamden, 2019). One person's terrorist remains another person's freedom fighter.

A definition of terrorism that is widely cited in research is the 1998 US Department of State definition of terrorism as 'premeditated, politically motivated violence perpetrated against non-combatant targets by subnational groups or clandestine agents, usually intended to influence an audience' (US Department of State Archive, n.d; Hudson, 2018; Taylor, 2018). Thus, the US Department of State considers violence intended to influence an audience to be terrorism.

A United Nations Security Council Report defines terrorism as 'criminal acts, including against civilians, committed with the intent to cause death or serious bodily injury, or taking of hostages, with the purpose to provoke a state of terror in the general public or in a group of persons or particular persons, intimidate a population or compel a government or an international organization to do or to abstain from doing any act' (United Nations Security Council, 2004). Thus, the United Nations stipulates that the violence must be intended to cause death or serious bodily harm. These are just two possible definitions of terrorism in a field where upwards of 200 definitions exist (Gavin, 2019).

The lack of consensus in defining terrorism is problematic because it muddies the waters and it does not help government and military bodies deal coherently with terrorist threats. However, it is probably not entirely accidental that by retaining the power to define what terrorism means, each government around the world can formulate a definition that fits with their own goals and objectives (Cottam, Dietz-Uhler, Mastors, & Preston, 2010).

In broad terms, terrorism is about the application of violence to a political context. Motivation and intention are critical factors. The people who perpetrate terrorist attacks are generally non-state actors who are in conflict with a more powerful adversary. A prominent goal of terrorists is to provoke extreme violence from their opponent. Those who commit acts of terror do so because of its usefulness in mobilising and polarising their audience.

Terrorist organisations are not usually powerful enough to pose a threat of annihilation to their enemies. Few would have thought, for example, that the Irish Republican Army (IRA) was going to destroy the British state. In order to successfully counteract terrorism, states need to respond in a way that inhibits the capacity of terrorism to polarise. Ideas of 'us' and 'them' are the oxygen that allows terrorist conflict to burn.

Many terrorist acts can be understood as 'events that alter how people, groups, and institutions, think, feel, and act in relation to their security' (Innes & Levi, 2017, p. 457). At heart, it is the political focus of violence targeted at non-combatants that marks terrorism as distinct from the general criminal violence that manifests in other guises (Taylor, 2018).

THE HISTORY OF TERRORISM

The word 'terrorism' dates from 1795, when it was first used to describe the behaviour of the French regime during the 'Reign of Terror' in post-revolutionary France. The term 'terrorism' was coined by the Anglo-Irish politician and writer Edmund

Burke in a written attack against the French revolutionaries, whom he referred to as 'those Hell Hounds called Terrorists' (Millington, 2018). For Millington, terrorism is only as old as the discourse that invented it. It is the discourse that gives it meaning. Elsewhere, Chaliand and Blin (2016) disagree with Millington and suggest that terrorism is likely to be as old as war itself, whatever label is applied to it.

I agree with Millington. To illustrate the importance of discourse, consider the Maquis, the rural guerrilla bands of the French Resistance, who fought against Nazi occupation during the Second World War. Describing them as 'terrorists' seems not only wrong but inaccurate, besmirching a worthy group of freedom fighters. This perception is, of course, nothing to do with the Maquis, but rather a function of our contemporary discourse around terrorism. Dháibhéid (2017), for example, suggests that the French Resistance engaged in 'political violence', defined as 'terrorism that has 'worked'. Context is crucial, and history is always viewed from the present.

If we accept that terrorism cannot exist apart from the discourse around it (for the sake of transparency, this is wholeheartedly my position), then that portion of the history of terrorism with relevance to contemporary criminology and forensic psychology seems to narrow.

But not so fast. While accepting that discourse of necessity limits, I argue that in order to achieve the best understanding possible, we need to try to keep our net cast wide. Although attacks perpetrated by the Zealots against the Romans in ancient Israel might seem of little use in understanding contemporary terrorist attacks perpetrated by the likes of Isis, the Zealots are still worth thinking about. It is interesting to note that the term 'Zealot' means 'one who follows or is an admirer of God' (Hamden, 2019, p. 7). It is also interesting to note that the ancient Zealots chose to stage a mass suicide rather than surrender to the besieging Romans at the fortress of Masada (Hamden, 2019).

In a similar vein, it is worth keeping half an eye on historic understandings and theory. Freud (1920/1990) proposed that human aggression stems from an innate 'death instinct'. This psychodynamic line of thinking is perhaps particularly interesting when applied to understanding aspects of Isis, which has been described as a 'death cult' (e.g. Ibrahim, 2019).

In the late nineteenth century and early part of the twentieth century, politically motivated terror groups began to emerge. Anarchist terror posed a significant threat. 'French anarchist Emile Henry, "ignited the age of modern terror," with his 1894 bombing of a Parisian restaurant' (Millington, 2018, p. 4). In the period up to about 1920, in the United States, the Galleanists, a group of militant Italian anarchists, introduced tactics and strategies that are still widely used today in the world of terrorism. They had a structure similar to that of Al-Qaeda, they used the media to promote their agenda, to find new supporters and to distribute propaganda. They attacked Wall Street, sent letter bombs and tried their best to spread chaos (Simon, 2008). After the Second World War, the Red Army Faction launched a wave of terror in West Germany (e.g. Bielby, 2010) and in South America the FARC guerrillas brought left-wing terrorism into the twenty-first century.

Another type of terrorist group with roots in the nineteenth and early twentieth centuries also remains with us today. Nationalist terror groups (Hamden, 2019) emerged from a period when national identities became increasingly important to people in different territories. People who believed that their state had been over-taken by others saw nationalism as a worthy cause and, in turn, there were those who saw violence as a legitimate means to achieve their political goals. Contemporary groups with nationalist roots include the Real Irish Republican Army (Real IRA), the Tamil Tigers in Sri Lanka and ETA in Spain (Cottam et al., 2010).

The final epoch in the history of terrorism is our current one, 'global terror'. While the roots of global terror can arguably be traced back to the hijacking of an El Al flight from Tel Aviv to Rome by the Popular Front for the Liberation of Palestine (PFLP) in the late 1960s (e.g. Hamden, 2019), the watershed moment in our contemporary consciousness is the attacks on the World Trade Center and Washington, DC that took place on 11 September 2001. More than 3,000 people had died and Islamic terrorism had now entered the public discourse in an unprecedented way. Public consciousness of terrorism was changed forever (Cottam et al., 2010).

TYPES OF TERRORIST

When our state of knowledge is poor it is incumbent upon academics to be up-front about it. Taylor (2018, p. 339) reports that 'unlike many areas of forensic application, the study of terrorism generally lacks substantive evidence-based research, and in particular has attracted relatively limited psychological analysis'. Sageman (2014, p. 565), in the opening words of his wonderfully titled paper 'The stagnation in terrorism research', reports that we are currently 'no closer to answering the simple question of "What leads a person to turn to political violence?"'.

One way of thinking about terrorism is to classify individual terrorists on the basis of information elicited about their activities. Hamden (2019) suggests that 30% of terrorists are of a psychopathic type, 30% are of an ethnogeographic reli-gious type, 25% are of an ethnogeographic political type, and 15% are of a retribu-tional type. We will now explore each of these types in more detail.

Psychopathic Terrorists

Hamden (2019) describes the psychopathic terrorist as possessing traits that are associated with antisocial personality disorder in DSM-5 (American Psychiat-ric Association, 2013). These traits include a disregard for the rights of others, a capacity to manipulate people in order to achieve one's ends, deceitfulness, a lack of remorse, a disregard for obligations and commitments, and an attraction to risk-taking or thrill-seeking behaviours. Impulsivity is high in this cohort and psychopathic terrorists also tend to be narcissistic, with little capacity for inti-macy or empathy with others. Psychopathic terrorists will show little moral or ethical understanding. As a consequence of their lack of an internal belief system, psychopathic terrorists will tend to be indiscriminate in their choice of victim. They will typically be male and have a deep-seated need to feel superior to others.

Psychopathic terrorists are very unlikely to involve themselves with any type of suicide action or plot with a high probability of death – they regard themselves as too good for sacrifice. The Unabomber, Ted Kaczynski and Nezar Hindawi (whose cases feature in individual chapters in this section) are presented by Hamden (2019) as terrorists of the psychopathic type. Kaczynski felt entitled to kill in order to publicise his ideas, and Hindawi put his pregnant Irish girlfriend onto an Israeli flight carrying a bomb that she did not know he had planted in her luggage.

Ethnogeographic Terrorists

Ethnogeographic terrorism comprises two subtypes: religious terrorists and political terrorists (Hamden, 2019). Both types have a fundamentalist mindset which dictates that they engage with the world through the exclusive prism of their own ideology. In a sense, this is a very modern (as opposed to postmodern) stance. Born of Enlightenment-style rationality, the world is understood in a black-and-white fashion where 'facts' are supreme and reality exists independently of any representation of it.

The problem for those of us who are not fundamentalist is that those who are believe that they directly perceive reality in a way that the rest of us either cannot or choose not to. The fundamentalist mindset is thus experienced as more than a little irritating to those on the 'outside'. I include myself among this number.[1] Fundamentalist terrorists are trapped within a very narrow frame, be they Marxists, white supremacists or Islamic fundamentalists (Hamden, 2019). For this group of terrorists, ideology is the determinant of behaviour because it links immediate behaviour, for example planting a bomb or detonating a suicide vest, with distant outcomes, such as the creation of a utopian state or a place in heaven (Taylor, 1991).[2] To the fundamentalist religious terrorist, murdering another can be constructed as something approaching an act of kindness; death in their cause will gain everlasting rewards whether one is victim or volunteer (Hamden, 2019).

Retributional Terrorists

Thanks to Hollywood, many of us are familiar with this last type of terrorist. Brad Pitt's character Frankie McGuire in the movie *The Devil's Own* is a good, fictional, example of this type. Frankie grows up and is motivated to join the IRA because as an 8-year-old boy he witnessed his father being shot for being an Irish republican sympathiser.

---

[1] 'Common sense' is the only thing that even remotely challenges a fundamentalist mindset for its capacity to irritate. The Westboro Baptist Church offers an excellent example of fundamentalism if you want to fray a nerve.

[2] Isn't it interesting how close the religious and secular fundamentalist can appear to be to outside eyes? In my view, there is nothing to separate the secular utopia and the religious heaven.

The retributional terrorist is a person who is seeking revenge against somebody, some group, or some nation, who deprived them of a loved one, a way of life, or a community. These types of terrorist are unlikely to show any signs of psychiatric or psychological disorder and they are unlikely to hold to any given political or religious ideology (Hamden, 2019). Loss and pain are the drivers of retributional terrorism. Trauma is the foundation from which it springs.

THEORIES OF TERRORISM

One way to think about terrorism is in terms of aggression. Relevant to the 'aggression' view are things like psychopathology, abnormality and individual differences (Taylor, 2018). A second way to think about terrorism is in terms of sociological understanding. Black's (2004) ideas about physical proximity and social distance are particularly useful in this regard. A third way to consider terrorism is in a criminological framework. In criminology, there are three factors that are generally considered necessary to the labelling of an act as terrorism: political violence, communicative violence and an asymmetry of power (Liebling, Maruna, & McAra, 2017). Last, but not least, terrorism can be considered in the context of social identity theory (Tajfel, 1982), a social psychological theory that focuses on the importance of intergroup relations (Haslam, Reicher, & Platow, 2011). These perspectives will be briefly considered next and then further expanded upon in the chapters that follow as they apply to each case.

Aggression

It is important to begin by noting that terrorists are not necessarily radical and that radicals are not necessarily terrorists. It is also worth restating that contemporary psychology is poor at identifying who is a terrorist (Taylor, 2018). One way of understanding terrorism is as 'the handling of a grievance with aggression' (Black, 2004, p. 16).

Some would define aggression as including pushing, shoving and striking. Others might include threatening speech, verbal insults or facial expressions. What we consider to be 'aggressive' is a function of the cultures that we belong to. Among Amish communities, the bar that determines aggression might be considered as being set very low. Shunning is understood to be an extremely harsh treatment. By contrast, in street gangs, the bar is much higher, with physical mutilation and murder being relatively commonplace. Even the definitions that scientists use are a function of the values that are held by individual scientists and differ from researcher to researcher (Hogg & Vaughan, 2018). There is a plethora of operationalisations of 'aggression'. These include, for example, punching an inflatable plastic doll (Bandura, Ross, & Ross, 1963).

Biological theories of aggression include psychodynamic theory, ethology and evolutionary psychology. From a psychodynamic perspective, Freud (1920/1990) proposed that human aggression stems from an 'innate death instinct', Thanatos.

This death instinct is constituted in opposition to our life instinct, Eros. According to Freud, Thanatos is initially turned inwards towards self-destruction, although later in its development Thanatos becomes directed outwards, towards other people. Similar to the sexual urge, which stems from Eros, the aggressive urge stemming from Thanatos builds from bodily tensions and needs to be expressed. Later psychodynamic theorists, building on Freud's theorising, came to think of aggression as a more natural, but still an innate, process. From the psychodynamic perspective, people seek a release for a type of primitive survival instinct that humans share with all animal species (Hogg & Vaughan, 2018).

In the 1960s, ethological researchers argued for the instinctual basis of human aggression on the grounds of a comparison with animal behaviour. One key text was Konrad Lorenz's *On Aggression* (1966). In common with the neo-Freudians, ethologists focused on the functional aspects of aggression. However, the ethologists also realised that while the potential for aggression may be innate, aggression is brought out by specific stimuli in the environment (releasers). Lorenz argued that aggression has survival value and that human beings are born with a fighting instinct. Human beings have some important differences from other species that we need to bear in mind. Human beings do not have sharp teeth, claws or other appendages that can usefully be applied to fighting others. As a species, we are also lacking in recognisable appeasement gestures, for example we don't lie down and turn our bellies up (as, say, a dog might) in a recognisable act of submission.

This lack of innate fighting appendages and submission gestures gives rise to two key implications: first, when we start being violent we do not seem to know when to stop; second, in order to kill, because we don't have sharp teeth or claws, we generally need weapons. This has resulted in a situation whereby the killing of others can be accomplished over very large distances. Bombs, for example, can be detonated by a phone call from a different continent. Furthermore, technology now enables killing with weapons such that the perpetrator receives no feedback pertaining to the anguish experienced by the victim. The person who detonates a suicide vest at a music concert full of teenagers does not get to see the devastation they wreak (Hogg & Vaughan, 2018).

The argument from evolutionary psychology is a provocative one: specific behaviours have evolved because they promote the survival of genes that allow the individual to live long enough to pass their genes on to the next generation. Aggression is regarded as adaptive because it would seem to be linked to the capacity to live long enough to procreate. For human beings, aggression may be adaptive because its goals can include rewards such as social and economic advantage, either in terms of defending the resources that we have or in acquiring new ones.

Biological theories have a certain appeal – I think mostly because they fit neatly with lay understandings of violence as being part of human nature. In the seventeenth century, the English philosopher Thomas Hobbes famously said that human lives are 'nasty, brutish, and short'. However, there is a circularity in these arguments that aggression is based on instinct. It is also the case that aggression relies on causal explanations for which there is no evidence. Instinct depends on an energy that is unknown. It is also the case that biological explanations are of very little use in the prevention or control of aggression and/or human behaviour (Hogg & Vaughan, 2018).

A Sociological Understanding of Aggression

Black (2004) tells us that terrorism is the handling of a grievance with aggression. In his paper, Black makes some interesting points. He regards terrorism as collective violence, a group project, and in this regard, according to Black, terrorism resembles rioting, lynching and vigilantism. Terrorism is mass violence that is one-sided rather than reciprocal. Unlike conventional warfare, terrorism is unilateral and covert rather than bilateral and overt. Black (2004) also argues that we shouldn't regard terrorism as purely criminological because terrorism is highly moralistic behaviour.

The most interesting argument that Black (2004) makes is that terrorism arises with a large degree of social and cultural distance. In conflict where there is cultural, social and physical proximity between the parties, if there is violence, the result is guerrilla warfare, not terrorism. Black argues that terrorism is a product of the twentieth and twenty-first centuries because technology, rapid transport and electronic communications have shrunk the physical world. In many cases, for example, immigrant communities live in parallel to their indigenous neighbours. They are physically close but separated by a social gulf. Technology has not (yet!) shrunk the social world. Terrorism by and against civilians requires physical contact between people separated by enormous chasms in social space.

On the positive side, Black (2004) also argues that the lifespan of terrorism is limited because of the implosion of physical and social space over recent history. The conditions that gave rise to terrorism, he argues, will also lead to its downfall – shrinking social space and increasing interconnectedness will eventually put an end to terror. As people continue to intermingle and technology develops, the conditions that are conducive to terrorism will die.

Criminology and Terrorism

In criminology, the three factors that are generally considered necessary to describe an act as terrorist are political violence, communicative violence and an asymmetry of power (Liebling et al., 2017).

Horgan (2005) and Atran (2010) argue that most people who become involved in terrorism are fairly 'ordinary'. Social networks are important (Sageman, 2014) and the social groups that individuals belong to can be harnessed to radicalise people and draw them into terrorism (Atran, 2010). Others in criminology direct our focus towards theology, and it does seem that religious fundamentalism seems to play a part (e.g. Wiktorowicz, 2006). Wiktorowicz's idea of 'culturing' highlights how the impact of a combination of theological, social psychological and social devices are employed to foster group membership and then shield these same group members from counter-influences.

Suicide bombings have also been considered in the criminological literature. Evidence suggests that suicide bombers are generally young unmarried men. Only about 15% are reported to be women. Suicide attackers do not generally display depression or diagnosable mental conditions. They tend to be well educated when compared to their peers and they tend to hail from relatively high social backgrounds (Gambetta, 2006). Notwithstanding recent attacks, suicide bombing remains relatively rare.

SOCIAL IDENTITY THEORY

In the social identity literature, Haslam, Reicher and Platow (2011, p. 91) suggest that 'extremists are much more likely to exert influence over a group when that group is locked into conflict with a clearly defined out-group, so that for members of that group the world is defined starkly in "us and them" terms'.

Social identity was defined by Tajfel (1982) as an individual's knowledge that they belong to certain social groups and that membership of these groups has emotional and value significance for them. It focuses on the 'we's' people ascribe to and how when 'we' self-categorise as a group member 'we' interact with 'them'. 'According to social identity theory, striving of group members for enhancement of their social identity may be resolved through individual mobility [...] or by social change [...]. Individual mobility may only be achieved when group boundaries are *permeable*; social change is only feasible when group status is *unstable*.' (Ellemers, van Knippenberg, & Wilke, 1990, p. 233, original italics). Terrorism can be understood as violent, instrumental acts designed to destabilise intergroup relationships and facilitate social change.

CONCLUSION

It is worth pointing out that it is not universally accepted that the world is becoming a more violent place. Stephen Pinker (2011) argues that the world has actually become a less aggressive place than it used to be. The chapters in this section will look at specific cases of terrorism in order to explore and understand the drivers and theories relevant to terrorism, but such an understanding does not need to elicit despair.

7

THE HINDAWI AFFAIR

LEARNING OBJECTIVES

By the end of this chapter you should be able to:

- Describe the main points of the Hindawi plot
- Detail some considerations of passenger profiling in the aviation industry
- Discuss the relevance of attribution theory to our understanding of terrorism
- Outline the relevance of intergroup relations and social identity theory to understanding the Hindawi plot

SYNOPSIS OF THE CASE

In 1986 Nezar Nawwaf al-Mansur al-Hindawi sent his pregnant fiancée, Anne-Marie Murphy, to board a flight to Israel with 375 other passengers and, unknown to her, there were 1.5 kilogrammes of Semtex explosives in her bag. The Lord Chief Justice stated that it was as horrible a crime as could possibly be imagined. This chapter considers the importance of passenger profiling and the usefulness of applying a social psychological analysis to our understanding of this crime.

DESCRIPTION OF THE CASE

Nezar Hindawi

Nezar Hindawi, convicted terrorist and founder of the Syrian-backed Jordanian Revolutionary Movement, was born in 1954 near the village of Baqra, close to the Jordan River. The Hindawi family were a well-to-do Palestinian clan. Historically, the Hindawis had been comfortable farmers but, like many in Palestine, they were forced off their land as a consequence of the birth of the state of Israel. Despite their loss of property, when they resettled in Trans-Jordan, the Hindawis were able to maintain their social standing, and when Nezar Hindawi was growing up during the 1960s and 1970s, two of his uncles served in the Jordanian government.

As a young man, and in common with the offspring of many well-connected families, Nezar Hindawi gravitated towards a career in journalism. In his early 20s, Nezar obtained a journalistic post in the Jordanian capital, Amman. By 1980, Nezar had fallen out with the Jordanian authorities because of his anti-Hashemite views.[1] As a result, he had moved to London. His move must have been somewhat eased by the fact that, at that stage, one of Nezar's brothers and his father were living in London as permanent residents. Nezar's other brothers, sisters and mother remained living in Jordan.

In London, Nezar Hindawi began to work as a reporter and he enrolled on several English language courses. On one of these courses, Nezar met his wife, Barbara Litwiniec, a Polish woman. However, the falling out with the Jordanian authorities was problematic because it meant that the Jordanian government would not renew Nezar Hindawi's Jordanian passport.

At around this time Nezar Hindawi was recruited as an agent by the Syrian government, possibly by the Syrian ambassador to the UK. Shortly after his recruitment, along with his new wife Barbara, Nezar Hindawi moved to Poland. This move to Poland may have been coincidental, but it does seem relevant that the newly employed Syrian agent ended up in Poland, which, like Syria, was at the time firmly in the orbit of the Soviet Union.

Over the next few years Nezar Hindawi would come and go from Poland as a function of his 'journalistic' assignments. In Poland, Barbara's father is reported as remembering Nezar as a 'good boy' who would help out with the apple harvest during his visits. Interestingly, Barbara's mother was sceptical of her son-in-law because of his fondness for eating pork, reportedly referring to Nezar Hindawi as a 'pork vacuum cleaner'.

Anne-Marie Murphy

Anne-Marie Murphy is from Sallynoggin, a working-class area of South Dublin. She was 29 years old and working as a chambermaid at the Hilton Hotel in Park Lane, London, when she first met Nezar Hindawi in 1984.

---

[1] The Hashemites, also known as the House of Hashim, are the ruling family of Jordan.

Anne-Marie grew up in an Ireland that was deeply conservative as the fifth of ten children. In the 1980s birth control and abortion were illegal in Ireland and sex outside marriage was considered taboo. Anne-Marie's family did not have a lot of money. Her father was a truck driver and she left school at 14 to take up a job at the Glen Abbey hosiery factory near her home. Anne-Marie worked at Glen Abbey from 1968 to 1979, when she took redundancy. Coming from Ireland myself, in my mind, this period seems like a suffocating and claustrophobic time in a repressive and conservative society. It cannot have been easy for a young person like Anne-Marie.

Five years after leaving Glen Abbey, Anne-Marie was still without regular work, a not uncommon scenario during these years. In common with many of her contemporaries, she was drawn to the bright lights of London in search of a better future. Shortly after her arrival in London, Anne-Marie's friend, Theresa Leonard, found her a job at the Park Lane Hilton. This was Anne-Marie's first time in London. It was 1984.

Not long after her arrival in London, Theresa Leonard made a fateful introduction: she introduced Anne-Marie to Nezar Hindawi, a flatmate of Theresa's boyfriend. Nezar Hindawi was a man who must have appeared sophisticated and suave to the recently arrived immigrants from Ireland. He was a heavy drinker and a man who enjoyed the high life in London. By Christmas 1984, Anne-Marie was pregnant by Nezar. At this point, Hindawi vanished. When Hindawi reappeared in Anne-Marie's life during February 1985, Anne-Marie had lost her baby and was recovering from the miscarriage. Hindawi came and went during this period and the couple were mostly apart. When Hindawi came back from a stint abroad in November 1985, he found that Anne-Marie was pregnant by him for the second time. But Hindawi was not a happy expectant father; he wanted Anne-Marie to terminate the pregnancy.

The Plot: Execution and Apprehension

In 1985, following directions given by Syrian intelligence, Hindawi went to Damascus for military instruction at a training camp under the command of Abu Nidal.[2] Later, in early 1986, Hindawi met with Muhammed al-Khuli, head of Syrian Air-Force intelligence. It was agreed at this meeting that Hindawi would make a strike against an Israeli passenger aeroplane. He was to be paid US$250,000 on the 'successful' completion of his assignment.

Hindawi's designated handler was Colonel Haythem Sa'id, who organised some cash and a passport for Hindawi in the name of 'Isam Sha'r'. Hindawi then made dummy runs to the UK, using this alias and a cover story presenting himself as a procurement officer seeking to obtain spare parts for Land Rovers. Hindawi's practice of deception had now begun in earnest. Following the first dummy run,

---

[2] Nidal was a well-known Palestinian terrorist and founder of militant group Fatah – The Revolutionary Council.

on Hindawi's return to Damascus, Sa'id trained Hindawi in the preparation of that old terrorist favourite, the suitcase bomb. As part of this training, Hindawi was instructed to identify himself as a drug runner if he was apprehended by the security forces. In the event of his arrest, Hindawi was also instructed to hide any connection with the Syrian government and informed that, should he fail to adhere to these instructions, one quarter of his family would be executed the day after his failure.

On 29 March 1986, the first concrete terrorist operation associated with Nezar Hindawi came to pass: the bombing in Berlin of the German-Arab Friendship Society, which the Syrian authorities believed was in league with Israeli intelligence. Nine people were injured in the attack. Ahmed Hasi, a brother of Nezar Hindawi was subsequently convicted of the bombing.

In the wake of the Berlin attack, Hindawi, using his false passport, landed in London on 5 April 1986. Posing as a Syrian Airlines employee, he spent two nights in the Royal Garden Hotel in a room paid for by Syrian Airlines. On 6 April 1986, Hindawi was given a bomb intended for use in the attack on an El Al jet. Colonel Sa'id ordered Hindawi to use a woman to carry the El Al bomb. 'Luckily' for Hindawi, Anne-Marie Murphy was to hand. It seems likely that the relationship between Hindawi and Anne-Marie was ordered by Syrian intelligence from the outset.

When Anne-Marie Murphy had found herself pregnant for the second time in November 1985, Hindawi was not interested and wanted her to have an abortion. As a result, Anne-Marie began planning her return to Ireland. Given her circumstances, and the intolerant attitude towards single mothers then prevalent in Ireland, you can imagine Anne-Marie's surprise, and probably her relief, when Hindawi came back into her life with declarations of love and a proposal of marriage on 7 April 1986.

Hindawi told Anne-Marie that he planned a marriage in Jordan for them. His plan was for the couple to travel to the wedding ceremony in Jordan via 'the Holy Land'. According to Hindawi, the couple had to travel separately because his employers had paid his fare on a different flight. Hindawi stressed his wish that Anne-Marie did not tell anyone of their plans. He was especially helpful in preparing Anne-Marie for their trip. He organised her passport, bought her ticket, new clothes and a brand new wheeled suitcase. The suitcase had a false bottom and a hidden compartment containing three and a quarter pounds of semtex explosive. The device was virtually undetectable to the x-ray technology available at the time.

On 17 April 1986, Hindawi inserted a detonator into the suitcase bomb before taking Anne-Marie Murphy to the airport to catch her flight to Israel. When Hindawi dropped Anne-Marie at the airport, he kissed her on both cheeks before returning to the Royal Garden Hotel. His plan was to return to Syria on a Syrian Airlines flight that same afternoon, while Anne-Marie's flight was intended to explode at approximately 39,000 feet somewhere between Italy and Greece. Thankfully, the suspicions of El Al security agents at Heathrow were aroused after Anne-Marie checked-in, and the lives of the 395 passengers and crew on the New York–London–Tel Aviv flight that Anne-Marie was scheduled to travel on were spared.

On arrival at Heathrow, security officers questioned Anne-Marie as part of their routine checks. She then passed through the airport screening checkpoint and made it as far as the departure gate. However, several factors aroused the suspicions of security staff. She told security staff that she would be staying at the Hilton in Tel Aviv, but she did not have the money on her to cover her stay. Anne-Marie had no access to money aside from a cheque guarantee card, she was heavily pregnant, travelling alone, her tickets had been re-booked, and she had not packed her suitcase herself. The security agents decided to search Anne-Marie's bag. They found it to be significantly heavier than would be expected. Inside the case, they discovered a false bottom with a bomb connected to a timing device. The timer/detonator was a Commodore scientific calculator which Hindawi had given to Anne-Marie for her to work out how much local currency she would need in Israel. What a peachy fiancé he was!

News of the foiled El Al bombing quickly emerged from Heathrow. Instead of boarding a flight to Syria, Hindawi was directed by his intelligence contact to the Syrian embassy where he was to hand a sealed envelope to the Syrian ambassador. On arrival at the embassy, Hindawi was taken to the ambassador, Loutouf al-Haydar, who complimented him on his 'good work'. On reading the contents of the envelope, the ambassador sent Hindawi, accompanied by two guards, to a safe house in West Kensington, where he spent the night. The following morning, when two guards arrived to accompany him back to the embassy, Hindawi thought that he was about to be murdered and ran. Shortly afterwards Hindawi was arrested by the police.

Nezar Hindawi was brought to trial at the Old Bailey where he was found guilty of trying to blow up the El Al flight and sentenced to 45 years in prison for what the judge described as a 'foul and horrible act of terrorism'. This is believed to be the longest fixed-term sentence handed down by a British court. On the same day that Hindawi was convicted, Britain cut diplomatic ties with Syria and ambassador Loutouf al-Haydar was given seven days to shut the embassy and leave.

Anne-Marie Murphy went on to give birth to a healthy baby girl and moved back to Ireland. She was the chief prosecution witness at her fiancé's trial. In court, Anne-Marie looked directly at Hindawi and asked, 'You bastard, you. How could you do that to me?' How indeed?

LINKS TO THEORY AND RESEARCH

Discussion

The Hindawi case raises some interesting issues. It illustrates the vital importance of airport passenger screening and raises a question as to whether passenger profiling remains a useful tool more than 30 years after the foiled plot. The case is also useful in considering the role that attributions play when we think about terrorism – terrorists tend to be understood in terms of bad people doing awful things. The Hindawi case is, perhaps, useful in that it can illustrate how easily we overlook background and contextual factors when considering terrorist crime.

Airport Profiling

Passenger profiling in aviation was introduced during the 1980s by the Israeli Security Agency. The Israeli approach centres on identifying dangerous people rather than seeking to identify dangerous objects (Levy, Ziegler, & Koch, 2014).

Profiling in the aviation passenger context can be defined as 'the observation, recording, and analysis of individuals or groups for the purpose of predicting future behaviour' (Whitaker, 2010, p. 373). Whitaker describes profiling as a risk management tool that relies upon data collection and prior modelling. Usefully, Whitaker (2010) also points out, and examines, a critical flaw in an important assumption underlying profiling. This is the idea that collected data can always be used to predict the future. Whitaker uses the example of Cold War spies to illustrate his point. During the early Cold War years, five British citizens with senior positions in the diplomatic and intelligence services were identified as Soviet spies. These spies became known as 'the Cambridge ring' and they created a profile of the typical Soviet spy as an ideologically motivated traitor who was university educated and belonged to the upper echelons of the British public service. In contrast, during the middle and later period of the Cold War money was a more likely motivator than ideology, and the Cambridge profile was the root of a counter-intelligence failure.

In a similar vein, it is worth bearing in mind that terrorists facing counter-terrorism measures in our post 9-11 world are likely to be conscious of profiling, and profilers need to remain cognisant of this fact (Whitaker, 2010). Being conscious of potential shortcomings does not, however, render profiling redundant. Far from it. The Israeli security services, and others, use multi-layered security approaches. Canadian airport security, for example, focuses on identifying irregular or suspicious behaviour and does not rely on ethnic or racial profiles (Whitaker, 2010). This was precisely the case when Israeli security profiled Anne-Marie Murphy at Heahrow.

Attribution

> Many myths surround terrorists and terrorism, but surely one of the most widely held is that terrorists are crazed fanatics: psychopaths who are completely immune to the suffering of their victims and who always remain committed to their cause. Like many myths, this one is easy to believe yet is almost always completely untrue. (Silke, 2003, p. 29)

As human beings, we are all preoccupied with trying to impose order on the world about us in order to understand that world, and in order to act on that world in an adaptive way. Having an understanding of other people and their behaviours is especially important in this regard, and it is fair to say that *everyone* behaves as a 'naïve' psychologist as they navigate their world (Hogg & Vaughan, 2008).

Attribution theory (Heider, 1958) comes into a particularly sharp focus when we are trying to understand, and find causes for, behaviours and events that come unexpectedly. This is perhaps especially so when the events in question are of a negative nature and it certainly applies to instances of terrorism. In such cases, we try to understand whether the cause for an event or behaviour lies within the person whose behaviour we are trying to explain, or whether the cause lies externally to them. According to Heider, we are all biased to prefer explanations of internal causality over explanations of external causality. This preference for internal or dispositional attributions even holds sway when there is evidence for external, or situational, causality. Psychologists are not immune from this.

The consensus (with which I concur) seems to be that Nezar Hindawi is a very bad man. In sentencing Hindawi, the then Lord Chief Justice described Hindawi as 'very dangerous due to his use of "extreme violence … callousness … lack of remorse and untrustworthiness"' and his plot as a 'foul and horrible act of terrorism' (Gardham, 2011, n.p.).

However, we should not lose sight of the fact that Hindawi was not a loose cannon or a lone wolf. He was a Syrian agent acting on behalf of the Syrian government and he received support and was facilitated by both the military and diplomatic arms of the Syrian state. Geoffrey Howe, the then British Foreign Secretary, said in Parliament that the evidence presented during the Hindawi trial demonstrated the 'plain involvement' of Syrian government agents in the bomb plot. The Foreign Secretary also said that 'It is, quite frankly, absurd and untenable to argue that a government is not responsible and accountable for the actions of its intelligence services and its ambassador' (Clines, 1986, n.p.).

Intergroup Factors

Pipes (1989) considered why the Syrian government might sponsor terrorism of the sort perpetrated by Nezar Hindawi. In his view, intergroup dynamics were at the heart of the Syrian motivation. Pipes asserts that since President Assad took power in Syria in 1970, the goal of the Syrian administration has been to retain power. A potential barrier to the Assad government's retention of power was (and is) that the Assad regime is predominately Alawi, a small religious community that is generally despised by the Sunni majority in Syria. In addition to their specific religious differences, the Alawi have prospered disproportionately under the Assad regime. Alawi privilege generates fear within the Alawi community as to what might happen should the Sunni majority wrestle power away from them.[3]

---

[3] These factors remain as relevant to the contemporary Syrian situation as they were when Pipes authored his paper in the late 1980s.

Conflict with Israel provides a banner under which Alawi and Sunni can unite in Syria – a common cause and the perception of a shared enemy. However, Israel was (and is) too strong to confront head on. Therefore, unconventional conflict is needed in place of conventional warfare. In this context, terrorism 'becomes a useful instrument of statecraft. It is inexpensive; it permits actions of a sort which a state could not possibly back openly; and it intimidates opponents' (Pipes, 1989, p. 18).

A problem that we often have in psychology is that we tend to see things in a binary way. Hollway (2007b, p. 201), for example, makes the argument that binaries make for widespread difficulties in Western thought. Hollway goes on to argue that binaries present a problem of particular relevance to social psychology because the discipline is defined by dualism – the study of individuals in social contexts.

If we were to consider the explanation for Nezar Hindawi's behaviour in a binary manner, it must be either internal or external. In contrast, a more holistic approach can consider both of these components. It is likely that there is some element of Hindawi's behaviour that is attributable to internal factors: for example, it is possible that Nezar Hindawi is a psychopath. Hindawi's record and behaviour would certainly seem to fit with Sammons and Putwain's (2019) observation that while psychopathic individuals might be drawn to terrorist activities, they tend to make poor terrorists as they generally lack commitment to ideals and causes and also lack the capacity to act in self-sacrificing ways. However, in addition to internal individual factors and traits, it is indubitably the case that there is utility in considering situational factors when attempting to understand Hindawi's crime.

There can be little question but that the Middle Eastern political climate at the time provided an important context and backdrop to the Hindawi plot. 'Us' and 'them' factors are never far from the surface in relation to any aspect of human behaviour. We are, after all, inherently social creatures (Lieberman, 2013). It is the suggestion of this chapter that there were several significant groups at play in the Hindawi plot – Arab, Israeli, Syrian, Jordanian and Palestinian identities are immediately apparent. Gendered identities, i.e. men and women as placeholders for 'us' and 'them', may also have been important.

Social Identity Theory

The social identity approach is a psychological meta-theory incorporating social identity theory (SIT) and self-categorization theory (SCT) (Haslam, Reicher, & Platow, 2011). The social identity perspective is conspicuous in social psychology because it embarks on analysis from a unique position. Rather than starting with 'the individual in the group', it proceeds from the understanding that one must begin with a consideration of how the group influences the individual (Reicher, Spears, & Haslam, 2010). Social identity was defined by Tajfel (1982) as an individual's knowledge that they belong to certain social groups and that membership of these groups has emotional and value significance for them.[4] The approach focuses on the 'we' that people ascribe to and how, when 'we' self-categorise as a group member, 'we' interact with 'others'. SCT has a focus on the shift behind people's self-categorization from idiosyncratic individuals to individuals as members of collective groups. It is interested in how we behave and how others behave towards us based on our group memberships or social identities. There are useful conceptual tools to consider here in contemplating Nezar Hindawi and the plot to bring down an El Al jet.

It is worth noting at this point that the term 'identity' has multiple meanings in psychology. A given person's identity, in a given context, can be understood as being made up of both individual and collective (or personal and social) components. Sometimes people see themselves, and others, as discrete individuals and at other times we see people as interchangeable members of social groups.

The concept of depersonalisation is key to understanding how people behave towards others as interchangeable members of social groups. Depersonalisation refers to the process whereby an individual shifts from thinking about themselves and others in terms of personal identity (as a discrete 'I') to thinking about themselves and others as interchangeable group members. Depersonalisation is the psychological process behind group-based phenomena such as social stereotyping, ethnocentrism, social influence and social norms (Turner & Oakes, 1986). Moreover, identities and identification processes are active and dynamic. Identities are fluid rather than fixed things and depend upon context. The subjective importance of these components to ourselves, and others, vary as a function of salience (Simon, 2004).

The concept of salience outlines when and why people come to see themselves in terms of a given social identity – for example, as a man, a Jordanian, a Syrian agent, etc. In short, the salience of an identity is a function of fit – whether a given self-categorisation makes sense in the context and as a function of perceiver readiness, and whether they are predisposed to define themselves in terms of a particular identity.

If we think for a moment about the groups that were salient in the Hindawi affair, a couple spring straight to mind in terms of 'them' and us'. There are the Arab and Israeli groups. There are also Palestinian, Jordanian and Syrian groups. There are Syrian agent and freedom-fighter identities. All of these should be considered in trying to understand the actions of Nezar Hindawi – how he understood both himself and Anne-Marie Murphy in the context of the plotted attack is crucial. Depersonalisation, thinking of both himself and Anne-Marie Murphy as interchangeable members of their respective social groups, would seem to have some explanatory utility.

However, thinking in terms of social groups and social identities raises an important question as to which were the salient identities. One particularly

---

[4] For example: I am Irish, a sports fan, an academic, etc.

important identity that I do not believe has been considered in the context of the Hindawi plot is that of gender. Considering gendered identities raises a question as to whether this attack was, in part, an act of misogyny? Smith (2019) raises a question as to whether there is a link between a background of domestic violence and subsequent involvement in terrorist violence. This theme will be revisited in upcoming chapters, but it is interesting to note that Hindawi's parents were living in separate countries on separate continents at the time of his attack. I do not know what his family history is, or was. It would be most interesting to find out.

CONCLUSION

Zimbardo (2007) argues that the belief that there is a gulf between 'good' and 'bad' people is comforting for two reasons. First, 'badness' is given an essence that is present in some people and not in others. Second, dispositional 'badness' allows all of us who understand ourselves as being 'good people' off the hook. 'We' generally understood terrorism in terms of the groups that we belong to, most often in terms of our national groups. If terrorists are grotesque individuals, we can have had no part in creating their badness because their badness is intrinsic to them as perpetrators of terror.

Social psychologists, such as Zimbardo, and socially minded psychologists, such as myself, wonder about the role of situational, social and environmental factors in creating terrorists. It goes without saying that acknowledging the impact of 'the social' in our analysis of terrorism, and other crimes, in no way excuses such crimes. Nor does such an approach make them any less immoral. What a social analysis does facilitate is the useful consideration of a wider range of variables and a fuller engagement with the social forces at play in these heinous crimes.

REFLECTIVE QUESTIONS

1. How do we go about understanding the behaviour of other people, particularly when they have committed acts of terror?
2. What motivates people to commit acts of terror?
3. Why did Nezar Hindawi put his pregnant fiancée on a plane with a bomb?

FURTHER READING

www.shabak.gov.il/english/heritage/affairs/Pages/Anne-MarieMurphyCase.aspx

Syed, M. H. (2002). *Islamic Terrorism, Myth or Reality*. Delhi: Kalpaz Publications.

8

MICHAEL STONE, THE MILLTOWN MASSACRE AND THE CORPORALS' MURDERS

LEARNING OBJECTIVES

By the end of this chapter you should be able to:

- Discuss the relevance of social identity theory to intergroup conflict
- Describe the relevance of self-categorisation to 'the Troubles' in Northern Ireland
- Apply a social identity understanding to a consideration of crowd behaviour

SYNOPSIS OF THE CASE

In Milltown Cemetery, Belfast, on 16 March 1988, Michael Stone, a loyalist paramilitary, carried out a gun and grenade attack on the funeral of an IRA volunteer who had been shot dead by security forces. The attack in Milltown Cemetery resulted in the deaths of three people and injuries to approximately 50 more.

About a week later, when one of those shot dead in 'the Milltown Massacre,' as it subsequently became known, was being buried, two off-duty soldiers strayed into the path of the funeral. The soldiers were attacked by a crowd and murdered shortly afterwards. The attack was captured by TV crews on the scene and by an army surveillance helicopter.

Following these incidents, Hunter, Stringer and Watson (1991) wanted to explore how the Protestant and Catholic communities in Northern Ireland understand political violence. Participants from both communities were shown newsreel of both events and asked to explain what had happened, and why. Each community attributed the violence of their own side to contextual causes and the violence of the other side to internal causes (e.g. 'they were psychos' and 'bloodlust'). These findings, and their implications for understanding terrorism will be considered via a social identity framework.

DESCRIPTION OF THE CASE

The events of March 1988, which culminated in one of the most terrible fortnights of 'the Troubles' in Northern Ireland, can be traced to an ambush that took place in the village of Loughall, County Armagh, Northern Ireland, on 8 May 1987.

Loughall Ambush

Loughall RUC (Royal Ulster Constabulary) base was a part-time, rural, police station that opened twice a day, between 9 and 11 in the morning, and 5 to 7 in the evening. Teams of three constables operated the base. Shortly after 7 pm on 8 May 1987, an IRA unit drove a digger, with a large bomb in its bucket, through the police station's perimeter fence. The digger was followed by a van carrying IRA men armed with automatic weapons. The IRA team detonated the bomb and attacked the police station with gunfire.

The British Army Special Reconnaissance Unit (SRU) and RUC Special Branch had obtained detailed information about the IRA plan and, almost immediately, a hidden British Army SAS (Special Air Services) unit, along with police and troops inside the station, opened fire. The eight IRA members attacking the RUC base were killed. It was the biggest loss of life suffered by the IRA in a single action during the Troubles. Security forces also killed a civilian, who inadvertently drove into the ambush, and another civilian, travelling in the same car, was seriously injured.

The Loughall ambush in 1987 constituted a significant setback for the IRA. In response, a 'spectacular' operation was planned which would restore morale among the IRA membership and their support base.

Gibraltar: Operation Flavius

The intended 'spectacular' target was the Royal Anglian Regiment. The IRA plan was to attack the regiment, using a car bomb, at the changing of the guard ceremony that takes place weekly at the Governor's residence in the British territory of Gibraltar.

The Royal Anglian Regiment had recently completed a tour in Northern Ireland at the time of the planned attack in Gibraltar. Operation Flavius is the codename the British military gave to the counter-terrorist operation, conducted on 6 March 1988, by the SAS, in which three unarmed members of an IRA cell were shot dead. The IRA personnel were Mairéad Farrell[1] (31 years of age), Seán Savage (23) and Daniel McCann (30). Had the IRA unit succeeded, there would have been significant casualties.

It is noteworthy that all three IRA members were unarmed at the time of their deaths. Farrell, Savage and McCann were shot dead by plainclothes SAS soldiers on Winston Churchill Avenue in Gibraltar. Their car, a white Renault 5, in which they had travelled to Gibraltar, did not contain a bomb. However, using keys found in Mairéad Farrell's handbag, police subsequently found a Ford Fiesta which did contain a bomb, shrapnel, timers and detonators in Marbella, about 50 miles from Gibraltar. In the wake of the killings, the security forces stated that they believed that the IRA members had been about to trigger a remote device at the time of their death.

The Milltown Massacre

Following the killings in Gibraltar, the bodies of the three IRA members were returned to Ireland on 14 March for burial at the Milltown Cemetery in Belfast. When the aeroplane carrying the remains landed at Dublin airport, a large crowd met the coffins and then accompanied the procession to Belfast. At the border between the Republic of Ireland and Northern Ireland, a large military and police force met the funeral cortege, causing tension between the authorities and mourners. That same evening, security forces were deployed in the neighbourhoods of the three dead IRA members, and IRA member Kevin McCracken was killed as he tried to engage British forces. Tensions were at fever pitch.

The funeral of Mairéad Farrell, Seán Savage and Daniel McCann took place at the Milltown Cemetery in Belfast on 16 March 1988. Loyalist, Michael Stone, had decided to use the ceremony as an opportunity to murder leading Irish Republicans,

---

[1] A *New York Times* review of the *Frontline* documentary programme, *Death of a Terrorist*' (O'Connor, 1989), contains the following thought-provoking contribution: 'In the end, Miss Farrell's story offers valuable but not very encouraging insight into the seemingly intractable situation. The program leaves us pondering the obvious conclusion: "To the people of Falls Road she was a patriot. To the British she was a terrorist. To her family she was a victim of Irish history."' (Source: www.nytimes.com/1989/06/13/movies/review-television-an-ira-member-from-several-angles.html)

Gerry Adams and Martin McGuinness. Stone went to the funeral mass at St Agnes Church in Andersonstown, Belfast. Unable to get near McGuinness and Adams at the church, Stone decided instead to stage his attack at the cemetery while the coffins were being interred.

In the period immediately preceding the IRA funerals, the Anglo-Irish Secretariat[2] warned the British Government that emotional and difficult scenes were highly likely at the funerals and they requested that security forces be sensitive in their handling of the proceedings. As such, fearing that they could potentially provoke riots, police pulled back from the funerals of the Gibraltar three and this gave loyalist attacker Stone more space than he might otherwise have been allowed.

Stone had made his way to Milltown Cemetery with the funeral cortege and, once there, mingled with the crowd. As the third coffin was being lowered into the grave, Stone attacked mourners with hand grenades and an automatic pistol. By the time Stone ran out of ammunition three people were dead: civilians Thomas McErlean and John Murray, and IRA member Caoimhín Mac Brádaigh. More than 60 other people had been wounded.

In the wake of the attack, Stone attempted to escape on foot but he was caught by mourners. Stone was beaten unconscious and only the timely arrival of RUC officers saved his life. The gun and grenade attack were captured by TV cameras present at the cemetery to cover the funerals.

The Corporals' Murders

Three days after the funerals of the IRA members killed in Gibraltar, the funeral of IRA volunteer Caoimhín Mac Brádaigh, murdered by loyalist Michael Stone, took place. As Mac Brádaigh's funeral cortege travelled up the Andersonstown Road in Belfast, a grey Volkswagen Passat carrying a driver and a passenger drove straight at the head of the funeral procession. The Volkswagen then mounted the footpath but could not get through the funeral procession as the exit was blocked. The car driver then put his vehicle into reverse and tried to escape backwards, away from the crowd. The two soldiers in the car failed to escape at this point because the crowd blocked their way.

The crowd then set on the car. There was a very brief respite when the driver fired a single shot from his handgun. It later transpired that the two men in the car were British Army corporals from the Royal Corps of Signals – Derek Wood and Derek Howes. Howes had been in Northern Ireland for one week. The corporals were dragged from their car, both were carrying service revolvers and British Army identification. They were next taken a couple of hundred yards to the Casement Park sports ground where they were shot dead. TV and British army cameras captured events as they unfolded.

It remains unclear why the corporals drove towards the funeral in the first place.

---

[2] The 1985 Anglo-Irish treaty gave the Irish government an advisory role in Northern Ireland's government, which was represented by the Anglo-Irish Secretariat.

LINKS TO THEORY AND RESEARCH

Recounting the events of March 1988 for the pages of this chapter, I recalled the feelings of bleakness and incomprehension that accompanied many, if not most, news programmes during those days and how, as a teenager, I tried to make sense of what was going on. Why did three young Irish people travel to the shores of the Mediterranean to blow up an apparently innocuous ceremony? Why were they seemingly executed? Why would anyone attack a funeral with hand grenades? And why were those soldiers shot dead in cold blood?

Psychology, and indeed academia generally, has been struggling to make sense of the conflict in Northern Ireland since hostilities began. Gough, Robinson, Kremer and Mitchell (1992) report how, in the 1970s psychiatry sought explanations for the sectarian violence in individual psychopathology. However, the psychiatric perspective, and its associated individualism, was not useful. Freudian psychodynamic perspectives or sociological, economic or political theories could not explain in a satisfactory manner the events that were broadcast with depressing regularity on evening news shows.

As such, many researchers, from the late 1970s on, began instead to apply social identity theory, building on the work of Henri Tajfel (e.g. Tajfel, 1978; Tajfel & Turner, 1979). Tajfel, a Polish Jew who had lost his family to the Holocaust, survived the Second World War because as a member of the French Army he was categorised as a prisoner of war rather than as a Polish Jew. 'Social categorisation and its consequences had an existential personal significance for Tajfel' (Hogg, 2016, p. 4). This focus on intergroup dynamics, the impact of social categorisation and understandings based on 'us' and 'them' provided researchers with a useful box of conceptual tools to tackle the unfolding events in Northern Ireland.

Discussion

The events and killings of March 1988 took place in the context of the prolonged conflict that was 'the Troubles' in Northern Ireland. Northern Ireland is a small place, home to about 1.5 million people. One can describe Northern Ireland as neither a nation nor a state. The six counties that comprise Northern Ireland are politically a part of the United Kingdom, but geographically a part of the island of Ireland (Gough et al., 1992).

Since the Norman invasion, 900 odd years ago, Ireland has been a place where conflict has been sustained, although violence has not always been present (Cairns, 1987). In 1801, the Act of Union declared the Kingdom of Great Britain and Ireland, which persisted to 1921 when the Government of Ireland Act partitioned the island of Ireland into the six counties that constitute Northern Ireland and the remaining 26 counties which constitute the Irish Free State. Partition in Ireland led to a situation where the population of Northern Ireland was, and remains, at odds with itself. Nationalists perceive the inhabitants of the island of Ireland as one nation divided by Britain. Unionists perceive the island as hosting distinct populations and believe the conflict as rooted in a nationalist failure to recognise this fact (Ferguson & McKeown, 2016). In the late 1960s, conflict between nationalists and unionists escalated, with 'the Troubles' beginning in 1968. Between 1968 and the 1998 ceasefire, roughly 3,600 people died in the conflict and some 40–50,000 more were injured. While it is often argued by some that Northern Ireland is now a post-conflict society, at the time of writing, politically motivated violence has not disappeared from the landscape of Northern Ireland and there has been a reported deterioration of community relations and a hardening of oppositional identities (Ferguson & McKeown, 2016).

Social polarisation and stark divisions between 'us' and 'them' characterised the conflict in Northern Ireland. Polarisation is an intrinsic part of drawn-out conflicts and research has shown that social identities perform a central role in both causing and maintaining conflict (Muldoon, 2003). When psychologists refer to social identity, they are referring to who it is that people understand themselves, and others, to be on the basis of shared group memberships. Social identities are crucial in understanding the Milltown massacre and the corporals' murders. Social identities associated with the murders perpetrated by Michael Stone and the deaths of the two British Army corporals include Irish republican identity, loyalist identity, as well as broader British and Irish identities.

It is important to note, for the purpose of this discussion, that the social identity approach is 'situated within a tradition that argues that the operation of psychological processes always depends upon social context. … What good psychology does is to tell us what to look for in our social world. It most definitely does not provide a pretext for ignoring the social world and looking only inside the head' (Haslam, Reicher, & Platow, 2011, p. xvii).

Before going any further, you should note four things with regard to social identity:

- Our sense of self is a function of the groups we belong to. Social identity theorists refer to this sense of self as our social identity.
- The way that groups of people behave towards each other is a function of the norms and values associated with the social identity they derive from their group memberships.
- When social identities are salient, group outcomes are more important to people than outcomes for themselves as individuals.
- What constitutes a group, and how any group behaves, is always linked with social context.

Taking Haslam, Reicher and Platow's (2011) advice on board, important social psychological factors, and normal psychological activities, that contribute to the process of social identity are social categorisation, social identification, and stereotyping the outgroup. These three factors all feed into the salience of a conflict identity and the behaviours associated with a conflict identity (Muldoon, 2003).

Social Categorisation

Some of the earliest academic research that was applied in the context of 'the Troubles' looked at social categorisation and self-categorisation (Jahoda & Harrison, 1975). Jahoda and Harrison employed a colour versus form sorting task to investigate the impact of ethnocentrism in a group of 60 Belfast children aged between 6 and 10. The participants were boys, half from a Catholic background, and half from a Protestant background. All were from areas of the city that were regarded as troubled. A similar 'control' sample was recruited in Edinburgh. The researchers asked the children to take part in a series of game-like tasks. In these types of tasks, children usually shift from sorting items based on colour to sorting items based on shape. This type of shift represents 'normal' developmental enhancement. However, in the Jahoda and Harrison (1975) research, older Belfast children did not make the expected switch from colour sorting to shape sorting. Instead, the Belfast children persisted in sorting on the basis of either red or blue *or* green and orange – the colours of Britishness and Irishness that mark distinction between unionist and nationalist, Protestant and Catholic. Almost half of the boys who took part in the research spontaneously mentioned what their choices meant in terms of political symbolism – many of them reporting that you can't put Catholics with Protestants. This persistence of colour sorting over shape sorting is at odds with consistent findings elsewhere in Europe and North America (Ferguson & McKeown, 2016).

In order to think in terms of 'them' and us' it is first necessary to know who 'they' are. Harris (1986 [1972]) made the argument that, in the context of Northern Ireland, it was crucial to know the identity of others before conversing:

> So important is it … to be able to determine the allegiances of strangers that many Ulster people seem to have developed an extreme sensitivity to signs other than explicit badges that denote the affiliations of those that they meet. Each looks automatically for slight indications from another's name, physical appearance, expression and manner, style of dress and speech idiom to provide the clues that will enable the correct categorisation to be made. (Harris, 1986 [1972], p. 148)

Among the most frequently employed cues used to 'tell' who a person is are the person's address, the school they went to, their names (both first name and surname), and the manner of their speech in terms of both content and accent. For example, whether the city by River Foyle is referred to as 'Derry' or 'Londonderry' is a clear marker as to whether a person is from a nationalist or unionist background.

Thus, 'telling' plays an important role in the management of day-to-day sectarian alienation in Northern Ireland. As suggested by Harris (1986 [1972]) and Burton (1978), in face-to-face interactions, telling can be used as a way of avoiding embarrassment and offence. However, a potentially more sinister significance of telling is that it can be used to determine the identity of another for military, political or criminal activity (Finlay, 1999).

Social Identification

In order to explain the events of March 1988, social identity theory is crucial because the actions of all involved are a function of how the actors identified both themselves and others. Muldoon, McLaughlin, Rougier and Trew (2008) have shown that ingroup identification provides an explanation as to why people engage in paramilitary violence. Having pride in, and love for, the community one identifies with is a key factor for those who make a decision to take part in political violence (Ferguson & Binks, 2015).

As outlined in Chapter 7 when discussing the Hindawi case, the social identity approach is a psychological meta-theory incorporating social identity theory (SIT) and self-categorisation theory (SCT) (Haslam, Reicher, & Platow, 2011). Social identity is defined as an individual's knowledge that they belong to certain social groups, and that this belonging to a group conveys emotional and value significance to them (Tajfel, 1982). Nominal group memberships are not important. It doesn't matter what boxes other people might ascribe one to. What matters are those group memberships that are valued by given individuals in a given context. Social identification pivots on a feeling of belonging.

When the IRA Active Service Unit travelled to Gibraltar to attack the Changing of the Guard ceremony, they weren't attacking other people's sons, they were attacking the British Army. They were indifferent to the personal identities of the targeted soldiers. In Milltown Cemetery, what mattered to the loyalist killer Michael Stone was that 'they' were all nationalists. He wanted to kill and maim, and it didn't matter who in terms of particular individuals, provided it was one of 'them'. Similarly, when the corporals were murdered, the crowd did not see either of the Dereks who died that day as individuals or young men. Rather, the crowd understood the two corporals in terms of their British Army identities. With catastrophic consequences. This tragedy offers a clear example of a situation where social categorisation had life and death significance (Hogg, 2016).

Stereotyping

A stereotype is defined as a 'widely shared and simplified evaluative image of a social group and its members' (Hogg & Vaughan, 2008, p. 47). Stereotypes are, arguably, at the heart of inter-group conflict. Hunter, Stringer and Watson (1991) produced one especially informative study of the events of March 1988, in which the researchers considered the effect of intergroup attributional bias in maintaining intergroup conflict. In psychology, the term 'attribution' describes the processes whereby people assign causes to their own behaviour and the behaviour of others (Hogg & Vaughan, 2008). Hunter et al. (1991) were interested in the effect of intergroup attributional bias in maintaining intergroup conflict. In order to investigate intergroup attributions, and by extension intergroup stereotypes, Hunter et al. recruited 26 Catholic and 21 Protestant students who were attending the University of Ulster. Participants were shown footage of the Michael Stone (loyalist) attack on the funerals of the Gibraltar Three in Milltown Cemetery. Participants were also shown footage of the corporals being attacked at Caoimhín Mac Brádaigh's funeral. Analysis showed that both Catholics and Protestants were between two and a half and four times as likely to attribute the violence of 'the other' group to internal causes. 'They' were understood to commit violence because 'they' were 'psychopaths' or had a 'bloodlust'. This pattern is almost completely reversed when participants describe the violence perpetrated by 'our' side. Ingroup violence was explained in terms of external causes, where phrases like 'retaliation' and 'fear of attack' were prominent.

Hunter et al. (1991) have convincingly shown that attributions for ingroup violence of the type perpetrated against mourners at the Mac Brádaigh funeral and the two British Army corporals serve to absolve ingroup members from responsibility and to justify ingroup perpetration of violence in a way that lays the blame for ingroup violence at the door of the outgroup. After all, 'their' inherently negative characteristics are ultimately the cause of the violence. If 'they' didn't have a 'bloodlust', 'we' wouldn't need to defend ourselves.

Understanding 'the Crowd'

Given the circumstances of the corporals' murders, a final, important aspect of the crimes discussed in this case requires consideration, namely, 'the crowd'. Much of our contemporary understanding regarding crowds is traceable to the seminal work of Le Bon (1995/1895), which argues that crowds are irrational, mindless and uncivilised. The basic idea is that crowds afford individuals anonymity. This anonymity is in turn understood as facilitating the manifestation of antisocial behaviours. These antisocial behaviours spread contagiously, like a wildfire, through the crowd (La Macchia & Louis, 2016). Theorists in the Le Bon tradition understand anonymity as also being behind a perceived stripping away of responsibility and accountability for one's actions. Anonymity thus allows primitive and aggressive instincts an outlet (Hogg, 2016).

This is not a useful way of understanding crowds. A considerably more pragmatic, and useful, way of understanding crowds can be achieved through the application of social identity theorising. Reicher (1996) places social identity and self-categorisation at the heart of crowd behaviour. Social identity and self-categorisation dictate who takes part in crowd behaviour. One has to feel a sense of belonging to the crowd to act as one with the crowd. Social identity in turn dictates the limits of crowd behaviour via group norms.

Depersonalisation is another important concept for understanding the behaviour of crowds, and indeed the behaviour of groups generally. Depersonalisation means that people see themselves, and others, as a category representative rather than in terms of any personal identity. If depersonalisation is behind antisocial and aggressive behaviour, it is only because people have identified with a group that subscribes to these types of behaviour (Hogg, 2016). When soldiers are taking aim, for example, depersonalisation is crucial. Depersonalisation is certainly a useful concept in attempting to understand all of the events described in this chapter, from the ambush on Loughall RUC station to the deaths of the corporals in Belfast.

CONCLUSION

The evidence presented in this chapter shows that social identity plays a key role in instigating and maintaining conflict. Social identity is thus an extremely useful concept to those who want to understand terrorism, war and struggle, not least because it shifts the focus of attention away from individuals and offers a social psychological framework.

Moreover, social identity allows analysis that extends beyond merely describing and understanding. Tajfel (1972) conceived groups to be significantly more than the cause of social problems. He understood groups as custodians of the solution to social problems (Reicher, Spears, & Haslam, 2010). In essence, social identity theory is a theory of social change. There is an optimism intrinsic to social identity theory because the approach appreciates that social change occurs when people mobilise together on the basis of shared social identity: 'The approach is about both understanding the world and changing it. In a period where we are all too often told that we are at "the end of history", social identity theories insist not only that our unequal society can be challenged but also how that can be achieved' (Reicher et al., 2010, p. 61).

In the context of the Northern Ireland conflict, social identity theorists recognise the central role identity can play for those who would negotiate adversity via a process of meaning making (Muldoon & Lowe, 2012). Groups are not static things. Rather, they evolve over time as a consequence of social and contextual factors, their trajectories determined by a constant working on 'who we are' (Wakefield, Bowe, Kellezi, McNamara, & Stevenson, 2019). In essence, this working on who we are, understood as an active process of identity entrepreneurship, is what leadership, political and otherwise, is about (Haslam, Reicher, & Platow, 2011). Groups can actively and/or strategically extend their boundaries to render themselves more inclusive (Wakefield et al., 2019). This is knowledge that indeed offers the potential to change the world. For the better.

REFLECTIVE QUESTIONS

1. Are the crimes described in this chapter explicable in terms of individual psychology?
2. Why would anyone attack a funeral with hand grenades?
3. Is the concept of depersonalisation one that could be generalised to other crime contexts?

FURTHER READING

Reicher, S., Spears, R., & Haslam, S. A. (2010). The social identity approach in social psychology. In M. Wetherell & C. Talpede Mohanty (Eds.), *The Sage Handbook of Identities*. London: Sage.

Stott, C., Drury, J., & Reicher, S. (2016). On the role of a social identity analysis in articulating structure and collective action: The 2011 riots in Tottenham and Hackney. *The British Journal of Criminology, 57*(4), 964–981. doi:10.1093/bjc/azw036

9

THE MANCHESTER ARENA BOMBING

LEARNING OBJECTIVES

By the end of this chapter you should be able to:

- Outline a brief history of suicide bombing
- Discuss radicalisation
- Describe the role of terror management in suicide bombing
- Discuss the role of social and contextual factors in suicide attacks

SYNOPSIS OF THE CASE

On the night of 22 May 2017, 22 people were killed and at least 800 more were injured in the Manchester Arena terrorist attack, when a lone suicide bomber detonated explosives as mostly teenage fans were leaving an Ariana Grande concert. The bomber, Salman Abedi, was a local man of Libyan descent. He came from quite a religious background and was known as a quiet boy; albeit a quiet boy whose attitude wasn't the best. Religious fundamentalism seems to have played a crucial part in his crime. One useful perspective that has a bearing on this case is Black's (2004) sociological view that physical proximity in tandem with social distance creates a space in which terrorism can exist.

DESCRIPTION OF THE CASE

Salman Abedi was 22 years old, from Didsbury in Manchester, born to Libyan refugees who had escaped the Gadaffi regime. On the evening of 22 May 2017, Abedi walked into the foyer of the Manchester Arena and blew himself up. In doing so, he murdered 22 people and injured 800 more. Abedi's targets were an audience of predominantly young girls attending an Ariana Grande concert.

Abedi's father, Ramadan, had been a security official in Tripoli. When Ramadan fell foul of the Libyan authorities, the family fled their homeland, first to Saudi Arabia, and then on to Manchester via London. It is reported that the Abedi children were raised as 'strict' Muslims by their father. As a youngster, Salman was apparently a good football player and a boy who loved sport. He supported his local football team and enjoyed cricket.

Abedi had an older brother, Ismail, a younger brother, Hashim, and a younger sister, Jomena. All of the Abedi children attended local schools in Manchester and the Abedi family attended the moderate Didsbury mosque. The facts, as we have them, about the youthful Salman Abedi, seem pretty innocuous. He was not exceptional at school. It appears that he was bullied and nicknamed 'Dumbo' because of his sticking-out ears.

In 2011, the Arab Spring protests and uprising spread to Libya. At this time, Salman's father returned to his native Libya in order to join the fight against the Gadaffi regime. Salman was 16 or 17 years of age. Acquaintances of the Abedi family have said that in his father's absence, Salman Abedi fell in with some 'pretty wild' company. It is reported that Salman was a heavy cannabis user, smoking weed on a daily basis. He also had a taste for vodka and enjoyed clubbing. In a sense, this Salman Abedi was a 'Dr Jekyll'-type character, a young man apparently rebelling against his strict religious background. But there was also a distinctly 'Mr Hyde' side to Salman Abedi. Following his father's departure for Libya and the conflict there, in 2011 Salman and his brother Hashim were invited to visit Libya several times. The teenage Abedi boys were photographed with weapons and the pictures were distributed both personally by the boys and on social media. It is likely that they were not shielded from the conflict. Indeed, the probability is that both boys witnessed the horrors of the Libyan civil war up close.

So, the teenage Salman Abedi was clubbing and smoking weed in Manchester and, at the same time, visiting a Libyan war zone. In Libya, Abedi encountered a version of Salafist Islam that was hard-line and aggressive. One extraordinary aspect of this case is that, given their frequent travel to a war-zone, no member of the Abedi family was ever referred to Prevent, the British government's counter-terrorism agency tasked with preventing vulnerable people from becoming terrorists or supporting terrorism.

It is notable that Salman Abedi has been recalled by acquaintances as a young man who had issues with women, especially female staff at the college he was attending. In 2012, he punched a young woman in the head because he considered her skirt was too short. He was able to avoid prosecution because the case was dealt with through restorative justice, a process whereby perpetrators and victims are brought together to discuss the impact of the offence. By owning up to issues with his anger, Abedi avoided conviction, and it may be that he also avoided a referral to Prevent.

As time passed, Salman Abedi continued to visit Libya from his Manchester home. In one of those strange twists of fate, the Abedi brothers were rescued, in 2014, from heavy fighting in Tripoli by the British Navy, when British nationals were evacuated aboard *HMS Enterprise*. In 2017, Salman Abedi was again back with his parents in Libya. His father was unhappy about the company Salman was keeping in Manchester and took Salman's passport away. The passport was only returned when Salman told his father that he planned to go on pilgrimage to Mecca. In mid-May 2017, Salman Abedi left Libya, flying back to Manchester via Dusseldorf on 19 May. That Friday evening Abedi bought the rucksack he would subsequently pack with explosives.

The following Monday, Abedi travelled to Manchester Arena where Ariana Grande's 'Dangerous Woman' tour was playing to 14,200 concert goers. At 10.31 pm Salman Abedi detonated the improvised explosive device (IED) he had packed into his rucksack. The device was packed with nuts and bolts, intended to act as shrapnel to wound and kill as many people as possible. People up to 20 metres from the explosion were killed. The survivor closest to the blast was Martin Hibbert, who was left paralysed from the waist down as a result of 22 shrapnel wounds. Martin had largely shielded his daughter, Eve, from the blast. However, the bomb still left Eve with a catastrophic brain injury. These were just two of the 800 injured; 22 others were dead. Saffie Roussos, aged 8, attending the concert with her mother and sister, was the youngest to die.

LINKS TO THEORY AND RESEARCH

One of the biggest problems facing those wishing to study acts of suicidal terrorism, and those who perpetrate it, is that the individuals who commit such acts are no longer alive and researchers must depend on secondary material (Taylor, 2018). One useful place to begin thinking about suicide terrorism is with a consideration of the tactic and its history.

The History of Suicide Bombing

The murder of Tsar Alexander II in St Petersburg on 1 March 1881 was the world's first suicide bombing. Prior attempts to assassinate the Tsar had shown that Alexander II was not an easy man to kill. Russian revolutionaries had concluded that the only way to succeed was to detonate an explosive device so close to the Tsar that the assassin would die in the attempt (Overton, 2019).

On his final day, the Tsar was returning from reviewing his Imperial Horse Guards in a secure coach when Nykolai Rysakov threw a homemade bomb under the hooves of the horses pulling the coach. The bomb exploded, fatally wounding two of the coach party, but the Tsar only suffered a slight cut to one of his hands.

While Alexander II was inspecting the damage to his carriage, Ignaty Grinevitsky threw a second bomb at the Tsar's feet. The ensuing explosion was fatal for both men. The device that killed Tsar Alexander II weighed 5lbs and had a blast range of one metre. The Narodnaya Volya revolutionary group, to which both Rysakov and Grinevitsky belonged, is thus the first terrorist organisation to successfully employ suicide as a means to murder. Ostensibly socialist and secular, there is an argument that these Russian revolutionaries were continuing 'religion by other means: after all, the destruction of one world to create another is a hallmark of faith' (Overton, 2019, p. 22).

Religious belief was certainly a factor in the suicide bombings conducted by the Japanese military in the Second World War. Between October 1944 and August 1945 more than 3,000 Japanese pilots undertook Kamikaze attacks. Many more soldiers and sailors used suicide vests and submarine bombs as a conveyance to the hereafter, as they hurled themselves at Allied Forces. Reverence towards the Emperor was key. Many Japanese troops prayed to the Emperor daily, facing towards the Imperial palace as they did so (Overton, 2019).

Suicide attacks became integrated into military strategising as a means for materially and numerically inferior forces to level the odds against stronger foes. In the 1980s, suicide attacks began to be used by terrorist groups striving to gain a strategic advantage. In 1983, an attack by two suicide bombers driving trucks loaded with explosives at the US Marine Corps barracks in Beirut killed hundreds of troops (Harmon, Mujik, Kaukinen, & Weir, 2018). Attacks like this one demonstrated that low-tech suicide missions could take many lives for the cost of a few.

In the period between 1982 and 2013, 40 distinct organisations carried out suicide attacks. Until 2000 the Liberation Tigers of Tamil Eelam (LTTE) were behind more suicide attacks than any other organisation (Harmon et al., 2018). It is noteworthy that the Tamil Tigers were a secular organisation and that it is they who perfected the suicide belt. In the 1980s and 1990s, most suicide attacks were directed against military targets. Only 17.2% of targets were civilian.

September 11, 2001 and the Al-Qaeda attacks on the World Trade Center was a watershed moment in the history of suicide bombing. Overnight, hijacked aeroplanes had become the most lethal weapons of suicide attack. The rate of suicide attacks also exploded in 2001. Between 2001 and 2005 there were more suicide attacks than in the previous 30 years (Harmon et al., 2018).

Another crucial change in suicide terrorism was that whereas in the period 1991–2001 only 25% of suicide attacks across the globe were perpetrated by Sunni militants, in the ten years after 9/11, 98% of suicide attacks were perpetrated by Sunni Salafists – 3,155 suicide attacks in total. 'A rise so extreme that today, the suicide bomb is a metonym for Sunni Islamist terror, a dark icon for the twenty-first century. In the minds of many, an entire religion has been tainted by a small sector of a small group of one strand of Islam' (Overton, 2019, p. 193).

The distinguishing quality of all terrorism, including suicide terrorism, is that it has a political context that other crimes generally lack. Furthermore, as mentioned elsewhere in this volume, the terms 'terror' and 'terrorist' lack universally agreed definitions and tend to be used for pejorative rather than descriptive purposes (Taylor, 2018). The psychology of terrorism is political.

One useful way of defining terrorists is as groups of people, usually small in number, who use violence or the threat of violence to attain political goals: 'Acts of terror are symbolic, that is, the targets of terrorists are symbols of the state or of social norms and structure' (Cottam et al., 2010, p. 264). The goal of terrorism is to gain change by violence. Suicide terror attacks are about killing as many people as possible in order to advance the cause of the perpetrators. Maximisation of lethality is seen as key (Overton, 2019) and language is crucial to a legitimising construction of suicide bombing (Gill, 2007).

Radicalisation

The word 'radicalisation' is often used to describe the origins of terrorism in those who commit and are associated with it. We can think of 'radicalisation' as exposure to, and sympathy with, radical ideology. A problem with the term is that, when using it, commentators often don't distinguish between holding radical views and expressing these views through violence. It is important to note that while we can identify factors that seem to relate to vulnerability to radicalisation, there is insufficient evidence at present to definitively resolve the issue (Taylor, 2018).

Looking at Islamic radicalisation, those who become involved in Islamic terror tend to believe that Islam is under attack, that the attack is a form of crusade, and that the attack is led by the USA. Jihadists, referred to as 'terrorists' by the West, are defending Islam against this attack. The actions taken by jihadists are believed to be in defence of Islam. Acts of Islamic terror are believed to be proportional, just, and have religious sanction. Furthermore, it is understood to be the duty of good Muslims to support these actions (Taylor, 2018).

Individual Factors

In terms of individual psychology, three of the most significant radicalisation factors relating to ideology are the dehumanisation of the opponent, enhanced group identification (e.g. with the Ummah, or the global Muslim community) and a focus on martyrdom. This is perhaps also important with other groups, such as the Tamil Tigers (Taylor, 2018).

Social Factors

In terms of social context, the most significant factor of radicalisation is the presence of a strong peer group. The peer group can be either real or virtual (Nesser, 2004). This peer group offers a sense of belonging and it confers a sense of meaning on those who are radicalised. The peer group also offers a space where people can express a reaction to perceived (by the peer group) injustices elsewhere (Slootman & Tillie, 2006).

It is important to note that identification with a group which perceives itself as a victim can radicalise a person who has not themselves directly experienced any grievance (e.g. Masuda et al., 2016). This would seem to be the case with Salman Abedi.

Leaders and Charismatic Figures

Research indicates that social involvement with charismatic leaders within peer groups can be a significant factor in radicalisation. For example, jihadis returning from Afghanistan, Pakistan, the Balkans and Somalia often play important roles as inspirational peer group figures in families, mosques and community settings (Change Institute, 2008). Indeed, 'the current phenomena of jihadist salafist networks may be analysed as a social movement in itself as well as one expression of broader, highly diverse and globalised social movements' (Change Institute, 2008, p. 21).

Transformative Events

A transformative event can be significant in a person's pathway towards radicalisation, and it is worth noting that this transformative event does not necessarily have be a violent one (Taylor, 2018). It is also the case that personal grievances do not generally lead to violent terrorist action unless such grievances are understood to be part of a larger group grievance (McCauley & Moskalenko, 2008).

It is also important to note that, taken individually, the factors outlined above do not offer much by way of predictive value. These factors cannot in themselves explain why people become terrorists. However, taken together, they can help us to contextualise an 'openness' to involvement with terrorism or radicalisation.

In their efforts to radicalise potential recruits, groups generally deploy euphemistic language when describing those who conduct suicide attacks on their behalf. The language of martyrdom and sacrifice is common (Routledge & Arndt, 2008). For those of us who believe that the language of murder is more appropriate than the language of martyrdom, there is a war of understanding with regard to suicide attacks that has yet to fully play out. Attempting to counter a martyrdom narrative with a murder narrative seems a useful place to start. There is also an argument that governments and authorities need to support and empower voices that challenge terrorist rhetoric (Change Institute, 2008, p. 25).

The Link between Foreign Policy and Group Threat

It is important to note that Salman Abedi was a Manchester boy. Homegrown jihadists pose a lethally problematic puzzle to the governments of liberal Western democracies. Jihad is more often associated with ideology than grievance, but in order to understand homegrown jihadists' grievances, Western foreign policy must be considered (McCauley, 2018).

The invasion of Iraq by Coalition forces convinced many people that Osama bin Laden's contention that Islam was under attack by the West was correct. The Iraq war showed that foreign and domestic policies are linked, and undoubtedly motivated some young British Muslims to become involved in terror (Manningham-Buller, 2011).

Radicalisation as a function of perceived threat has two important aspects to consider. The first aspect is domestic, and the second originates overseas. Domestically, the marginalisation of Muslim immigrants has created a space in which jihadi ideas can thrive and mobilise (Renard & Coolsaet, 2018). Anti-immigrant sentiment, prejudice and discrimination with regard to housing, employment and educational opportunities have caused significant numbers of young Muslim immigrants in Western countries to identify as Muslim rather than as citizens of the countries in which they reside. Second-generation Muslims often have weak ties with the countries of their forebears. If the wider population of the nations in which second-generation Muslims are born – France, Belgium or the UK, for example – see these second-generation citizens as 'Muslims' rather than as fellow French, Belgian or British nationals, it is hardly surprising that these same individuals see themselves as part of the global Muslim community rather than as French, Belgian or British (Roy, 2017). Hence, when individuals who identify with the Ummah perceive the Ummah to be under attack, it is unsurprising that they perceive themselves as also being threatened. The 'war on terror' is seen as a war on Islam and the perceived suffering of the Ummah is harnessed as a justification for violence.

Islam and Suicide Bombing

Group identities and identification with threatened groups play a role in suicide bombing. But what about the attitude of the groups in whose name suicide bombers act? It is notable that about one-third of US Muslim respondents believe that the war on terror is a war on Islam (Fajmonova, Moskalenko, & McCauley, 2017) and about 10% of those US Muslims surveyed believed that suicide bombing was justified. In practical terms, considered at a population level, 10% of US Muslims translates to some hundred thousand people.

Polling of European Muslim opinion with regard to suicide bombing is scant. McCauley (2018) reports that what information is available suggests that extremist opinions among European Muslims are on a par with those of US Muslims. As with the US, a small percentage in population terms quickly translates to significant numbers of people.

This coming together of identification and support gives space for a narrative to develop where the perceived suffering of the Ummah is a vehicle which malcontents can harness in order to cobble together a Walter Mitty-like tale where the disaffected can play the role of hero and saviour in dramas of their own making. There might be a certain charm to this if it were not for the trail of devastation and innocent lives lost that these deadly but deluded and unhappy individuals leave in their wake. The perceived suffering of the Ummah allows the 'individual zero to become an avenging hero' (McCauley, 2018, p. 5).

An analysis conducted by Roy (2017) of homegrown French jihadists describes the typical Islamic terrorist as a young second-generation immigrant or convert. According to Roy, the typical jihadi is generally a person with a background in petty crime and little or no religious education. Their conversion, or reconversion, has tended to be rapid and is more likely to have been with a group of friends, or online, than in a mosque. The new-found religiosity is worn ostentatiously and exhibited loudly, 'but does not necessarily correspond to immersion in religious practice' (Roy, 2017, p. 32). Furthermore, according to Roy, the link between the jihadi and 'their people' is often an imaginary one. Although he wrote before the Manchester attack, Roy could have been talking about Salman Abedi.

Islam and Suicide

An aspect of suicide terror that is all too easy to overlook is the suicide itself. Among the general population, most people who kill themselves will have experienced some type of psychiatric disorder (Holmes, 2010). On average, Muslims commit suicide less than non-Muslims. This is perhaps a function of the strict Islamic law regarding suicide (it is forbidden) and the expectation that those who do commit suicide will potentially be facing eternity in hell (Chel'loob, 2019). However, there is one, but only one, way for the believer in Islam to kill themselves without the threat of eternal hellfire – that is if they kill themselves in 'defence' of Islam (Chel'loob, 2019).

Terrorism and Mental Illness

In looking at terrorism generally, there is a consensus that approaches which frame terrorism in terms of psychopathology, abnormality or personality traits are unhelpful in understanding or predicting terrorist behaviour (Taylor, 2018). In a similar vein, the view that suicide bombers are suicidal has been challenged by psychologists, who argue that identity processes, rather than psychopathological or demographic factors, are the source of motivation for suicide terrorism (Cottam et al., 2010). It seems likely that attribution errors, whereby we explain other people's behaviour in dispositional terms, are at play in the many studies of terrorism where observers' expectations, based on observed individual behaviour, dominate the frame (Ward, 2018). Thus, coming full circle, we return to social, contextual and situational factors.

Terror Management Theory

One site where the social and the psychological can usefully be brought together is in thinking about suicide bombing as terror management. All human beings eventually become aware that death is inevitable. Terror Management Theory (TMT) states that people turn to cultural belief systems in order to deal with the certainty of their own deaths. The idea is that people can gain a sense of their own immortality by investing in a group that will outlast their own lives: 'A symbolic sense of self that transcends mortality' (Routeledge & Arndt, 2008, p. 532). One way that people can build a self-narrative around suicide is through ideas of 'self-sacrifice' for one's country or group. Self-sacrifice through participation in war is one meme with which we are all familiar in the West: dying for one's country. In a relatively recent study, Routledge and Arndt (2008) were able to show that self-sacrifice is, at least in part, a way for individuals to defend against the awareness of death. At this point, we return to the important war of understanding, introduced earlier, with regard to suicide attacks, which has yet to fully play out. This war of understanding, whereby we attempt to counter a martyrdom narrative with a murder narrative, has a long and worthy history. Following the opening of the New Menin Gate, built and opened in 1927 to commemorate the 54,896 British and Commonwealth soldiers whose bodies were never found following the Battle of Ypres in the First World War, the English war poets Siegfried Sassoon and Wilfred Owen wrote famous and moving poems ('On Passing the New Menin Gate' and 'Dulce Et Decorum Est' respectively) that critiqued the idea that it is an honour to die for your country. It is the same old lie, albeit in modern garb, that we need to argue against in terms of martyrdom.

Domestic Violence and Misogyny

It is a striking fact that the vast majority of suicide bombers are men. Yet, gender is a factor that is seldom considered in the discourse around terrorism. Smith (2019) reports that five of the six who perpetrated the attacks on Westminster Bridge and Finsbury Park in London and at the Manchester Arena had a history of attacks against women relatives. Salman Abedi, as outlined above, had assaulted a young woman in his college because of his views about her clothing. Smith (2019) argues that although it is not surprising that violent men commit violent acts, we should regard those who perpetrate domestic violence, in their 'private' spheres, as being further along the path to committing public acts of violence. Smith argues that a history of domestic violence is relevant to the consideration of terrorists and terrorism. Furthermore, Smith argues that terrorism should be considered in terms of gendered, male violence. It is certainly the case that the Manchester Arena attack seems to fit the profile of a misogynistic act of terror.

CONCLUSION

Black (2004) argues that terrorism, and the use of violence generally, is about social control. Those who commit acts of terror, according to Black, see themselves as representing an aggrieved group. Moreover, Black regards terrorists as civilians who attack other civilians, when the other civilians are perceived as belonging to superior social groups. From this view, terrorism, including suicide terror, is about social control from below (Baumgartner, 1984).

For my part, I think it is important to distinguish between radical ideas and radical actions. Abedi's sister claims that witnessing Muslim children dying on TV had a big impact on her brother. That's fair enough. Many millions of people share grievances of one kind or another and many of those grievances are, in my opinion, justified. What is not justified, under any circumstances, and regardless of opinion, is murder. No religion or government anywhere permits murder. Political activism is perfectly acceptable and is more likely to succeed than violence ever will (McCauley, 2018). Because of that fact, the focus of our argument should be against violence rather than against grievance. As such, we need to find ways to shift the discourse from martyr to murderer.

Black (2004) says that terrorism can only exist where there is physical proximity and, at the same time, social distance. At present, because of the physical proximity between people separated by social gulfs, terrorism has a space in which to thrive. The internet and affordable air travel have enormously shrunk the physical space of our world. As the social space between us also shrinks, so will the conditions that foster terrorism begin to dissolve. As people continue to intermingle, the social space between polarised groups must weaken and eventually disappear. According to Black, the eventual, and inevitable, fate of terrorism is sociological death. We should attempt to hurry the process along by arguing as vigorously as possible against violence. It is simply not as effective as activism.

REFLECTIVE QUESTIONS

1. Is suicide bombing about suicide?
2. Was the Manchester Arena attack a misogynistic attack?
3. Should we look to individuals, context, or both when seeking to understand suicide attacks?
4. Has 'Islamic' terror got anything to do with religion?

FURTHER READING

Black, D. (2004). The geometry of terrorism. *Sociological Theory, 22*(1), 14–25. doi:10.1111/j.1467-9558.2004.00201.x

Overton, I. (2019). *The Price of Paradise*. London: Hachette UK.

Smith, J. (2019). *Home-Grown: How Domestic Violence Turns Men into Terrorists*. London: Riverrun.

10

THE UNABOMBER

LEARNING OBJECTIVES

By the end of this chapter you should be able to:

- Make an argument as to why ethics are important in psychological research
- Discuss the role of insanity and mental health with regard to terrorism
- Consider the importance of profiling in apprehending the Unabomber

SYNOPSIS OF THE CASE

'Ted' Kaczynski, aka the Unabomber, killed three individuals and wounded 23 people over a period of almost 20 years in one-man terrorist attacks against society. In 1995, after decades of terrorist activity, Kaczynski demanded that his 'manifesto' be published verbatim – or the bombings would continue. The *New York Times* and *Washington Post* printed his rant against modern technological culture, but his brother David recognised Kaczynski's writing style, and this ultimately led to the Unabomber's arrest and conviction.

This case is a good illustration of the important role of psychopathology in understanding some terrorist crimes, since a range of forensic psychologists and psychiatrists diagnosed Kaczynski as suffering from mental illness. The potential impact of Kaczynski's participation, as an adolescent, in research conducted by the controversial psychologist Henry Murray will also be considered, as will offender profiling.

DESCRIPTION OF THE CASE

The Unabomber is a name, given by the Federal Bureau of Investigation, to a domestic American terrorist, Ted Kaczynski. The Unabomber name derives from the fact that the bomber's early victims were associated with either universities or airlines.

Theodore (Ted) Kaczynski was born in Chicago on 22 May 1942 into a working-class Polish family. His brother, and only sibling, David was born two years later. Ted's father, also Theodore but known as 'Turk', worked in the family sausage business. Both Ted's parents were unusual in the Polish community of the time as a consequence of their love of books and their agnosticism. Turk, in particular, but also Ted's mother, Wanda, were noted for their enthusiasm for learning and both were ambitious for their children.

It seems that Ted Kaczynski had quite a 'normal' childhood:

At age two, his paediatrician wrote that he 'plays well with other children'. At eight, the medical records noted that Kaczynski, then attending nearby Sherman Elementary School, was 'healthy' and 'well adjusted'; at nine, that he 'plays well with children in school and [the] neighbourhood. Very happy'; at ten, 'appetite, activity and general adjustment are all quite good'; at eleven, he 'presents no behaviour problems'; at twelve, he 'does well socially'. In the fifth grade, after the school guidance counsellor, Vera Frye, had given him an IQ test, she observed that Ted was entirely normal, telling his mother (as Wanda told the *Washington Post*) that 'he had a strong sense of security, which surprised me. … She said he could be whatever he wanted to be. … He was the cat's whiskers.' (Chase, 2003, p. 161)

Ted's life changed for ever soon after his fifth-grade assessment. The IQ test administered by Vera Frye delivered Ted a 'genius' score of 167. As a consequence, and with both parental and school authority consent, Ted was skipped straight into the seventh grade. His life never recovered. Ted became the youngest boy in his class and he instantly became a social outsider. Ted's intellect became a badge of honour for his parents and they pushed him relentlessly. Unsurprisingly, Ted's academic performance was negatively correlated with his social integration. The more Ted succeeded academically the more isolated from his peers he became socially.

Then it happened again. During his sophomore year, the high school administration at Evergreen Park High recommended that Ted skip his junior year. His parents agreed. Ted Kaczynski was now two years younger than most of his classmates and even more of an outcast. Regarded by many of his peers as a 'freak', according to his own account, Ted's social isolation was mushrooming.

At 16 years of age, Ted won a place at Harvard University, majoring in mathematics, where he began his studies in September 1958. Harvard, at the time, was an impersonal place where 'preppies', privately schooled students from privileged Ivy League backgrounds, rubbed along uncomfortably with 'wonks', lowly high school graduates. Ted had moved to a world of patricians and plebs where former high school students were particularly isolated, with most of them coming from other states, in contrast to the former prep school students who tended to have grown up nearby. Yet, Ted seemed to be doing OK. During his freshman year, his grades evidenced a balanced student who was on-track to realise his potential. The health services doctor who performed the medical exam that all freshmen underwent, reported: 'Good impression created. Attractive, mature for age, relaxed. ... Talks easily, fluently and pleasantly ... likes people and gets on with them. ... Exceedingly stable, well integrated and feels secure within himself. Usually very adaptable. May have many achievements and satisfactions' (Chase, 2003, p. 184)

Thus, we have a sense of Kaczynski as a somewhat conflicted figure. At 16 years of age, Ted was an outsider who was perceived as integrated, capable and well-adjusted by the educational authorities that he encountered. He was a child of the Cold War. He was much younger than most of his classmates, he had skipped two years at school, he was a loner and a mathematician. There are many people who share some or all of these characteristics.

An unusual aspect of Ted Kaczynski's time in Harvard was his participation in a series of experiments entitled 'Multiform Assessments of Personality Development among Gifted College Men', conducted by a team of psychologists under the leadership of Professor Henry A. Murray of the Department of Social Relations. In common with others who took part, Kaczynski was recruited from his Harvard class, as a sophomore, and continued to participate in Murray's research over a period of three years. Each participant contributed about 200 hours to the research.

Henry Murray, born in New York City, was a Harvard professor of psychology, famed for his classic 1938 work, *Explorations in Personality*. During the Second World War, Murray had served with the Office of Strategic Services (OSS), the precursor to the Central Intelligence Agency (CIA), where he had held the rank of Lieutenant Colonel and was responsible for the selection of secret agents. Following the Second World War, the aristocratic Murray, who had both a medical degree and a PhD in biochemistry, returned to his academic career at Harvard. Here, Murray became a Cold War warrior, focused on serving America's defence interests, paying particular attention to 'brainwashing'. It was in this context that Murray's path crossed with the ill-starred and very young Ted Kaczynski.

'Brainwashing' is the idea, originating in the Cold War, that the thoughts and beliefs of another person can be altered, against that person's will, through the application of psychological techniques. The CIA believed that the Soviets had developed these techniques and, consequently, the Americans needed to master them too. In the context of national defence, social science, including psychology, became a vehicle whose purpose was not merely to understand humanity, but to control it too. To this end, the CIA and US establishment pumped huge amounts of money into psychological research. Professor Henry Murray and the Harvard Psychological Clinic were among the beneficiaries of this funding.

The purpose of Murray's research was to harness standardised tests and projective measures with intensive study of social interaction, responses to stress, and memory in order to further understand personality in a manner that was useful to the armed forces. The Rockefeller Foundation funded the research, which began in 1949 and built on prior research that had commenced in 1941. Murray recruited 20 students, all men, from each of the Harvard cohorts of 1942, 1952, 1955, 1959 and 1962. One of these recruits was the 16-year-old Ted Kaczynski[1].

It is now apparent that the research in which Ted Kaczynski participated was deeply unethical. When the extent of Nazi medical experimentation in the Second World War became known, the Allied forces sent those Nazi doctors involved in murderous human trials, including high altitude, hypothermia and seawater experiments, for trial at the International Military Tribunal at Nuremberg. One important outcome of the 'Doctors' Trial' was the publication of the Nuremberg Code, which is probably the most important document in the history of the ethics of medical research. The first article of the code states that 'The voluntary consent of the human subject is absolutely essential'.

In the autumn of 1959, Ted Kaczynski received the an invitation to take part in the research: 'Would you be willing to contribute to the solution of certain psychological problems (parts of an ongoing program of research in the development of personality) by serving as a subject in a series of experiments or taking a number of tests (average about 2 hours a week) through the academic year (at the current College rate per hour)?' Those who volunteered were given a battery of tests. The researchers were seeking to recruit a proportion of very well-adjusted students, a group of average students, and a group of very alienated students. Screening identified Kaczynski as the most alienated student of the cohort. It is noteworthy that Kaczynski was not enrolled on the psychology course where recruitment was advertised, and it may be that Murray was aware of Kaczynski's isolation and alienation, and considered him a prime candidate, going out of his way to recruit Kaczynski.

The consent form used in the Murray study did not say that the study would last three years, it did not say that the students would be deceived, and it did not say anything about the possible effects of the study. The study asked participants to write an essay about their personal philosophies. Researchers then measured physiological responses while confederates used the essays as a basis to launch personal attacks and insults on participants with the specific aim of humiliating and denigrating participants. Ted Kaczynski took part in this research for more than 200 hours and there seems little doubt that participation had a deleterious impact on his mental health and emotional well-being.

Notwithstanding his participation in the Murray studies, Kaczynski graduated from Harvard with a degree in Maths in 1962, going on to gain a Master's and a

---

[1] It may be that the Harvard research that recruited Kaczynski was part of a wider programme of research, indemnified by the American government, into mind control that was called the MK ULTRA project. If you are interested in true conspiracies, this is well worth investigating.

PhD in the same subject from the University of Michigan. In 1967, Kaczynski became the youngest assistant professor in The University of California, Berkeley. He worked at Berkeley for two years, teaching calculus, before retiring without explanation in June 1969.

Ted Kaczynski then drifted for a couple of years, finally settling near Lincoln, Montana, in 1971, where he built a log cabin (10 × 12 feet) and set out on a reclusive, self-sufficient and 'returned to nature' lifestyle. He hunted, farmed and worked in a range of odd jobs, supplementing his meagre earnings with parental handouts.

By 1975, Ted had become increasingly frustrated with the developments he saw around him. His response was a violent one. Kaczynski 'spiked' trees, driving a metal nail into a tree at a point where a logger's chainsaw would be likely to hit it, resulting in exploding chainsaws and flying shrapnel. 'Monkeywrenching' was another pursuit, where he would pour sugar into the petrol tanks of bulldozers and other machinery. His initial targets were machinery rather than people, but that was not to last.

According to his own diaries, Kaczynski then moved on to attacking the holiday homes of his neighbours, shooting at helicopters and stretching wire between trees in the hope of decapitating dirt bikers or snowmobilers. His activities were ostensibly in defence of the environment, although according to the diaries, 'revenge' was also a significant motivating factor. The violence quickly escalated. In 1978, Kaczynski began using mail bombs. His first target was a Northwestern University professor of engineering. The professor escaped injury when he refused the package as it was marked 'return to sender' and he recognised that he had not sent it. Rather, it was the unfortunate security guard who was injured when he opened the package and the bomb exploded.

By the end of the following year, Kaczynski had attempted two more bombings, one at Northwestern and another targeting an American Airlines flight, where the bomb was armed with a pressure trigger that caused it to explode at altitude. Had this bomb detonated correctly, it was sufficiently powerful to have destroyed Flight 444, a Boeing 727 flying from Chicago to Washington. This bombing was a watershed in so far as it brought the Unabomber to the attention of the FBI. Airline bombing is a federal crime. In 1980, an attack on the president of United Airlines resulted in the FBI forming the UNABOM task force.

As time went by, the Unabomber's devices became increasingly lethal. In December 1985, the Unabomber killed his first victim. Hugh Scrutton, the owner of a computer shop in Sacramento, died when he was eviscerated by a Kaczynski device. A second computer shop owner was targeted in Salt Lake City, but the intended victim survived the blast. This time, a witness saw Kaczynski planting his device and they were able to give a fairly accurate description of him to the FBI. It must have given him a fright because despite the fact that he kept on testing his explosives, there was a six-year hiatus before his next attack.

In 1993 the Unabomber attacked two more professors in San Francisco and Connecticut. In December 1994 and April 1995, Kaczynski struck again, with deadly consequences. Just before Christmas in 1994 Thomas J. Mosser, a 50-year-old advertising executive, died when he opened a package that was addressed to him. In April 1995, Gilbert Murray, a Californian Forestry Association official, was murdered by a device similar to the one that had killed Mosser. Gilbert Murray was so badly injured by the bomb that his family were only allowed to touch his feet and legs below the knee as a last gesture of goodbye. Gilbert Murray was the Unabomber's final victim. In total, before his apprehension, the Unabomber committed 14 attacks, used 16 bombs, murdered three people and injured 23 more.

In June 1995, the *New York Times*, *Washington Post*, and *Penthouse* magazine received a 35,000-word document entitled 'Industrial Society and Its Future'. The essay on the evils of technology came with a letter warning that if the essay was not published, someone would perish. If the essay was published, the Unabomber (who signed himself 'FC') would desist from further attacks. Following deliberation, the FBI's director, Louis Freeh, and the attorney general, Janet Reno, agreed that the article should be published.

On publication, Ted Kaczynski's brother David read the article and recognised his brother's writing. David alerted the FBI to his suspicions and allowed the FBI access to letters he had received from Ted over the years. On 3 April 1996, the FBI arrested Ted Kaczynski and searched his cabin. They found bomb-making equipment, diaries and a range of incriminating material, including a live bomb that was ready for the post.

Indicted by a Grand Jury in Apil 1996, Ted Kaczynski refused the advice of his lawyers to plead insanity and instead pleaded guilty to 10 counts of illegally transporting, mailing and using bombs, as well as three charges of murder. He is currently incarcerated at a Supermax prison in Colorado with no possibility of parole.

LINKS TO THEORY AND RESEARCH

We know that 'traumatic events experienced during childhood … can massively increase the risk of developing schizophrenia' during adulthood (Field & Cartwright-Hatton, 2015, p. 149). In order to understand the Unabomber, we need to consider both his experience of trauma and particularly his experience of participating in Henry Murray's studies at such a crucial stage of development – adolescence – and its effects on his subsequent mental health.

The Unabomber was diagnosed as a paranoid schizophrenic (Magid, 2009). As such, the relevance of abnormal psychology to understanding both Kaczynski's actions and his subsequent trial and sentencing will be considered. Finally, the role of profiling in capturing serial killers will be discussed.

Ethics: The Murray Studies

It is easy to be blasé about ethics. As an academic who coordinates a large undergraduate research unit, I see hundreds of research ethics protocols and applications on an annual basis. I know from first-hand experience that it is all too easy to lapse into a 'what's all the fuss about' mindset regarding ethics. But that is a very slippery slope.

Between 1939 and 1945, German scientists were conducting horrific research on concentration camp prisoners without their consent. In the early 1960s Stanley Milgram was able to demonstrate that many people will behave in ways that they consider morally wrong. In a period between the late 1950s and 1980, Krugman, Giles and other medical researchers conducted studies exploring the impact of hepatitis. Disabled children were intentionally infected with the disease and then the researchers recorded its natural progression (Salkind, 2012). This is the unhappy tradition into which the Murray studies fit. In a Cold War context, social science was, in the hands of those like Professor Murray, a tool of mind control. It is a fact that Kaczynski was not deluded in holding the view that scientists were trying to control his mind. His lived experience of Murray's experiments was that scientists were, in fact, attempting to control his mind.

Ted Kaczynski is the living manifestation of all the ethical shortcomings of Murray's research. Murray's experiments were at the root of Kaczynski's theory that technology and science were destroying individual liberty. 'The system', in Kaczynski's lived experience, was actively developing techniques intended for the behavioural control of populations (Chase, 2003). This is the very 'system' that infuriated the Unabomber, the system that he targeted, and the system that he wished to destroy.

Cruel and dangerous experiments were, to some degree, standard fare during the Cold War period. In Canada, the MK ULTRA experiments, which probably included the US study in which Ted Kaczynski participated, have resulted in compensation payments to participants for the long-term mental damage they caused. In Canada, Dr Ewan Cameron used drugs, including LSD, electro-convulsive therapy (ECT), sensory deprivation, sleep deprivation and isolation to 'break' participants (Gunn, 2006). We may, thankfully, have only one Unabomber, but the impact of unethical research is wide and its victims numerous.

Gunn (2006) argues that most offenders are victims themselves and that we need to understand human development if we wish to understand the origins of crime and antisocial behaviour. This certainly seems to be the case with regards to the Unabomber, and it is undoubtedly the case with crime generally. For those of us involved in research, the importance of conducting any research in an ethical fashion should be self-evident. We know that 'Murray's experiment, despite the protests of his allies, was indeed unethical. Like so much research by Cold Warriors of that era, his violated the Nuremberg Code's requirement of "informed consent"' (Chase, 2003, p. 285). Moreover, the Murray studies did real harm. In deceiving his participants, he eroded their trust in authority. Even trust in legitimate authority was damaged. Murray himself reported that Kaczynski was more severely affected by his participation in the studies than any of the other participants.

One aspect that made Kaczynski especially vulnerable to the Murray experiments was his age. Erik Erikson, the lifespan developmental psychologist famous for his theory of psychosocial development, identified adolescence, a period that coincided with Kaczynski's then development, as a key stage. Adolescence, the period between approximately 14 and 20 years of age, is when young people form their adult identity and social roles in life. A disruption or confusion between a person's sense of themselves or their identity and their social role can result in an adolescent identity crisis (Sugarman, 2001). The societal manifestation of the adolescent identity crisis is ideology.

Kaczynski was in precisely this developmental phase when Murray recruited him to the 'Multiform Assessments of Personality Development among Gifted College Men' studies. 'The danger of this stage is identity diffusion or role confusion – uncertainty about who one is and what one is to become. To counteract such uncertainty, or to bolster a still fragile sense of identity, the young person might temporarily over-identify with a clannish subgroup of peers and/or particular cults or individuals. The development of self-destructive or socially unacceptable identity might be preferable to no identity' (Sugarman, 2001, p. 96). This Eriksonian view certainly seems to chime with Kaczynski.

Allely, Minnis, Thompson, Wilson and Gillberg (2014) outline how psychological abuse was a pervasive characteristic of serial killers' childhoods. Rejection, humiliation and narcissistic injury are all listed as relevant factors in the case histories of serial killers, and all are present in the Unabomber's life history. Particularly so in the Murray experiments, conducted when Kaczynski was little more than a child.

Another possible neurodevelopmental and psychosocial risk factor that has been identified in serial killers and mass murderers is the presence of autistic spectrum disorder (ASD) (Allely et al., 2014), and it seems likely that Kaczynski is on the autistic spectrum. However, it must be noted, and acknowledged, that the gaps in knowledge within this area are huge, and that while ASD is a variable of interest to researchers, significantly more work needs to be conducted before any definitive statements can be made regarding any relationship between ASD and serial killing.

Mental Health: Schizophrenia and Paranoid Schizophrenia

Dr Sally Johnson diagnosed Ted Kaczynski with paranoid schizophrenia (Magid, 2009). Schizophrenia is an illness that usually develops in early adulthood at a time in people's lives when they may be facing a novel range of experiential stresses without family support (Holmes, 2010). Again, this chimes with the particulars of the Unabomber's experience.

The DSM-5 (American Psychiatric Association, 2013) criteria for schizophrenia are the presence of two (or more) of the following: (1) delusions, (2) hallucinations, (3) disorganised speech, (4) grossly disorganised or catatonic behaviour, and (5) negative symptoms. Each item must be present for a significant period of time during a one-month period (less, if successfully treated), with at least one of these items being delusions, hallucinations or disorganised speech.

Following his arrest, Ted Kaczynski refused to enter a 'not guilty by reason of insanity' defence and instead pleaded guilty to the charges against him. Kaczynski's refusal to enter an insanity defence, and his refusal to be examined by psychiatric experts, is notable because it was, prior to the trial, probably his only possibility of escaping the death penalty. Interestingly, taking this position was evidence of Kaczynski's diagnosis with schizophrenia. A severe lack of insight lies behind most cases of people with schizophrenia, who, as defendants, have an apparently irrational need to demonstrate their 'sanity' in spite of the threat to their life (in states with the death penalty) of doing so. Again, this would seem to be the case with Ted Kaczynski. It appears that Kaczynski was not trying to manipulate the court or behave defensively by refusing to engage with psychiatry. Rather, the evidence suggests that his refusal was itself rooted in brain dysfunction. He was demonstrating anosognosia, a neurological condition that results in an unawareness of one's deficits (Amador & Paul-Odouard, 2000).

Insanity Defence and the Unabomber

Baele (2014) makes the point that our definition of insanity is rooted in law rather than in any diagnostic criteria. This may be obvious, but its implications are significant. Insanity is a legal category, not a psychiatric category or a psychological category.

Insanity is at one end of a dichotomous grouping. Legally speaking, individuals are judged by courts to be either 'normal' or 'insane'. There is no middle ground here. To be considered insane, a person must prove that they acted impulsively and irrationally. They must show that they did not *understand* what they were doing and that they did not know *what* they were doing was morally wrong. Moreover, the person must not know *why* they are doing what they are doing at the time of the offence (Baele, 2014). Ted Kaczynski was/is not legally insane – 'insanity' is not compatible with any kind of carefully planned action undertaken as part of a political programme (Baele, 2014). The Unabomber's campaign was nothing if not carefully planned and political.

There is a further problem, on top of the difference between legal and psychiatric understandings of insanity: the legal concept of insanity has been challenged in the philosophy of law and jurisprudence. The DSM diagnoses are no better. The diagnosis criteria are reflective of social norms and are thus conceptually and scientifically problematic. Psychiatric opinions diverge widely (Baele, 2014), orthopaedic opinions less so. Ergo, there is something conceptually questionable about the concepts of insanity and DSM classifications.

So there are conceptual problems with both insanity and DSM criteria with regard to terrorism. But there are other instruments available that do show some promise. One such instrument is the TRAP-18 (Terrorist Radicalisation Assessment Protocol), an instrument designed to facilitate structured professional judgements for the assessment of people who may constitute a risk in terms of lone-actor terrorism. The instrument is made up of eight proximal warning characteristics and 10 distal characteristics.

Meloy and Gill (2016), in their study of 111 lone-actor terrorists, like the Unabomber, found that the top four 'red flag' characteristics, or warning behaviours, in the TRAP-18 are:

- 'Leakage' (85%, i.e. the terrorist communicates their intention to do harm in an attack)
- 'Pathway warning behaviour' (80%, i.e. planning, preparing or implementing an attack)
- 'Fixation' (77%, i.e. becoming increasingly preoccupied with a person or a cause in a pathological way)
- 'Identification' (77%, i.e. the terrorist believes that they are a soldier or agent acting for a particular belief system)

The top three distal characteristics of the TRAP-18 are:

- 'Framed by an ideology' (100%, i.e. believing in things that provide justification for terrorism, including religious and political beliefs)
- 'Changes in thinking and emotion' (88%, i.e. people's thoughts and expression become more strident, absolute and simplistic; anger shifts to contempt and disgust of a sort that creates a willingness to kill)
- 'Failure of sexual-intimate pair bonding (84%, i.e. the terrorist has had no lasting sexually intimate relationship)' (Meloy & Gill, 2016, p. 46).

At first blush, Ted Kaczynski certainly seems to tick the boxes of the TRAP-18. It seems difficult to regard Kaczynski as insane; it also seems difficult to argue against his diagnosis of paranoid-schizophrenia. It might be that he is simply an individual with a particular array of characteristics that make him more likely to commit 'lone terrorist' crimes. As such, at this point it is timely to consider the role of profiling in the case of the Unabomber.

Profiling

For anyone who has read about the Unabomber on the internet or watched the *Manhunt: Unabomber* series, mention of the Unabomber is likely to prime thoughts of profiling. Particularly with regard to Jim Fitzgerald, the FBI profiler who played a key role in the Kaczynski investigation. Profiling has been described as the examination of every behavioural detail of unsolved crimes where the crime scenes show evidence of psychopathology (White, Lester, Gentile, & Rosenbleeth, 2011). Within profiling, a distinction can usefully be drawn between behavioural profiling and linguistic profiling. Behavioural profiling began with the FBI when psychologists and criminologists came together to consider the behavioural characteristics of criminals who were yet to be identified.

Behavioural profilers build their criminal profiles based on research data, personal experience, previous crimes and psychological theory. Of necessity, behavioural profiles are subjective, somewhat of an art, and perhaps subject to confirmation bias – after all, the behavioural profilers are working from a theory to the facts as they seek evidence that will support their profile. Indeed, it is fair to say that profilers generally begin with little in terms of evidential data. However, behavioural profiling is considered useful in some cases and is generally regarded with respect in criminology (Shuy, 2014).

Linguistic profiling is different from behavioural profiling. 'The sole focus of linguistic profiling is to point out the sociolinguistic features about suspects that their own language use suggests' (Shuy, 2014, p. 75). Where behavioural profiling builds on the comparisons of the behavioural characteristics of unidentified perpetrators with the behavioural characteristics of past similar crimes, linguistic profiling builds on known written, or spoken, language evidence.

The Unabomber provided a plethora of solid linguistic data, not least in his manifesto. Other sources of linguistic Unabomber data included letters that he had written to newspapers and magazines as well as the messages that were sent with his bombs. Roger Shuy was Professor of Linguistics at Georgetown University in 1994 when a serving FBI agent attended one of his graduate seminars. This agent was in contact with the FBI's Unabomber task force, and felt that they might benefit from the type of linguistic profiling that was being advocated at the seminar (Shuy, 2014).

Ultimately, the goal of linguistic profiling is not to come up with a 'this is your man!' level of perpetrator specificity. Rather, linguistic profiling seeks to aid investigators by narrowing the list of suspects (Campbell & DeNevi, 2004). From May 1995, Professor Shuy was working with the FBI on the Unabomber case. Previous, but at the time the most recent, FBI profiles suggested that the Unabomber was in the 40–50 age bracket, had a high school education and some trade school and college training (Shuy, 2014).

Shuy was able to show that the Unabomber's spelling of common words matched those used by the *Chicago Tribune* newspaper in the 1940s and 1950s. For example, he used the spellings 'wilfully' rather than 'willfully', and 'clew' rather than 'clue'. As well as suggesting the bomber's age, these clues provided a possible geographical biography. When the manifesto's author wrote about going out into 'the sierra', he gave away that he had spent part of his life in Northern California. The absences of other western American words, such as 'ranch', 'gulch', 'fork' (in a stream), 'range' or 'mesa', indicated that the author was not a native of the western United States. The inclusion of a religiously informed lexicon suggested a Catholic background – the overuse of 'sin', for example, as well as 'God's will', 'cradle to grave' and 'unclean thoughts'. The content of the Unabomber's correspondence suggested a high level of academic achievement. However, the poor editing suggested (correctly) that such education had been in the 'hard' sciences rather than in arts or humanities (Shuy, 2014).

CONCLUSION

The dividing line between politically/socially/religiously based terrorism, criminal acts, and acts of violence resulting from severe psychological disturbance are not always clear. … Should such acts be categorized as terrorist acts or as acts of violence related to mental illness? (Schouten, 2010, p. 370)

The Unabomber case raises more questions than answers. The case straddles the boundary between terrorism and mental illness, although clearly, and correctly, the courts decided that Kaczynski's mental illness (i.e. paranoid schizophrenia) did not render him insane. What his case does do is illustrate a gulf between legal and psychiatric understanding of 'sanity' that needs to be addressed. Where should the line be drawn between legal understandings of 'sanity' and psychiatric/psychological understandings of mental illness?

Furthermore, Kaczynski's case throws up an uncomfortable mirror to the society that 'nurtured' him. From a twenty-first-century perspective, a multiplicity of societal failings is immediately evident – skipping grades at school, unethical research being pursued by powerful institutions and narcissistic academics, class, fears of imminent global catastrophe and a hankering for simpler times. These are among a myriad of shortcomings apparent to even the most cursory engagement with this case. But what lessons can we learn from Kaczynski that might apply to the lone-wolf terrorists of our own era? Alienation and anomie are not without currency in contemporary societies. The Unabomber case is a deep rabbit hole for those who explore it. I encourage you to take a look.

REFLECTIVE QUESTIONS

1. Historically, there was an issue with research ethics. Do we need to worry about research ethics today? Why or why not?
2. Did Kaczynski's experiences in adolescence contribute to his becoming a terrorist?
3. What, if any, role does mental health play in understanding terrorism?

FURTHER READING

The Unabomber's manifesto, as published in the *New York Times*, is available at: https://archive.nytimes.com/www.nytimes.com/library/national/unabom-manifesto-1.html

The Nuremberg Code can be found at: https://history.nih.gov/download/attachments/1016866/nuremberg.pdf?version=1&modificationDate=1589152811742&api=v2 or www.nejm.org/doi/full/10.1056/NEJM199711133372006

The FBI's account can be found at: www.fbi.gov/history/famous-cases/unabomber

Chase, A. (2003). *A Mind for Murder: The Education of the Unabomber and the Origins of Modern Terrorism*. New York: W. W. Norton & Co.

PART III
SEXUAL CRIMES

11

PARAPHILIA AND SEX CRIMES: AN OVERVIEW

Few topics arouse more attention of people than sex and sex crimes. The sex offender is viewed by many as a moral degenerate and one who preys upon moral citizens at an alarming rate with relative impunity. The crimes committed, such as rape, lust murder, and child molestation, appal and disgust, but they attract and fascinate at the same time. (Holmes & Holmes, 2009, p. xiii)

Any society with a criminal justice system must codify and formally state what behaviours are, and are not, to be considered criminal (Hollin, 2013). The law regarding sexual behaviour gives priority to the concept of consent. As a general rule, unless sex is between consenting partners, there will be illegality associated with the behaviour (Gavin, 2019). Sexual offences include rape, indecent exposure, sexual activity with a child, harm to animals, illicit watching of sexual activity, and many more. The list is a long one.

PARAPHILIA

DSM-5 (American Psychiatric Association, 2013, p. 685) defines paraphilia as 'any intense and persistent sexual interest other than sexual interest in genital stimulation or preparatory fondling with phenotypically normal, physiologically mature, consenting human partners'. According to Vella-Zarb, Cohen, McCabe and Rowa (2017), it is common for people to present with more than one paraphilia. Paraphilias vary in their level of intrusiveness into individuals' thoughts, and people who experience paraphilias experience them as having an impulsive quality. There are varying estimates of prevalence, but the American Psychiatric Association (APA) (2013) suggest a highest possible lifetime prevalence rate of 2–12%, depending upon the paraphilic focus. Onset of paraphilia normally occurs during adolescence, prior to age 18, and men are more likely to be affected than women, by a factor of 20:1. Paraphilia tends to peak when individuals are in their 20s (Ragan & Martin, 2000).

The medical model of sex and sexual deviance builds on the idea that problems arising from sexual aspects of the mind and sexual behaviours can be explained as diseases. These diseases present problems which are amenable to solutions. In essence, the medical model of sexual deviance posits that there are identifiable causes, which can be treated, underlying sexual deviance and sexual offending (Gavin, 2019).

There are, however, some issues with the definition of paraphilia presented in DSM-5 that it are worth being aware of: the DSM-5 definition of paraphilia is such that only a 'very narrow range of sexual behaviours is normophilic' (Moser, 2016, p. 2183). For example, Moser (2016, p. 2183) suggests that if a man 'prefers to stimulate his penis by contact with his partner's genitals, that is not a paraphilia. … If he prefers to stimulate his penis by contact with his partner's feet, that does seem to be a paraphilia. There is no research basis to support this distinction. If there is a logic behind this distinction, the APA has chosen not to share it'.

Moser (2016) points out that the idea of a phenotypically normal partner is also confused. Not least because both men and women spend considerable effort, and resources, in altering their appearance in ways that are not phenotypically normal. Examples that Moser gives include tatooings, piercings, shaving and silicone augmentation. Moser also expresses his doubt at the idea that the APA intended to categorise those who eroticise the above characteristics as having a paraphilia.

Considered on their own, the distinction between paraphilic and normophilic sexual interests is not clear. Moreover, it is not clear why such a distinction might be important. Moser (2016, p. 2183) suggests that the APA is focused on coitus as 'normal' and that this focus seems to say more about 'the sexual concerns of the APA than it does about any nosology of sexual interests based on scientific or psychiatric data'.

Where the paraphilias do seem to come alive with relevance is in a consideration of sexual crimes. The concept of paraphilic disorders is key to this.

PARAPHILIC DISORDERS

In preparing DSM-5, the APA Working Group sought to distinguish the atypical human behaviour that manifests in paraphilia (e.g. a foot fetish) from behaviour that causes mental distress to others (e.g. voyeuristic disorder) or behaviour that makes the person a serious threat to the psychological and physical well-being of others (e.g. sexual sadism disorder). The medical approach to paraphilic disorders, as manifest in the DSM-5, is about understanding the offender as a patient and treating the underlying disorder (Gavin, 2019). The paraphilic disorders have a unique position in DSM-5 in so far as forensic considerations occupied a central role in the formulation of diagnostic criteria and accompanying text (First, 2014).

The concept of paraphilic disorder, is defined by the APA (2013, p. 686) as comprising at least two criteria: 'Criterion A specifies the qualitative nature of the paraphilia … and Criterion B specifies the … distress, impairment or harm to others.' The APA also state that 'A paraphilia is a necessary but not a sufficient condition for having a paraphilic disorder and a paraphilia by itself does not necessarily justify or require clinical intervention'.

The paraphilic disorders set out in the DSM-5 manual are as follows:

…voyeuristic disorder (spying on others in private activities), exhibitionistic disorder (exposing the genitals), frotteuristic disorder (touching or rubbing against a nonconsenting individual), sexual masochism disorder (undergoing humiliation, bondage, or suffering), sexual sadism disorder (inflicting humiliation, bondage, or suffering), pedophilic disorder (sexual focus on children), fetishistic disorder (using nonliving objects or having a highly specific focus on nongenital body parts), and transvestic disorder (engaging in sexually arousing cross-dressing). These disorders have traditionally been selected for specific listing and assignment of explicit diagnostic criteria in DSM for two main reasons: they are relatively common, in relation to other paraphilic disorders, and some of them entail actions for their satisfaction that, because of their noxiousness or potential harm to others, are classed as criminal offenses. The eight listed disorders do not exhaust the list of possible paraphilic disorders. Many dozens of distinct paraphilias have been identified and named, and almost any of them could, by virtue of its negative consequences for the individual or for others, rise to the level of a paraphilic disorder. The diagnoses of the other specified and unspecified paraphilic disorders are therefore indispensable and will be required in many cases. (American Psychiatric Association, 2013)

SEX CRIME

Of course, closer examination throws up some significant problems and anomalies arising from this application of the medical modelling to sexual offending. One major anomaly is that the DSM does not include rape among the paraphilic disorders (Moser, 2016). This may be because, historically, women were understood as property and rape was considered a crime against property, or chastity, rather than as a crime against the person. The rape of a virgin, for example, was considered a more significant crime than the rape of a wife or a widow. Indeed, in some cultures, the rape of a prostitute was not considered a crime because her chastity was not harmed (Gavin, 2019). However, it is hard to understand why rape is not pathologised by the contemporary DSM. Indeed, rape has not been mentioned by the DSM since DSM-I in 1952 (American Psychiatric Association, 1952). Moreover, this omission does not seem to be a passive one. Moser (2016) reports that a proposal to insert a variation of rape, Coercive Paraphilic Disorder, that was made in the preparatory period for DSM-5 also was rejected. It is also noteworthy that the DSM-5 criteria for paraphilias isolate mental disorder from context.

Part 1 of the Sexual Offences Act (2003) sets out the sexual behaviours that are prohibited by law in England and Wales. These include:

Rape
Assault by penetration
Sexual assault
Causing sexual activity without consent
Causing or inciting a child under 13 to engage in sexual activity
Sexual activity with a child
Sexual activity with a person with a mental disorder impeding choice
Causing a person with a mental disorder to engage in or agree to engage in sexual
    activity by inducement, threat or deception
Indecent photographs of persons aged 16 or 17
Soliciting prostitution
Causing or inciting prostitution for gain
Trafficking for sexual exploitation
Administering a substance with intent
Committing an offence with intent to commit a sexual offence
Trespass with intent to commit a sexual offence
Exposure
Voyeurism
Intercourse with an animal
Sexual penetration of a corpse
Sexual activity in a public lavatory

As can be seen from the above, sexual offending covers a wide and varied range of behaviours. The range of crimes runs from non-contact offences, such as taking indecent photographs of underage individuals or indecent exposure, to extreme acts of physical violence, such as rape (Hollin, 2013). It is noteworthy that commission of a sexual offence does not necessarily mean that the perpetrator is suffering from a mental disorder. It is also notable that problems around legal definitions of crime are compounded by the fact that the legality of behaviours that constitute sexual offences vary from country to country. This last fact also makes it difficult to compare rates of sexual offending between countries.

THE HISTORY OF PARAPHILIA AND SEX CRIME

One of the difficulties inherent in any definition of sex crime is that criminal law reflects society's moral values, and the moral values in any given society fluctuate over time (Hollin, 2013). Hence it is useful to consider the history of paraphilia and the history of sex crime.

The History of Paraphilia

The idea of sexual disorders has been with us for a very long time. In the early nineteenth century, Benjamin Rush included a chapter entitled 'Of the Morbid State of the Sexual Appetite' in his (1812) book *Medical Inquiries and Observations Upon the Disease of the Mind*. At the other end of the century, Krafft-Ebbing published his *Psychopathia Sexualis*, which included over 200 case studies of sexual disorders (Ragan & Martin, 2000). The term 'paraphilia' first appeared in the English language in 1925 in an English translation of Stekel's *Sexual Abberations* (Yakeley, 2018). The term 'paraphilia' was welcomed at the time as less a pejorative word than perversion. Perversion, however, is the starting point of our consideration of paraphilia.

Perversion, as an idea, has had currency in the field of mental health since Freud's early formulation of perversion as the negative of the neuroses in the *Three Essays* (Gonzalez, 2010). 'Perversion' comprises those human fantasies and behaviours, of a sexual type, that are considered perverse. However, nowadays, ideas of perversion are considered anachronistic in the Western world, where there has been a shift towards the normalisation and acceptance of sexual practices and orientations that were considered 'deviant' or 'perverse' in earlier times. The term 'perversion' is now generally considered to be pejorative and stigmatising of those whose sexualities do not correspond with traditional norms (Yakeley, 2018).

In 1980, the APA replaced 'sexual deviancy' with 'paraphilia' in the third edition of the DSM (American Psychiatric Association, 1980) and, over time, paraphilia became the preferred and accepted term for sexual deviance or perversion as a mental disorder (Yakeley, 2018).

The History of Sex Crime

One useful example for illustrating how an understanding of paraphilias and sex crimes has evolved is the case of homosexuality. Another example is marital rape, which is a sex crime although not a paraphilia.

Homosexuality was decriminalised in England and Wales in 1967, in Scotland in 1981, in Northern Ireland in 1982, and in the Republic of Ireland in 1993. In England and Wales, the age of homosexual consent was reduced from 21 years of age to age 18 in 1994, and reduced again to age 16 for both homosexual and heterosexual sexual behaviours in 2000 (Hollin, 2013). The homosexual behaviour that was illegal then is (rightly) nowadays no longer so. Similarly, until 1991 there was, in the UK, spousal immunity from rape prosecution. In the eyes of the law, a man could not, until this time, rape his wife (Leader-Elliott & Naffine, 2000).

Rape has never been included among the paraphilic disorders in the DSM. But what of homosexuality as a mental disorder? DSM-I, introduced in 1952, classified homosexuality as a mental disorder, as did DSM-II, introduced in 1968. The diagnosis of homosexuality was not removed from the DSM until the 1970s, lingering even longer in the World Health Organisation's *International Classification of Diseases* until 1990 (Drescher, 2015).

CONCLUSION

Thankfully the world has moved past a narrow view of what constitutes a 'healthy' human sexuality centred on reproduction and shifted to a wider and more democratic understanding of human sexuality rooted in concepts of consent, respect for others and sexual well-being (Giami, 2015). It may be that the DSM still has some catching up to do, but it is indubitable that it is to the public good that sexual behaviours that inflict distress and/or harm on others, or oneself, are pathologised and indeed criminalised.

The chapters that follow will consider cases of paraphilia, sexual assault and rape in order to illustrate contemporary understandings of sex crime. It may be that crime is socially constructed (Warner, 2015). The examples of homosexuality and marital rape certainly seem to evidence 'things' that are socially constructed. If this is the case, and crime is a social construct, it is incumbent on psychologists and other practitioners to follow the advice of the prominent social constructionist Ken Gergen and pursue, in knowledge terms, that which is useful (Gergen, 2001). In the case of sex crime, what is useful is the production of knowledge that will protect the vulnerable and foster both respect for others and a recognition of the importance of consent in sexual behaviour.

12

PRAMS AND HANDBAGS: A CASE OF FETISHISM

From whence came those extraordinary passions which are peculiar to certain men? (Descartes, 1649, cited in Raymond, 1956)

LEARNING OBJECTIVES

By the end of this chapter you should be able to:

- Describe paraphilia with reference to DSM-5
- Discuss fetishism with reference to DSM-5 and psychological treatments
- Make an argument for the idea that crime and mental illness are social constructions

SYNOPSIS OF THE CASE

The person at the centre of this case was 'turned on' by prams and handbags. He found them sexually attractive. The man in question was a 33-year-old married father who was registered as an outpatient with a psychiatric hospital. At the time his case was first reported in 1956, the man was being assessed for a prefrontal leucotomy (such an operation would never be considered today). His 'thing' seems to have started when, at 10 years of age, he first felt the impulse to attack and damage prams and handbags, doing so a couple of times a week thereafter. The 'man who was turned on by prams and handbags' first came to the attention of a wide audience through Raymond (1956), and subsequently Eysenck (1965) and Rolls (2010). He was treated with aversion therapy, based on the principles of classical conditioning, and this will be considered here. More broadly, the chapter will discuss the paraphilias, as set out in DSM-5 (American Psychiatric Association, 2013), and this will set the scene for an examination of the social construction of crime and mental illness.

DESCRIPTION OF THE CASE

In the *British Medical Journal* (BMJ), Raymond (1956) reported the case of a married man who had been referred to the outpatient department of an English mental hospital for consideration of a prefrontal leucotomy.[1] The man had been referred because of a recent, sexually motivated attack on a pram. The case reached a wider audience when Eysenck (1965) included 'The case of the prams and handbags' in a chapter entitled 'Therapy or Brain-washing?'. More recently, the case has penetrated the consciousness of a new generation, in Geoff Rolls' *Classic Case Studies in Psychology* (2010, 2019).

The pram attack, underpinning the patient's referral to psychiatry in November 1954, was the twelfth such incident perpetrated by this patient that the police were aware of. The pram attacks were, however, significantly more frequent than the authorities then knew. By the perpetrator's own account, the attacks were on a grand-scale and had been happening since he was 10 years of age.

On the occasion of his twelfth known attack, the perpetrator had followed a woman who was pushing her pram, which he attacked by smearing the pram with oil. A brief history of the man's odd, sexually motivated behaviour since first coming to the attention of police is as follows.

In September 1948, while serving as ground crew with the Royal Air Force, the man had slashed two empty prams at a railway station before setting them on fire and completely destroying them. The man – for the sake of ease let's call him Mr X – had also admitted five other incidents that involved either cutting or scratching prams. These incidents led to Mr X's conviction for malicious damage and, consequently, he was placed on probation with the condition that he accept medical treatment. Following his conviction, Mr X left the RAF and was put in the care of a mental hospital from March to April 1949. In April 1949 he was transferred to a neurosis unit, where he spent a further month. Medical opinion was that Mr X would not benefit from psychotherapy (it is hard to disagree with

---

[1] A prefrontal leucotomy was an operation (now considered an obsolete treatment and viewed as barbaric by many) that surgically severed connections between a patient's frontal lobes and other brain areas. This operation was also known as a lobotomy.

that conclusion), and that Mr X was potentially dangerous and should remain in a mental hospital.

However, contrary to medical advice, Mr X did not remain in a mental hospital, and on his release early in 1950 he again perpetrated a sexually motivated attack on a pram. This time, rather disgustingly, and also perhaps somewhat ominously, he smeared the contents of his (used) handkerchief onto a handbag. Mr X also, again, damaged a pram by scratching and cutting. He was not charged, but was once more taken to a mental hospital where he remained from February 1950 until June 1951.

In April 1952, in what was now the ninth incident that the police were aware of, Mr X deliberately rode his motorcycle (and sidecar) at a pram which this time had a baby in it. Although Mr X swerved at the last minute, he nevertheless crashed into the pram. As a direct result of this incident, Mr X was fined for careless driving. In August 1952, Mr X again came to the attention of the police. In this incident he damaged a pram and a woman's skirt and stockings by squirting oil on them. Charges of causing malicious damage were brought and Mr X was again fined. In 1953 Mr X was once more causing trouble on his motorbike. This time he deliberately rode his motorbike through a puddle, splashing a pram as well as the woman pushing it. Charges of driving without due care and attention were brought, but the court gave Mr X the benefit of the doubt. This was the eleventh incident that the authorities were aware of. Then there was the pram attack in September 1954, when Mr X was charged and convicted of causing wilful damage and put on probation, with the condition that he accept medical treatment.

During court proceedings, the prosecuting counsel, while stressing that the accused deserved sympathy, had said that Mr X was a menace to any woman with a pram. Counsel went on to speak of 'a real fear that he may cause serious injury to a baby or mother unless he is put under some form of restraint' (Raymond, 1956, p. 855). Mr X admitted that he had felt impulses to damage prams and handbags since he had been about 10 years of age. He admitted to having attacked several prams in a single day. On average, he guessed that he attacked prams two or three times every week. Mr X said that he was usually satisfied if he could scratch prams with his thumbnail.

Following many hours of analytical treatment Mr X is reported to have traced his behaviour to two childhood incidents. In the first, having been brought to a park to sail a toy boat, he had been impressed by 'the feminine consternation' he encountered from a mother when he struck the keel of his toy yacht against her passing pram. The second incident was when he became sexually aroused in the presence of his sister's handbag. He came to think that prams and handbags were, for him, 'symbolic sexual containers' (Raymond, 1956, p. 855).

Interestingly, Mr X's mother was a paraphrenic, that is she suffered from a type of late onset psychosis. She was certified at the age of 54 (when he was 12) and died aged 66. Mr X's father also died aged 66 (when he was 15 years old). It is also notable that Mr X's father was away from home for long periods when Mr X was growing up. Mr X had was one sister, 12 years older than him. According to Mr X, his sister had played a maternal role in his life, and he was devoted to her.

Personal History

As a child, Mr X's physical health had been good and had remained so until he left school at the age of 14. On leaving elementary school, Mr X progressed to technical school for three years before joining the RAF as an engine fitter. He served with the RAF for 10 years until he was discharged because of his fetishism. Mr X's behaviour towards prams had cost him his career. According to his discharge papers from the RAF, he had worked well in a job that required a degree of mechanical skill, he was industrious and successful, and he was well regarded by his employers.

According to his case report, Mr X had begun to masturbate at about age 10. He had fantasies of prams and handbags. In particular, he fantasised about damage being caused to prams and handbags by their owners. He first had sexual intercourse after his marriage at the age of 27. Mr X said that sexual intercourse with his wife was only possible with the aid of fantasies of handbags and prams. The couple had two children. Mr X's wife described him as a good husband and father. In what looks to the outside eye to be a particularly odd aspect of their marriage, household prams and his wife's handbags were not immune from Mr X's sexually motivated attacks. In particular, a handbag filled to capacity and bulging often provided Mr X with significant sexual arousal. It is notable that while handbags and prams aroused Mr X sexually, his attacks upon them were never accompanied by ejaculation, although he was usually conscious of a release of tension.

Mr X described himself, socially, as a good mixer, but said that being alone was never a problem for him, and he reported himself as having always been a daydreamer. Mr X liked reading, especially adventure and crime novels, and he was also keen on gardening and woodwork. Unsurprisingly perhaps, Mr X had an encyclopaedic knowledge of prams and handbags, and he devoted a significant proportion of his spare time to them.

Treatment

Mr X scored highly on intelligence tests and showed no psychotic abnormality. He reported dismay at a perceived likelihood that any intervention regarding his behaviour would be ineffective. However, it was noted by medical staff that Mr X spoke of his fetish with a certain amount of relish.

Aversion therapy, similar to that used in the treatment of alcoholism (at the time), was considered by clinicians to be appropriate for this case. It was explained to Mr X that the aim of his treatment was to change his attitude to handbags and prams by bringing him to associate prams and handbags with an unpleasant sensation, rather than thinking of them as erotic. A collection of handbags, prams and pictures of prams and handbags was put together and shown to Mr X following an injection of apomorphine to make him experience nausea. The treatment was given every two hours, day and night, no food was allowed, and at night amphetamines were administered to keep him awake. At the end of the first week, treatment was (temporarily) suspended and Mr X was allowed home for a short visit.

After an eight-day break, treatment resumed, and the patient reported (jubilantly) that he had for the first time been able to have intercourse with his wife without fantasising about prams and handbags. His wife said that she had noticed a change in his attitude to her, but that she could not define it.

Nineteen months after the first aversion therapy Mr X appeared to be doing well. He said that he no longer required the old fantasies to enable him to have sexual intercourse, nor did he masturbate with these fantasies. Mr X's wife said that she was no longer constantly worrying about him or about the possibility of the police knocking on the door because of his behaviour. Mrs X also reported that their sexual relations had 'greatly improved'. Mr X's probation officer said that he had made 'very noticeable progress' and that 'his general attitude to life, his conversation, and his appearance have all shown a marked improvement', and he had not been in any trouble with the police (Raymond, 1956, p. 856).

LINKS TO THEORY AND RESEARCH

Paraphilias

Today, because of his sexual fantasises and behaviours involving prams and handbags, the 33-year-old married man at the centre of this case would be diagnosed as a paraphilic. According to the American Psychiatric Association's DSM-5 (2013) most people with atypical sexual interests do not have a mental disorder. To move over the bar dividing atypical sexual interests into being diagnosed with a paraphilic disorder, DSM-5 requires that people with atypical sexual interests are distressed by their sexual interests in a way that goes beyond any concern about societal disapproval. This seems to have been the case with the man who was turned on by prams and handbags, who reported himself as depressed to medical staff.

Alternatively, the DSM-5 definition of paraphilia includes those who present with a sexual desire or behaviour that involves another person's psychological distress, injury or death, or a desire for sexual behaviours involving unwilling persons or persons unable to give legal consent. Again, this seems to fit with the man at the centre of this case. The incident outlined above, in which the man steered his motorcycle and sidecar towards a pram seems to be a particularly striking incident of behaviour that fits with this criterion.

The DSM-5 chapter on paraphilic disorders includes eight paraphilic conditions: exhibitionistic disorder, fetishistic disorder, frotteuristic disorder, paedophilic disorder, sexual masochism disorder, sexual sadism disorder, transvestic disorder and voyeuristic disorder. According to current DSM-5 criteria, the man who was turned on by prams and handbags was suffering from a fetishistic disorder (American Psychiatric Association, 2013). Key features of fetishism are intense and recurrent sexual fantasies, urges or behaviours that involve a non-living object (Comer, 2012). Prams and handbags certainly fit the bill. Fetishistic disorders generally begin in adolescence, as in this case, and are far more common in men than women. Almost anything can be the object of a fetish, but it seems that women's underwear, shoes and boots are particularly common. The objects of fetishism are often used in some way when the fetishist is masturbating or having sex. It is interesting, and noteworthy, that researchers have not as yet identified the causes of fetishism (Comer, 2012).

Psychodynamic theorists have attempted to explain sexual deviancy, of the type manifest in this case, in terms of weak superegos (morals) and powerful ids (sexual drivers) (Gavin, 2019). However, it has long been known that psychodynamic theory does not offer any efficacious treatments for paraphilic cases such as the one presented here (e.g. Eysenck, 1965).

Raymond (1956) used aversion therapy with his patient in order to treat the paraphilia and he claimed success for the treatment. The aversion therapy approach rests on the behaviourist assumption that fetishes are acquired through classical conditioning, that is learning through association (e.g. Dozier, Iwata, & Worsdell, 2011). Aversion therapy seeks to undo the learned association by linking an unwanted behaviour to an aversive outcome.

The man who was turned on by handbags and prams was able to trace his sexual interest in handbags to an incident in his late childhood/early adolescence when he had been taken to a park to sail his model boat. On this occasion, he had been aroused by the 'feminine consternation' manifest when he struck the keel of his toy yacht against a passing pram. The sexual interest in handbags was also traceable to an incident, again in early adolescence, when he became sexually aroused in the presence of his sister's handbag (Raymond, 1956, p. 855).

Raymond (1956) used emetics (i.e. induced vomiting) in his aversion therapy. Electric shocks have also been administered as part of aversion therapy. However, aversion therapies are nowadays considered controversial (Gavin, 2019) and it has been argued that use of such therapies have been marginalised since their application in cases of homosexuality, which was considered a mental disorder by the American Psychiatric Association until the 1970s (Reay, 2018). Ultimately, the value of therapy hinges on the efficacy of the therapy, and aversion therapy has been found to be ineffective in the treatment of many behaviours (Arlinghaus, Foreyt, & Johnston, 2016).

Comer (2012) outlines two other behavioural treatments for fetishism. The first is called masturbatory satiation. In this approach, which harnesses the concept of boredom, the client is advised to masturbate till the point of orgasm while fantasising about something appropriate. They are then encouraged to masturbate again while fantasising about the objects they fetishise about. The idea is that this will result in a feeling of boredom which will attach to the fetishistic object. The second behavioural approach to fetishism is orgasmic reorientation, whereby clients are taught to respond to new, appropriate, sources of sexual stimulation. Comer (2012) offers the example of a person with a shoe fetish. Such a person will be instructed to gain an erection while examining pictures of shoes. They will then be given a picture of a naked woman, considered to be a 'conventional stimulus', and asked to direct all their attention to the conventional stimulus as orgasm approaches. One wonders how such treatments will appear to the eyes of future generations.

Social Construction of Crime and 'Mental Illness'

Comer (2012) usefully cautions that our definitions of paraphilia and sexual dysfunction are a consequence of the norms of the society in which they are located. The key social constructionist thinker Ken Gergen makes an important point that is relevant to the consideration of paraphilia: what we take to be true is a function of our social relationships (Gergen, 2015). Gergen (2015) argues that entering the logic of social constructionism can change the world. If we understand that what people claim as real, true or moral as being human constructions, functions of culture and history, then we are likely to be more tolerant and curious about those from whom we differ. 'Nothing is real unless people agree that it is' (Gergen (2015, p. 5).

Applying this constructionist line of thought to a consideration of crime and mental illness is a useful exercise. Gergen (2015) suggests that whatever we call something grows from the tradition or community that we are part of. Whatever construction we make bears value. Social constructionism posits that there is no value-neutral description of the world. Social constructionism is a resource, a way of talking; it is not a belief system. Social constructionism shifts our focus from what is 'true' to what is being done in how we construct things.

Power

One element that plays a significant role in our construction of 'things' is power. The French philosopher Michael Foucault contemplated power and what he called 'disciplinary regimes' – those institutions that make claims to knowledge and whose values are embedded within these claims (Gergen, 2015). One such 'disciplinary regime' is medicine, including psychiatry. For Foucault, all social practices include both language and a doing element, so he attempted to overcome traditional distinctions drawn between what is said and what is done. According to Foucault, knowledge does not simply pop up in a value-neutral vacuum. Rather, he argues that effective knowledge is produced, disseminated and advocated by social groups who possess status, standing and power. Much of this knowledge is designed to serve the purpose of favouring the very group promoting that knowledge, and this link between power and knowledge has profoundly affected the law (Howitt, 2011).

The application of the medical model for studying social problems (including crime) is based on the idea that a disease, or pathological condition, is the cause underlying the social problem. This medical understanding explains the search for intrinsic characteristics and illnesses peculiar to criminals. Criminals are constructed as 'flawed' psychologically (Howitt, 2011). By constructing criminals as flawed, medicine and medical science positions itself as having privileged (on the basis of medical knowledge) access to the answers that society needs.

At the time Eysenck (1965) reported the case of the prams and handbags, homosexuality was understood as both criminal and 'deviant'. Indeed, in the very same chapter as the prams and handbags case, Eysenck categorises homosexuality, then recognised as a criminal disorder, and a 'perversion', alongside fetishism. This positioning of 'deviance' and 'disorder' is interesting because it speaks to the disease mindset of medical science. Szasz (2007) picks up on instances where sexual behaviours are labelled as 'diseases' because such labelling applies not only a description, but also a covert moral judgement. This moral judgement places power and control in the hands of the diagnosing physician.

As I see it, the primary problem that presents in the prams and handbags case was not that the man was sexually aroused by prams and handbags. If this sexual arousal did not negatively impact the man himself, I don't even see it as an issue – indeed, the current iteration of the DSM adopts pretty much this stance. The issue with the prams and handbags case was that the man's behaviour towards prams and handbags was at best unacceptable to others, and at worst, downright dangerous. The instance where he drove his motorcycle at a pram before swerving is a prime example.

In the case of the man who was turned on by prams and handbags, I argue that sexual arousal was not the problem, but his behaviour was. Szasz (2007, pp. 95–98) captures this point well when he argues that 'crimes are acts that we commit. Diseases are biological processes that happen to our bodies. Mixing these two concepts – and defining behaviours we disapprove of as diseases – is a bottomless source of confusion and corruption … a priest who commits sexual abuse is a criminal who should be imprisoned, not a patient who should be monitored by psychiatrists in the church's pay.'

CONCLUSION

Aversion therapy has been widely used in the treatment of alcoholism and homosexuality, although in the case of the latter it is no longer sanctioned by the American Psychiatric Association, or considered appropriate by society in general. Research has examined the effectiveness of aversion therapy (generally involving sleep deprivation or emetics) in the treatment of paedophilia, exhibitionism and transvestism. There is little robust evidence for the effectiveness of these treatments (Rolls, 2010).

REFLECTIVE QUESTIONS

1. Might it be more useful to think of 'sexual disorders' in terms of morality than mental disorder?
2. Are crimes associated with paraphilia best understood through a legal framework?
3. How should paraphilic offenders be treated?

FURTHER READING

Raymond, M. J. (1956). Case of fetishism treated by aversion therapy. *British Medical Journal*, *2*(4997), 854–857. doi:10.1136/bmj.2.4997.854. Also available at: www.bmj.com/content/2/4997/854

Gergen, K. J. (2001). Psychological science in a postmodern context. *American Psychologist*, *56*(10), 803–813. doi:10.1037/0003-066x.56.10.803

13
KIRK ANDERSON

LEARNING OBJECTIVES

By the end of this chapter you should be able to:

- Define and discuss the crime of rape
- Discuss the concept of consent as it applies to the crime of rape
- Consider the topic of rape myths
- Describe stalking and set out some stalking types

SYNOPSIS OF THE CASE

In 1977, Kirk Anderson, an 18-stone Mormon missionary, said that former beauty queen and cheerleader Joyce McKinney tied him to a bed for three days and raped him repeatedly. She said that wasn't possible. This case will be used to address a common source of misunderstanding about sexual arousal in cases of rape: the idea that sexual arousal equates with consent. The case will be used to address what Leader-Elliott and Naffine (2000) refer to as 'the language game of rape'. Stalking will also be considered.

DESCRIPTION OF THE CASE

In 2011, the movie *Tabloid* brought awareness of the salacious case of the 'Manacled Mormon' to a generation who were either too young to remember or had not been born when the events depicted took place. The film portrays a 1977 case when Americans Joyce McKinney and Keith May were arrested for the false imprisonment of another American, Kirk Anderson, and possession of a false 38mm revolver.

Mormon missionary Kirk Anderson claimed that he had been abducted at gun-point from the steps of a church meeting house in Surrey. The lurid details of the case were such that the tabloid press had a field day with the story, which became known as 'the Manacled Mormon' case, and was also known as the 'Sex in chains affair'.

Joyce McKinney, an only child, was born in August 1949 in the Appalachian mountains of North Carolina. Her father was a schoolmaster and she grew up in a traditional and religious household. McKinney, a beauty queen and cheerleader, converted to Mormonism in 1973 and moved to Utah. In Utah, in 1975, McKinney met the then 19-year-old Kirk Anderson, six years her junior, and the pair started dating. According to McKinney, she and Anderson slept together and planned to marry. But his family and the Mormon bishop would not agree to the marriage. Kirk Anderson, according to Joyce McKinney, was overcome by guilt and confessed to the Mormon elders that the couple had slept together. The elders put an end to the affair and sent Anderson away, first to California, then Oregon, and ultimately to the UK.

Joyce McKinney was upset by the Mormon authorities' reaction to the sexual affair that she and Anderson had had. She left Mormonism, but remained focused, with a striking single-mindedness, on Anderson. While in Oregon, in an effort to escape from McKinney's attention, Kirk Anderson adopted an assumed name. Then, in the summer of 1976, Anderson moved to England. McKinney employed a private detective to track him down.

McKinney, with accomplice and friend, Keith May, caught up with Kirk Anderson outside a Church of the Latter-Day Saints (Mormon Church) in Ewell, Surrey. Armed with chloroform and a fake pistol, the pair abducted Anderson, who was taken to a rented seventeenth-century cottage in Okehampton, Devon. In the cottage, Anderson, spread-eagled and naked, was handcuffed with mink-lined manacles to a bed.

While it's not clear what exactly took place over the three days Anderson was kept in the cottage, all parties agree that Anderson was tied to the bed while McKinney had sex with him multiple times in an effort to get pregnant. For McKinney, her claim has remained that it was bondage designed to ease any guilt Anderson may have felt over sexual enjoyment, whereas Anderson has always insisted that he was effectively raped.[1] In 1977, English law did not consider the rape of a man by a woman was possible. Miss McKinney pointed out that raping a man 'would be like trying to squeeze a marshmallow into a parking meter'.[2] When he was released from his bondage, Kirk Anderson went straight to the police, McKinney and May were arrested and charged with kidnap and assault. There was no rape charge because under English law such a thing was not possible.

---

[1] www.theguardian.com/film/2011/oct/16/mckinney-mormon-missionary-sex-tabloid

[2] www.theguardian.com/film/2011/mar/10/errol-morris-tabloid-joyce-mckinney

At their committal hearing, McKinney claimed that the three days of sex with Anderson were consensual. She claimed that she was in love with Anderson and that she was trying to save him from an evil brainwashing cult. Famously, McKinney said that for the love of Kirk Anderson she would ski nude down Mount Everest with a carnation up her nose. Naturally this quote made it verbatim into the tabloids. McKinney also said 'I have been played up as a wicked and perverted woman. It's not true. How could an eight-stone girl rape an 18-stone, 6ft 2in man?'[3]

After spending some time in prison on remand, McKinney and May were released while awaiting trial. Just before their trial, in May 1978, McKinney and May failed to report to West Hendon police station. Armed with false passports and posing as members of a deaf and dumb acting troupe, in order to avoid questioning by officials, McKinney and May caught a flight from London Heathrow to Shannon Airport in the West of Ireland. From Shannon they travelled on to Toronto, Canada. It subsequently transpired that Joyce McKinney had posed for S&M magazines and 'had offered unusual services to clients' (Tory, 2010, p. 65). Naturally, the tabloids again had a field day.

Interestingly, in 1984 McKinney was once more arrested after Kirk Anderson spotted her hanging around his place of work near Salt Lake City. On searching the boot of her car, police found a length of rope, a pair of handcuffs and a notebook detailing the by now married Anderson's movements. McKinney failed to turn up at a subsequent court hearing in Utah and the case was dropped.[4] Bizarrely, McKinney surfaced again in 2008 when she was reported to have paid $25,000 to a South Korean laboratory to clone her dead dog. Keith May died in 2004. Kirk Anderson has kept a low profile since the tabloid feeding-frenzy of the late 1970s, but reportedly went on to work as an estate agent.

LINKS TO THEORY AND RESEARCH

The fact that men can be raped is often treated with surprise or disbelief, particularly those who are raped by females. Such a response to rape is common. (Gavin, 2014, p. 164)

Rape and Sexual Violence

There is consensus that rape is a crime of violence, where the perpetrator employs sex as a weapon in the commission of their crime (Holmes & Holmes, 2009). In the public perception, rape is generally thought of as a crime perpetrated by men upon women. In addition, there is an awareness that male-on-male rape is not uncommon in certain contexts, such as prisons, where men and boys are dependent on other males and cannot easily escape violent attention and the risk of sexual assault.

---

[3] www.express.co.uk/news/world/635114/return-Joyce-kidnap-beauty-queen

[4] www.dailyrecord.co.uk/news/uk-world-news/beauty-queen-kidnapped-mormon-ex-12352307

Both men and women are victims and perpetrators of rape. But, because of reporting failures and other data collection problems, the number of people living with the consequences of rape is unknown, and probably unknowable. What is certain, is that rape is a horrific crime that is devastating to both survivors and their significant others (Holmes & Holmes, 2009). Some aspects of the crime of rape are less clear-cut. For example, Hollin (2013, p. 189) defines the act of rape 'as one in which a man intentionally penetrates with his penis the vagina, anus, or mouth of a non-consenting person'. This relatively recent and rather narrow definition, which is drawn from a psychology textbook, positions rape as a crime that can only be committed by men.

Gavin (2014) reports the surprise that is experienced by many people when women are found to be perpetrators of sexual offences. This surprise was certainly common in the late 1970s when there was a public perception of 'common sense' to Joyce McKinney's assertion that a woman could not rape a man because it 'would be like trying to squeeze a marshmallow into a parking meter'. The law has moved on significantly since 1978. It is now recognised that women can commit an act of rape, or sexual assault by penetration, if they engage a non-consenting man in penetrative sex. The widespread assumption, as voiced by Joyce McKinney in her marshmallow simile, that a woman cannot rape a man because the erectile function is voluntary is mistaken.

Sexual arousal in either male or female victims is, in fact, involuntary. In a review published in the *Journal of Clinical and Forensic Medicine*, Levin and van Berlo (2004, p. 82) state that 'A perpetrator's defence simply built upon the fact that evidence of genital arousal or orgasm proves consent has no intrinsic validity and should be disregarded'. People tend not to believe in male victims of female rape because they do not properly understand male sexual arousal and, in particular, the involuntary nature of erectile response (Gavin, 2014).

Under Section 4 of the Sexual Offences Act (2003), a woman can be prosecuted if she causes a man to participate in sexual activity without his consent. As with non-consensual penile penetration of the mouth, anus or vagina committed by a man, where a woman causes a man, without consent, to engage in sexual activity involving penetration of the moth, anus or vagina the maximum sentence under English Law is life imprisonment.

Section 2 of the 2003 Sexual Offences Act also introduced a new offence, 'assault by penetration', that is committed when one person sexually penetrates the anus or vagina of another with either a part of their body or an object. Assault by penetration carries the same sentence as rape – that is, life imprisonment. The intention of the 2003 Act was to make rape, and these types of offence, gender-neutral (Gavin, 2014).

Mens rea, the knowledge of wrongdoing, is an important element in rape law. For an assault to constitute rape, the perpetrator must be aware that the victim is not consenting or that they might not be consenting (Gavin, 2014). Other essential elements of forcible rape include proof that a sex act, as defined by the law, has taken place and proof that force or the threat of force was used to perform the sex act (Holmes & Holmes, 2009).

Types of Rape

If the 'Manacled Mormon' affair was reported today, it would be considered a case of a male being raped by a female because it involved non-consensual penetrative sex acts. Such rapes seem to be relatively unusual. Fisher and Pina (2013) report that data on female-perpetrated sexual assault is scant because of a tendency in psychology to focus on aggression as a male behaviour. However, Gavin (2014) reports that about 2% of all sexual offences are committed by women. Other types of rape include the rape of males by males, the rape of females by males, statutory rape (i.e. the rape of children by adults), acquaintance rape, spousal rape, gang rape and drug-facilitated rape.

Rape can have a negative impact on the physical health of both male and female victims. And, as with other forms of interpersonal violence, rape is strongly linked to post-traumatic stress disorder (PTSD), depression, sleep problems, substance abuse, anxiety and social difficulties (Tjaden & Thoennes, 2000). Furthermore, male victims of rape report issues around perceived loss of masculinity and sexuality. It seems that men are less likely to seek help following rape because of the reactions they believe they may encounter (Hamilton-Giachritsis & Sleath, 2018).

Looking to the psychological effect of rape, self-blame is a common problem for rape survivors. The main cause of self-blame is counterfactual thinking, whereby victims think that because they did not do things differently, they are at fault for being attacked. Victims can also feel that there is something intrinsic to them that is the cause of their being attacked. Both of these avoidance coping approaches serve to hold back the healing process (Gavin, 2014).

Classification of Rapists

Harkins, Ware and Mann (2018) set out a classification of rapists whereby offenders are divided into five categories: the opportunistic rapist, the non-sadistic sexual rapist, the vindictive rapist, the pervasively angry rapist and the sadistic sexual rapist.

Opportunistic rapists have pro-offending attitudes which include the belief that there is nothing wrong with having coercive sex. Rapes that fall into this category are typically impulsive and predatory attacks. Situation and circumstance play a larger role in these types of attacks than do explicit anger or sexual fantasies.

Non-sadistic sexual rapists usually have a high level of sexual fantasy before the offence. These fantasies tend to reflect sexual arousal and distorted attitudes about sex. In addition, non-sadistic rapists tend to display comparatively low levels of interpersonal aggression and to use instrumental forces to ensure victim compliance. This type of rapist seems to fit with the information pertaining to Joyce McKinney.

Vindictive rapists are driven by anger. The rape is characterised by behaviour that is designed and intended to humiliate, degrade and hurt their victim. These can be especially violent rapes and the violence may be such that it results in murder.

Pervasively angry rapists are driven by a fury that runs through all aspects of their lives. This type of rapist is likely to express aggression and have a long history of antisocial behaviour. Rape is another manifestation of anger and hostility in the lives of these offenders.

Lastly, there is the sadistic sexual rapist. These offenders have eroticised their anger and there is a fusion of aggression and sex in their attacks.

It is noteworthy that offenders who commit rape are no different from offenders generally or non-offenders (Harkins et al., 2018). Moreover, although rape is a serious crime that can be punished with a sentence of life imprisonment, it is not included among the paraphilic disorders (Moser, 2016). Thus, psychiatry does not *de facto* regard rapists as mentally ill.

Rape Myths

Rape myths are widely held and persistent beliefs that serve to place blame on the victim and vindicate the perpetrator (Fisher & Pina, 2013). Examples of rape myth are: 'victims falsely cry rape', 'only bad girls get raped', 'women ask for it' and 'rapists are sex-starved, insane, or both' (Burt, 1980, p. 217). Rape myths originated in the context of rape that was perpetrated against women, but in more recent times have been introduced into the male rape literature.

One such myth is that, because of size differences, women cannot rape men (Fisher & Pina, 2013). Rape myths were clearly evident in popular reactions to the so-called 'Manacled Mormon' and it seems that Joyce McKinney was evoking one such myth when she stated that 'I have been played up as a wicked and perverted woman. It's not true. How could an eight-stone girl rape an 18-stone, 6ft 2in man?' Another rape myth that plays a part in public perceptions of this case is that 'if a man obtained an erection while being raped it probably means that he started to enjoy it' (Sleath & Bull, 2009, p. 11). Again, this myth was played upon by McKinney when she stated that raping a man 'would be like trying to squeeze a marshmallow into a parking meter'. On the contrary, research has shown that men can become sexually aroused in situations where they are in a state of fear, and that sexual arousal is not synonymous with sexual pleasure (Fisher & Pina, 2013).

Rape myths, pertaining to both men and women, need to be confronted. Victims must be treated with respect and dignity, and offenders need to be brought to justice.

The 'Language Game' of Rape

'It is generally accepted that unless sexual activity is carried out between consenting partners there will be elements of illegality in the behaviour' (Gavin, 2019, p. 155). 'Consent' is a key concept in any consideration of rape, with most trials turning on the concept. We commonly refer to 'consenting adults' and 'the age of consent' without being sufficiently definite about what this consent might be. Consent implies that a person is fully aware of the consequences of their behaviour and that they assent to, in this case, sexual behaviour.

Consent has been conceived as a continuum, with positive consent at one end and reluctant agreement at the other. Consent to gendered sexual activity is very much the product of social construction, and this is problematic. The introduction of gender-neutral rape laws was intended to buttress sexual equality, but women particularly are 'still being committed to meanings that they do not intend' (Leader-Elliot & Naffine, 2000, p. 68). As such, 'the concept (of consent) remains poorly defined and curiously unstable' (ibid., p. 48). Fletcher (1995) usefully distinguishes between the inner moment called consent and the outward sign of consent. Leader-Elliot and Naffine draw out this distinction and highlight a reluctance on the part of judges and legal commentators to consider crimes of rape from the victim's point of view. This has resulted in a situation whereby 'silence may still be construed as consent ... a stated "no" may also be construed as consent ... [and] a "yes" which has been extracted by deception ... is also thought to be consistent with consent (Leader-Elliot & Nafine, 2000, p. 68). Confused? Me too. The apparent outward signs of consent can still trump that 'inner moment' of consent in a way that privileges the perpetrator over the victim. This remains an important issue that should be addressed.

The great twentieth-century Austrian philosopher Ludwig Wittgenstein coined the term 'language game' to capture the idea that 'only in the stream of thought and life do words have meaning' (Wittgenstein, 1967, p. 173). The idea of a language game is intended to convey that language is always embedded in a particular form of life and a set of agreed conventions in social relations. The case of Kirk Anderson was played out at a time when the language game of rape was more 'traditional' than it is today. A husband could not rape his wife because the law could not conceive it. Similarly, a man could not rape another man, nor could a woman rape a man. The rules of language, at the time, and the way the language game was played simply would not allow it. This is powerful knowledge. An awareness of the power of language games also allows us to unlock the liberating potential of language.

Stalking

'Stalking' is a term used to describe the 'unwanted and/or obsessive attention by an individual or group towards another person and includes harassment and intimidation' (Gavin, 2019, p. 185).

The word 'obsessional', when applied to stalking, is contentious because it implies that the stalker has repeated and intrusive thoughts about their target, and that these thoughts about their victim are the drivers of the stalking behaviour. The contentiousness lies in the fact that this assumption that intrusive thoughts drive stalking has yet to be scientifically tested (Dixon & Bowen, 2018).

Stalking is distinct from other forms of crime because of its extremely subjective nature. In order to be stalked, a person must recognise that they are being stalked. If a person does not recognise that they are being stalked, then stalking is not happening. Importantly, research indicates that there is a high level of consistency in what people regard as stalking behaviour. A fear for one's safety combined with unwanted and repeated harassment are generally agreed to form the basis of stalking (Dixon & Bowen, 2018). On the face of it, all these factors seem to have been present in the behaviour of Joyce McKinney towards Kirk Anderson. Furthermore, and again consistent with the Kirk Anderson case, people who are victims of stalking tend to be the current or former intimates of the stalker (Melton, 2000).

Zona, Palarea and Lane (1998) generated a three-category typology of stalking: erotomaniac stalking, simple obsessional stalking and love-obsessional stalking.

The erotomaniac stalker is an individual with the delusional belief that their victim loves them, despite the fact that their victim is unattainable to them. As such, the erotomanic's stalking behaviours are about making their stalking target aware of the stalker's presence. This type of stalking is more likely to be conducted by a female, often in pursuit of high-status males with whom they have had no previous relationship.

Simple obsessional stalkers are typically rooted in either an intimate relationship or a work/professional relationship. These types of stalker tend to be seeking either vengeance for previous perceived slights or the desire to restart a relationship. At first blush, this typology certainly seems to fit what we know about the Kirk Anderson case.

Love-obsessional stalkers know their target but there is no history or previous relationship between the stalker and their target. Their victims can include public figures and celebrities (Zona et al., 1998).

CONCLUSION

It may not have been possible for Joyce McKinney to rape Kirk Anderson in 1977 because language – through legal and commonplace understandings of rape – would not allow events to be construed in that way. However, to everyone's benefit, this has not been the case since the latter part of the twentieth century.

REFLECTIVE QUESTIONS

1. Are contemporary understandings of rape gender-neutral?
2. Might the concept of consent be refined?
3. Does the subjective aspect of stalking add or detract from our understanding?

FURTHER READING

Gavin, H. (2014). Crimes of a sexual nature. Chapter 8 in *Criminological and Forensic Psychology*. Thousand Oaks, CA: Sage.

Fisher, N. L., & Pina, A. (2013). An overview of the literature on female-perpetrated adult male sexual victimization. *Aggression and Violent Behavior*, *18*(1), 54–61. doi:10.1016/j.avb.2012.10.001

Leader-Elliott, I., & Naffine, N. (2000). Wittgenstein, rape law and the language games of consent. *Monash University Law Review*, *26*(1), 48–73.

A useful resource regarding consent can be found at: https://youtu.be/Efmm2s3LxAk

14
KITTY GENOVESE

LEARNING OBJECTIVES

By the end of this chapter you should be able to:

- Discuss the case of Kitty Genovese in the context of the bystander effect
- Appraise the bystander effect with reference to critical social psychology
- Describe the relevance of psychopathy and sexually motivated homicide with reference to the murder of Kitty Genovese

SYNOPSIS OF THE CASE

The rape and murder of Kitty Genovese in 1964 is generally introduced to psychology students in order to illustrate the 'bystander effect', when the presence of others discourages an individual from intervening in an emergency situation because of a 'diffusion of responsibility'. This chapter will address the social construction of crime and how socially constructing crime also extends to socially constructing what is not a crime. Cherry's (1995) rejection of the 'group inhibition' and 'diffusion of responsibility' accounts put forward by Darley and Latané (1968) will be presented, as will her consideration of the Genovese murder through the framework of sex/gender relationships and the larger framework of multiple structures of powerlessness (sex, race, age and class) that play out in the daily lives of many people.

DESCRIPTION OF THE CASE

For more than half an hour 38 respectable, law-abiding citizens in Queens watched a killer stalk and stab a woman in three separate attacks in Kew Gardens. Twice the sound of their voices and the sudden glow of their bedroom lights interrupted him and frightened him off. Each time he returned, sought her out and stabbed her again. Not one person telephoned the police during the assault; one witness called after the woman was dead. (*New York Times*, 27 March 1964)

So runs the version of events, published in the *New York Times* on 27 March 1964, recounting the murder of Kitty (Catherine) Genovese, a 28-year-old bar-worker in the city a couple of weeks earlier on 13 March. The *New York Times* report of March 1964 was not accurate – it was, however, extraordinarily impactful. The Kitty Genovese case, as reported by the *New York Times*, took hold of the public imagination and was seen as emblematic of urban disaffection, isolation and apathy. Rooted in the flawed reporting of a terrible crime, a wave of academic research was born in which the 'bystander effect', 'diffusion of responsibility' and other tales of urban callousness became a key part of the curricula of countless psychology, sociology and criminology students. It is hardly an exaggeration to say that the Kitty Genovese case is by now embedded in our collective consciousness. The facts were as follows.

In the early hours of 13 March 1964, Kitty Genovese was driving home from work to her home in Kew Gardens, Queens, which she shared with her girlfriend Mary Ann Zielonko. The area where they lived was considered quiet and peaceful. Kitty worked nearby as a bar manager at Ev's 11th Hour, a bar in the Hollis area of Queens, New York.

Unknown to Kitty, she had been randomly targeted by Winston Moseley, a 29-year-old married father of two, for murder and rape. Moseley had been driving around for more than an hour looking for a victim when he spotted Kitty. He tailed Kitty's car back to her apartment and then followed her on foot as she walked to her building. Kitty, seeing her assailant approaching, ran.

Moseley caught up with Kitty outside a local bookshop at Kew Gardens where he stabbed her twice in the back with a hunting knife. Kitty cried out 'Oh my God, he stabbed me! Help me! Help me!' An unknown number of people in nearby apartments heard her screams. One of these, Robert Mozer, testified that when he heard Kitty cry out 'I got up and looked out, and across the street a girl was kneeling down, and this fellow was bending over her. I hollered: 'Hey, get out of there! What are you doing?' He jumped up and ran like a scared rabbit. She got up and walked out of sight, around a corner.'

Moseley had not run far. In his confession, he reported: 'I had a feeling that this man would close his window and go back to sleep, and sure enough he did.' In court, Moseley said that he had realised, at this point, that he had left his car where it might be seen, so he decided to move it away from the crime scene. At the same time, Moseley changed his stocking cap for a wide brimmed hat that would hide his features. He then walked back to his victim because, as he testified in court, 'I'd not finished what I set out to do'. Moseley found the injured Kitty lying in a hallway at the back of the building. According to Moseley, Kitty was bleeding and crying for help when he found her. He stabbed her another dozen times before raping her and running away.

Moseley was caught by the police five days later in the act of committing a burglary – he had a thing for stealing TV sets. When arrested, he confessed to the murder of Kitty Genovese and to the murder of two other Queens' residents: Annie Mae Johnson, who was 24 years of age, and Barbara Kralik, who was 15 years old. Both Annie Mae and Barbara had also been sexually assaulted.

Moseley seems an unlikely serial killer. He had been born in Manhattan in 1935 and, as a child, had been fascinated with ants. He was a clever child, if somewhat troubled, but at the time of his arrest in 1964 he owned a business operating office machines and owned his own home. Moseley was without previous convictions at the time of his arrest. He had married for the first time in 1954, was subsequently divorced and then remarried in 1961. His wife was a nurse who worked night shifts, and care for their young family was shared by Moseley's mother, which, according to the police, facilitated his prowling and criminal activity.

Following his arrest, it transpired that Moseley was a necrophiliac serial killer who had murdered three women, raped eight women and perpetrated in excess of 30 burglaries. On his conviction of first-degree murder for the killing of Kitty Genovese, Moseley was sentenced to death, despite his plea of not guilty by reason of insanity. In 1967, the Court of Appeal reduced Moseley's sentence to life imprisonment on the grounds that evidence of his mental condition should have been allowed at his sentencing hearing. Moseley was never tried for the murders of Annie Mae Johnson or Barbara Kralik.

In 1968, Moseley escaped from prison for a short time. He took five hostages and committed another rape before being captured by the FBI. Moseley was sentenced to two 15-year terms for these crimes. Moseley also took part in the Attica Prison riot of 1971, which resulted in the deaths of at least 43 people, including 10 prison staff and 33 inmates. In 1977, he was awarded a degree in sociology and expressed his regret for killing Kitty Genovese. Many, including this author, see that expression of regret as part of a plan to seek release following later parole hearings. Moseley died in prison, aged 81, on 28 March 2016.

Epilogue

In April 2016, following Winston Moseley's death, the *New York Times* ran a piece on the Kitty Genovese case in which they highlighted the shortcomings of their initial reporting in 1964:

> While there was no question that the attack occurred, and that some neighbours ignored cries for help, the portrayal of 38 witnesses as fully aware and unresponsive was erroneous. The article grossly exaggerated the number of witnesses and what they had perceived. None saw the attack in its entirety.

Only a few had glimpsed parts of it, or recognized the cries for help. Many thought they had heard lovers or drunks quarreling. There were two attacks, not three. And afterward, two people did call the police. A 70-year-old woman ventured out and cradled the dying victim in her arms until they arrived. Ms. Genovese died on the way to a hospital. But the account of 38 witnesses heartlessly ignoring a murderous attack was widely disseminated and took on a life of its own...

LINKS TO THEORY AND RESEARCH

The case of Kitty Genovese is one of the most famous stories in social psychology. 'You may be shocked to learn that this story as told by Latané and Darley (and numerous textbook writers who followed on after them) simply is not true' (Stainton Rogers, 2011, p. 4). This chapter will revisit Latané and Darley (1968), with reference to Cherry's (1995) feminist critique. The chapter will also consider psychopathy, sexually motivated murder and the treatment of sex offenders.

Bystander Effect

The *New York Times* account of 38 people idly witnessing brutal murder in 1964 gave impetus to an avalanche of research in social psychology (Dovidio, 1984) which sought to establish the conditions under which people would come to the aid of others in emergency situations. Prominent among these social psychological researchers were Bibb Latané and John Darley. Darley and Latané (1968) began an extensive programme of bystander research with a paper, now considered a classic in social psychology, which linked bystander intervention in emergencies with diffusion of responsibility. Their attention had been caught by the Genovese case but, whereas media reports of the time framed explanations in terms of 'moral decay', 'dehumanisation' caused by the urban environment, 'alienation' and 'despair', Darley and Latané saw the potential impact of the presence of other people as being crucial. Darley and Latané hypothesised that the 38 witnesses would all have been aware that other people were watching the events, and that because of this awareness of the presence of others both individual responsibility and the potential for blame were diffused. In short, everyone expected that it was someone else's responsibility to call the police.

Following on from their initial theorising about diffusion of responsibility, and using a simulated epileptic seizure as an emergency exemplar in their experimental paradigm, Darley and Latané (1968) found that people did not stand idly by in emergency situations because of apathy towards the victims of emergencies. Rather, they found that the presence of other people served to reduce individual feelings of personal responsibility, a phenomenon that would became known as the 'bystander effect'. Darley and Latané found that as more people witness an emergency, the less likely it is that any given individual will help. Conversely, if a person believes themselves to be the only person witnessing an emergency, they will have a clear sense of their responsibility and intervene.

Following experimental social psychology's engagement with the Genovese case, and the resulting concepts of 'bystander effect' and 'diffusion of responsibility', it did not take long for critical social psychology to apply its lens to the Genovese case. Critical social psychology is psychology that is entwined with questions of politics, morality and social change. The starting point of critical social psychology is a concern with exploitation, oppression and human well-being. Moreover, critical social psychology questions the assumptions, practices and broader influence of psychology generally, and social psychology in particular (Hepburn, 2011).

One of the earliest feminist critics of the Kitty Genovese case was Brownmiller (1975), who saw Genovese's murder from an entirely different perspective from that of Darley and Latané (1968). Brownmiller highlighted the 'stubborn particulars' of gender in this case and made the crucial point that the Genovese case was not merely about bystanders; rather, a key feature of the case was men's violence towards women. This gendered aspect of Genovese's murder was eloquently picked up by Cherry (1995). In a feminist critique of the Darley and Latané account, Cherry argues that Darley and Latané present an example of 'culturally embedded theorising', and she faults their abstraction of social meaning in explaining bystander intervention. Cherry argues against the type of situational determinism then common in social psychology, that is those explanations for behaviour based on 'the situation', which were manifest in the Darley and Latané and similar studies. According to Cherry, at the time of Kitty Genovese's murder, American society did little to intervene in situations where violence was perpetrated against women. Indeed, American society, like many other societies of the time, did not have a name for, or recognise, widespread violence against women.

Cherry (1995) notes that the Darley and Latané studies stripped away factors like race and gender that were at the heart of Kitty Genovese's murder. In contrast, Cherry highlights perceptions of female and male relatedness. It is very interesting that, as Cherry points out, in the social psychological research that followed in the wake of the Genovese murder, the focus was turned away from the victim and the perpetrator and instead focused on the bystanders.

This aversion of gaze did not take place in a vacuum. Kassin (2017) reports how, in 1964, the police had an innocent man, the then 18-year-old Alvin Mitchell, in their sights for the murder of Barbara Kralik. The police had elicited a confession from Mitchell, following a 13-hour, all-night interrogation, a coerced confession which Mitchell subsequently recanted. Crucially, this confession was 'elicited' from Mitchell prior to Moseley's arrest for the Genovese murder and his confession to the killing of Barbara Kralik. Although Moseley's confession included details that only Kralik's murderer could have known, unperturbed, the police proceeded to prosecute Mitchell for the crime. He subsequently served a long jail term for the murder of Barbara Kralik, and Moseley was never tried for this murder.

The particular relevance of the Kralik murder, and Alvin Mitchell, to the Kitty Genovese story is this: in 1964, the local New York newspapers were aware that

Moseley had confessed to the Kralik murder and that Alvin Mitchell was claiming coercion by the police. Michael Murphy, the New York Police Department Commissioner, used the Genovese murder to deflect attention. When a *New York Times* journalist asked Commissioner Murphy about the claim of coercion, Murphy reportedly changed the subject, saying 'Brother, that Queens story is one for the books. Thirty-eight witnesses … this beats everything (Cook, 2014, p. 97; Pelonero 2014, p. 164). For the first time on record, Murphy injected into the story the now questionable claim that 38 witnesses had failed to act' (Kassin, 2017, p. 378). From here, the story grew a life of its own.

Serial Killing

Serial murder is a topic that gives rise to widespread public interest, as a quick perusal of any daily TV schedule or any given bookshop's ample crime section will attest. Winston Moseley was a serial killer who murdered at least three women. At his trial, Moseley admitted that he had a compulsion to kill women (Lurigio, 2015). I think that most of us would agree that Kitty Genovese's murderer was a callous, serial-killing 'psychopath'. But what does that mean? Adjorlolo and Chan (2014, p. 486) report that the term 'serial killer' is one of the 'least understood in the criminology literature. As such, the terms 'serial killer' and 'psychopath' warrant closer examination.

Serial homicide has been defined thus:

[it generally involves] three or more victims. What sets this category apart … is a cooling-off period between murders. The hiatus could be days, months, or years. In other words, the serial killer is not killing with frequency. Part of the reason is that the organized type of killer is not generally a risk taker. He wants to be sure that if he decides to commit a crime, he will be in a win-win position. Second, he does not have to kill often if he is taking mementos from the victim—some clothing or jewellery—so he can relive the crime and extend the fantasy. A serial killer usually goes after strangers, but the victims tend to share similarities such as gender, age, or occupation. Although he prefers a certain look or background, it does not mean he will not substitute another victim if he cannot find his intended target. At any given time, there are between thirty-five and fifty serial killers in the United States, and that is a conservative estimate. About a dozen serial killers are arrested each year. (Douglas, Burgess, Burgess, & Ressler, 2006, p. 461)

Psychopathy

Psychopathy is a term with wide contemporary currency among the public. In common parlance, we know what another person means when they speak of psychopathy. In a technical sense, however, matters are less clear-cut. Psychopathy, as a diagnosis, has never been included in the American Psychiatric Association's

Diagnostic and Statistical Manual (DSM). Nor has psychopathy ever been included in the World Health Organisation's *International Classification of Diseases* (ICD). Instead, the APA and WHO include Antisocial and Dissocial Personality Disorder in their respective manuals. These diagnoses share some, but not all, of the characteristics of psychopathy (Clark, 2014).

Hare and Cox (1978) present the clinical concept of psychopathy as one which rests on the assumption that some people share a particular set of symptoms and personality traits, for example, 'deviant' expressions of sexuality, and selfishness. In terms of its intellectual genealogy, a line can be traced from the concept of psychopathy back to the nineteenth-century musings of Cesare Lombroso about 'homo criminalis'. Psychopathy researchers often argue that 'the manifest behavioural signs of psychopathy are merely rough approximations of the more fundamental and true biological signs' (Jalava, 2006, p. 427).

Psychopathy should be understood as a clinical disorder characterised by a specific array of interpersonal, affective and lifestyle characteristics. Important among these characteristics are: glibness and superficial charm; a grandiose sense of self-worth; a need for stimulation; pathological lying; conning and manipulation; lack of remorse or guilt; shallow affect; lack of empathy; leading a parasitic lifestyle; poor behavioural controls; promiscuous sexual behaviour; early behavioural problems; a lack of realistic, long-term goals; impulsivity; irresponsibility; failure to accept responsibility for one's action; having many short-term relationships; juvenile delinquency; and criminal versatility. While the label 'psychopathy' includes the clinical features of several personality disorders, defining a given individual as a psychopath is 'not akin to rendering a clinical diagnosis. Rather, it is the acknowledgment that an individual exhibits behaviour and personality characteristics that are consistent with the clinical description of psychopathy' (DeMatteo, Fairfax-Columbo, & Scully, 2017, p. 2744).

There is notable circularity here, in the definition of the psychopath, that we should be aware of – psychopathy is inferred from antisocial behaviour while antisocial behaviour is at the same time explained by psychopathy (Jacobs, 1964). Understood in terms of psychopathy, it could be argued that because of the circumstances of Winston Moseley's murder of Kitty Genovese, and his other criminal behaviour, we can say that he was a psychopath. At the same time, it could be argued that Moseley murdered Kitty Genovese because he was a psychopath.

Sexually-Motivated Murder

Holmes and Holmes (2009) consider 'Lust Murder' in their chapter on sexually-motivated homicides, and outline how serial killers of a hedonistic type as well as power/control killers are driven by sex to kill. Holmes and Holmes suggest that John Gacy and Ted Bundy, among others, fit this typology. They might well add Winston Moseley.

Evidence from Kitty Genovese's murder indicates that Moseley was motivated by a hunger for sexual gratification, and it seems clear that he had made a connection between sexual gratification and fatal violence. Holmes and Holmes (2009) point out that lust killers often combine aberrant sexual practices, including picquerism (the sexually-driven interest in penetrating the skin of another person with sharp objects), flagellation (flogging or beating for sexual gratification), anthropophagy (cannibalism with sexual connotations), and necrosadism (committing murder in order to have sex with a corpse). The observations made by Holmes and Holmes certainly ring true in the case of Winston Moseley, as does their observation that sex is paramount in terms of motivation.

Treatment of Sex Offenders

Moseley expressed 'regret' for killing Kitty Genovese in 1977, 13 years after her murder. Considering what we know about psychopathy – that is, how manipulative psychopaths are, their loose relation with the truth, their failure to accept responsibility for their actions, and a lack of remorse or guilt – it is hard to see Moseley's 'regret' as anything other than an attempt to manipulate his parole board and regain his freedom. However, prejudices and 'gut feelings' are an insufficient basis from which to embark on a consideration of how convicted sex offenders might best be treated. More solid ground is needed. There are two crucial aspects to the treatment of sex offenders – rehabilitation and the assessment of risk (Gavin, 2019).

Rehabilitation

Since the 1990s accredited sex offender treatment programmes (SOTP) have been implemented across the UK. The Core SOTP builds on cognitive behavioural therapy (CBT) principles and uses strategies focused on deviant arousal, distorted thinking, reducing denial on the part of perpetrators, and promoting empathy for victims to try to prevent reoffending and to help offenders build the self-management skills needed to achieve this. Core SOTP treatment in the UK, on average, lasts for 180 hours. It is generally delivered via two-hour sessions that take place a couple of times each week. There are other treatments available, including pharmacological treatments and extended SOTP (Gavin, 2019).

Risk

There is a lack of evidence pertaining to the efficacy of sex offender treatment programmes. However, what evidence there is does indicate that sex offender treatment appears to be more successful with adolescents rather than adult offenders. Furthermore, in a meta-analysis of sex offender recidivism research, US-based researchers Kim, Benekos and Merlo (2016) found that surgical castration and hormonal medication have significantly larger effects compared to psychological SOTPs, which they report as showing small but significant effect sizes. Kim et al. also note the need for more rigorous studies with better research designs and, as such, recommend that their results be interpreted cautiously.

In the UK, a report commissioned by the Ministry of Justice indicates that the Core SOTP does not have the positive effect reported by earlier research (Mews, Di Bella, & Purver, 2017). Rather, according to Mews et al., treated sex offenders were more likely to reoffend with a sexual crime than matched non-treatment offenders.

In the Genovese case, Winston Moseley was judged by 15 parole boards to be ineligible for parole. It is hard to disagree with their judgement. Winston Moseley's death in jail, aged 81 years, seems to have been a fitting end.

CONCLUSION

Over the years, social psychology has shifted from being a solely predictive science to one that incorporates more interpretative aspects (Cherry, 1995). Over the same period, there had been an argument to reorient psychological science towards usefulness rather than truth (i.e. truth with a capital 'T'; truth understood as relative (small 't') rather than absolute (Gergen, 2001)).

The murder of Kitty Genovese was a terrible crime committed by a serial killer displaying psychopathic traits. But it is a useful and interesting case to consider for many reasons, not least because it is one of the few cases where the victim is better known than the perpetrator. The bystander paradigm led to the introduction of the 911 emergency service and a focus on the victims of crime. However, located as it was in the social psychology of the late 1960s, Darley and Latané's research trumpeted a 'hardcore situationalist message' (Kassin, 2017). It is no bad thing that psychology now has a more nuanced embarkation point in understanding crimes such as this.

Ultimately, the shift in social psychology from a predictive to an interpretative science is a powerful illustration of the truth (with a small 't'!) that theorising does not have one meaning for all time (Cherry, 1995). Ultimately, what counts is that which is both useful and aids understanding (Gergen, 2001).

REFLECTIVE QUESTIONS

1. Can you think of situations in your own experience where diffusion of responsibility has impeded someone receiving help?
2. Is psychopathy a useful concept? Why or why not?
3. Could the Kitty Genovese case happen today?

FURTHER READING

www.nytimes.com/1964/03/27/archives/37-who-saw-murder-didnt-call-the-police-apathy-at-stabbing-of.html

www.nytimes.com/2016/04/06/insider/1964-how-many-witnessed-the-murder-of-kitty-genovese.html

www.nytimes.com/2016/04/05/nyregion/winston-moseley-81-killer-of-kitty-genovese-dies-in-prison.html

Cherry, F. (1995). Chapter 2: Kitty Genovese and culturally embedded theorizing. In *Stubborn Particulars of Social Psychology: Essays on the Research Process*. London and New York: Routledge.

Kassin, S. M. (2017). The killing of Kitty Genovese: What else does this case tell us? *Perspectives on Psychological Science, 12*(3), 374–381. doi:10.1177/1745691616679465

PART IV
FIRESETTING AND HOMICIDE

15
FIRESETTING AND HOMICIDE: AN OVERVIEW

This chapter introduces a broad overview of firesetting and homicide, including some definitions, and serves to set the scene for the chapters to follow on firesetting (arson), genocide, mass killing, serial killing and murder-suicide. In our examination of homicide, we will consider the case of a serial killer who was also an arsonist; a lethal motorcycle gang rivalry, a reserve police battalion, comprised of middle-aged men, who murdered thousands of people; a former US marine who went on a shooting spree; a serial-killing PhD student of criminology; and a primary school headmaster who murdered his family before committing suicide.

In a sense, we are all like moths drawn to a flame when it comes to a consideration of arson and murder. There is something primitively entrancing about fire, the boom in horror movies and the appeal of true crime TV shows evidences an interest in illegal killing that is deeply embedded in the human psyche. This captivation with homicide is not a modern phenomenon. From the biblical Cain and Abel in prehistory, to Vlad the Impaler in the middle ages and Jack the Ripper in Victorian London, we can see that for as long as there have been people, there has been a fascination with murder. The Brothers Grimm knew well how to harness our fascination with the dark side in order to weave stories that entice, for folklore too plays on archetypes and fears that are part of what we are. It is little wonder that fire and murder continues its hold on our collective consciousness today.

FIRESETTING

The law generally refers to firesetting as arson, and arson is usually defined as the unlawful use of fire for the intentional destruction of property, although legal definitions do vary across jurisdictions. Definitional variations notwithstanding, most jurisdictions associate arson with three core components: intent underlying the arson; unlawful aims associated with the arson (e.g. to cause harm or to benefit fraudulently); and a stipulation that the arson must cause damage (Gannon & Pina, 2010). Rather than using the term 'arson', because of the definitional variability of the term across jurisdictions, Gannon and Pina (2010) instead employ the term 'firesetting', which incorporates all intentional acts of setting a fire. That is the definition we followed in this chapter.

In purely economic terms, arson is a much more significant problem than many people realise. The UK's National Fire Chiefs Council (NFCC) reports that arson is the country's single biggest cause of fire. In 2017/18, they report that of the 213,782 fires attended in the UK, 108,024 were set deliberately. Furthermore, the fire chiefs estimate that in 2017/18 the cost of arson to the UK economy was between £5.73 billion and £11.46 billion (NFCC, n.d.).

As with many crimes, there are distinct classifications of those categories of behaviour that constitute arson, both within and across professional boundaries. In line with the Criminal Damage Act (1971), the police record categories of arson as intentional or reckless damage to property; damage to property that endangers the life of another; and damage to property caused by fire (Daykin & Hamilton, 2012).

Psychological conceptualisations and taxonomies of arson, in contrast to the legally based police categories outlined above, see arson in terms of categories associated with (among other things) mental illness, sexual gratification, revenge, power, excitement, terrorism and fraud (e.g. Gavin, 2019). However, research pertaining to both arson and arsonists is scant at this time, so it is necessary to consider existing theory and what this theory has to say about firesetting (Gavin, 2019).

Psychological theories applied to firesetting include psychodynamic theories, biological theories, social learning theory, functional analysis theory, and dynamic behaviour theory (Gannon & Pina, 2010). These theories will be considered in Chapter 16 with reference to the specific case of Peter Dinsdale (aka Bruce Lee), an arsonist and serial killer responsible for more than 30 fires and convicted of the manslaughter of 26 victims (Gavin, 2019).

HOMICIDE

Homicide is without doubt the most serious manifestation of violent crime (Brookman, 2005). It is the taking of the life of another person or people. Interestingly, homicide is not, by definition, illegal. Some homicides, such as state-sponsored executions, are the purposive taking of the life of one person by another person but are not criminal.

The word 'homicide' is generally used to describe what should, strictly speaking, be reported as criminal homicide (Walters & Hickey, 2015). The range of crimes covered by the term 'criminal homicide' is diverse, from fatal road traffic accidents (e.g. vehicular homicide) to corporate killing (e.g. via unsafe work environments or contaminated foodstuffs) to serial killers (e.g. Ted Bundy). In Chapter 17 we look at homicide in the context of specific group membership and social identity theory. Some crimes simply cannot be understood at a solely individual level of analysis. The motorcycle murder, considered in Chapter 17, offers a clear example of a case where group identification motivates murder.

GENOCIDE

Let not one of them go free of sudden death at our hands; not the young man child that the mother carries still in her body, not even he, but let all of Ilion's people perish, utterly blotted out and unmourned for. (Agamemnon to Menelaus at Troy, *The Iliad*, Homer c. 850 BCE)

Genocide is not a new phenomenon. It has been a part of human experience from ancient times, as the opening quote demonstrates. Gavin (2019, p. 11) defines genocide as 'the killing of a group in order to eradicate that group's identity, ethnicity, race, or religion'. In recent years, we have witnessed genocide in Myanmar, where the Rohingya people have been targeted for rape, murder, brutalisation and eviction by government forces. Zimbardo (2007, p. 12) describes the twentieth century as the 'mass murder century' and reports that in excess of 50 million people were murdered in genocides during this time. This figure includes some 1.5 million Armenians, who were murdered by Turks, at least 6 million Jews murdered by the Nazis, alongside some 3 million Soviet prisoners of war, 2 million Polish citizens, and many hundreds of thousands of 'undesirable' people, including homosexuals, gypsies and Jehovah's Witnesses. Elsewhere, the Ba'ath party in Iraq, under the leadership of Saddam Hussain, murdered 100,000 Kurds, and in Rwanda, 800,000 people, including about three-quarters of the entire Tutsi population, were murdered by their Hutu neighbours in a period of about three months.

Milgram's obedience studies have been, and continue to be, widely taught in psychology (Dickerson, 2012). In part, this is because they raise a challenging question: What can explain the willingness of 'ordinary people' to do exceptional violence when ordered or asked to do so?

In Chapter 18 we examine the case of a German Reserve Police Battalion composed of middle-aged men from Hamburg. During World War Two, this unit carried out a central role in the implementation of the 'Final Solution' in Eastern Europe (Browning, 2001). This case study allows us to reflect on classic and contemporary psychological explanations of genocide, ranging from the early work of Tajfel (e.g. Tajfel, 1979) and Milgram (1963) to more recent research conducted by Haslam and Reicher (e.g. Haslam & Reicher, 2007).

MASS KILLING

Mass killing describes those homicides in which multiple people are murdered in a single event and in the same geographical area. The Dunblane massacre, in which Thomas Hamilton walked into a Scottish primary school in 1996 and murdered a schoolteacher and 16 children before killing himself, is one prominent example of this type of murder in the UK (Brookman, 2005). The shootings at Hungerford (in the UK) and Columbine (in Colorado, USA) are two more prominent examples of this category.

Mass killings, or mass murders, are also sometimes referred to as 'spree killing'. However, there are differences between mass killings and spree killings. Spree killings are spread across different geographical locations and can take place over a period of up to 30 days (Brookman, 2005).

In Chapter 19, our examination of mass killing will focus on one well-known mass killer, Charles Whitman. On 1 August 1966, while still a student, Charles Whitman murdered his wife and mother and then shot and killed 14 people and wounded 13 others. He was eventually shot dead by the police. An autopsy revealed that Whitman had a large brain tumour in the amygdala. The chapter will consider whether the explanation for Whitman's crime lies in the life of Charles Whitman or can be attributed to his brain tumour? Using the Whitman case as a basis, the relationship between neurobiology and criminal behaviour will be investigated.

SERIAL KILLING

Serial murder can be defined as the killing of three or more people by the same perpetrator over a period of time (usually more than 30 days), with a 'cooling-off' period between murders (Brookman, 2005; Gavin, 2019). Serial killers have been described as monsters, and there is little doubt that monsters, especially fictional ones, have a certain allure. Dietrich and Fox Hall (2010, p. 95) sensibly point out that 'serial killers in real life may not be as alluring as fictional ones, but they are at least fascinating in a terrifying way'. There is something about serial killers that we are driven to understand.

In Chapter 20, we look at the case of Stephen Griffiths, who was a PhD student studying criminology at Bradford University when he was tried and convicted of murdering three women. The well-known criminologist David Wilson, whose books Griffiths seems to have read, has looked in some depth at this case. Wilson suggests that Griffiths is a misogynist with a narcissistic personality disorder and believes that he set out to be recognised as a serial killer.

Canter (1994, p. 299) states that 'through his actions the criminal tells us about how he has chosen to live his life. The challenge is to reveal his destructive life story; to uncover the plot in which crime appears to play such a significant part'. Canter also argues that criminals are limited people and that their limited narratives share a common factor – the victim is regarded as less than human. The Griffiths case will be used to reflect on Canter's view of the importance of criminal narrative.

MURDER-SUICIDE

Murder-suicide is when a perpetrator kills one or more person and either kills themselves at the same time or shortly afterwards (Gavin, 2019). These cases are tragedies that often occur in a domestic context. Victims of murder-suicide are often the partners and/or children of the perpetrator and the motivation to commit these murders seems to be the same as those at play in cases of domestic violence (Gavin, 2019).

One particularly tragic case of murder-suicide was that perpetrated by Alan Hawe, the subject of Chapter 21. The circumstances surrounding Alan Hawe's murder of his family, and subsequent suicide at his home in Cavan, Ireland, in August 2016, share many characteristics found in other murder-suicides. Hawe, a deputy school principal, had been seen accessing pornography on his laptop while in school in the run-up to the atrocity. The killer was also facing allegations of engaging in an 'indecent act' in the school setting in relation to the same incident.

CONCLUSION

The chapters that follow will set out some of the psychological factors that are important to understanding cases of arson, murder, murder-suicide, firesetting, serial killers, mass killings and genocide through the use of high-profile cases. Taken together, these cases highlight the heterogenous nature of murder. Yet there is a theme that unites them. These awful cases all raise the same question – 'why'? Arntfield and Danesi (2017) suggest that murder and narrative are linked. Arntfield and Danesi also argue that narratives of murder transfix our species, inspiring loathing and fascination, often simultaneously. It certainly seems that firesetting, and homicide, touch some deep-seated need in our species – a need to understand. This section seeks to offer some detail appropriate to this endeavour.

16

PETER DINSDALE AKA BRUCE LEE

LEARNING OBJECTIVES

By the end of this chapter you should be able to:

- Distinguish between firesetting, arson and pyromania
- Set out some detail pertaining to the case of Peter Dinsdale/Bruce Lee
- Discuss psychopathology (especially antisocial personality disorder and psychopathy) in the context of arson
- Outline three theoretical perspectives on firesetting/arson
- Debate moral responsibility, in the context of arson, with reference to psychiatric diagnoses

SYNOPSIS OF THE CASE

Peter Dinsdale, aka Bruce Lee, is one of Britain's most prolific but least well-known serial killers. Currently serving a life sentence, he was convicted of 26 counts of manslaughter, 11 of which were later overturned, and he confessed to 11 counts of arson. Reported to have said that 'I am devoted to fire and I despise people', Dinsdale's case will be used to reflect on the psychology of firesetting.

DESCRIPTION OF THE CASE

In January 1981, *The Guardian* newspaper ran the headline 'The "twisted kid" who became mass arson killer' above the by-line 'Bruce Lee, aged 20, who spent most of his childhood in council care, admitted causing a series of fires in which 26 people died'.

Bruce Lee, born on 31 July 1960 in Withington, Manchester, was christened Peter Dinsdale. Peter was born into difficult circumstances and did not have an easy start in life. His mother, Doreen Dinsdale, was a prostitute, and there is no record of his father on Peter's birth certificate. Peter was born with several disabilities, including congenital spastic hemiplegia, a condition which means that the muscles on one side of the body are constantly contracted, and he also had learning difficulties. Peter suffered from epilepsy, and was recorded as having a below average IQ. Because of these factors, Peter attended special schools, mostly in Hull, where Peter grew up.

At the age of four, Peter had his first contact with the authorities when his mother abandoned him with a neighbour and he was taken into care by Humberside Social Services. Peter spent most of his childhood years between foster homes and social services providers. He was a difficult and troubled child, who was in the care of the council until he was 18 years of age. A massive fan of martial arts movie hero Bruce Lee, Dinsdale changed his name by deed poll to that of his idol in 1979.

The Guardian newspaper, in their 1981 report, cites a spokesman for the council who said that Mr Lee 'had an 'overriding desire throughout to live with his mother'. Time after time he went back to her, but he soon found himself back in care after yet another failure of the mother–child relationship'. The paper also reports that 'his relationship with his mother bordered on hatred as he grew older'.

Referred to by many who knew him as 'daft Peter' and 'Limpy Loo', Bruce Lee was a homosexual child sex predator, who, at the time of *The Guardian* article in 1981, had just been convicted of a series of arson attacks and identified as Britain's (then) most prolific killer.[1] He was then 20 years old.

Lee's first arson attack had taken place in 1973 when he was just 13 years of age. Over the course of his 'career', Lee admitted to the police that he had started 11 fires and killed 26 people. The police arrested Lee following a house-fire at Selby Street in west Hull on 4 December 1979, in which three brothers aged 15, 12 and 8, died. The dead children's mother survived after being pushed, by one of the children, from an upstairs window. Another child survived by jumping out of a bedroom window at the back of the house. Three other children were staying with neighbours on the night of the tragedy.

---

[1] Dinsdale's dubious 'record' as Britain's most prolific serial killer was subsequently surpassed by deviant GP, Dr Harold Shipman.

At the time of the fire, police interviewed Lee, but he was not arrested until six months later when he told Detective Superintendent Ron Sagar that he, Lee, was responsible for a series of arson attacks in Hull from 1973 onwards. It transpired that Lee had been motivated to attack the home at Selby Street, while its occupants slept, by revenge. Lee said that he had been involved in indecent behaviour with the 15-year-old boy who died in the attack. It is also reported that, according to Lee, the boy had demanded money in exchange for not telling the police about what had happened. Lee also told police that he was in love with a 16-year-old sister of the dead boys, but that the siblings regarded Lee as a hanger-on and an object of mirth and derision. In his confession, Lee described in detail how he had poured paraffin through the letterbox of the house in Selby Street, and after a couple of failed attempts, had lit some newspaper which he shoved through the letterbox, igniting the paraffin and setting the house ablaze. Lee's confession was in accordance with forensic evidence found at the Selby Street crime scene and convinced detectives that they had their culprit. Lee proceeded to confess to a string of other arson offences, including the killings of a 1-year-old baby, Andrew Edwards, who died following an arson attack in June 1976, and a 6-year-old boy who was killed in another Hull attack in June 1973.

Lee was tried at Leeds Crown Court in January 1981. He admitted to killing 26 people in 11 fires between 1973 and 1979, but he pleaded guilty to manslaughter on the grounds of diminished responsibility, not to murder. The trial judge accepted the plea on the basis that Lee was suffering from a psychopathic personality disorder and, in 1981, Lee was sentenced to be detained for life under the Mental Health Act. At the time of writing, Lee remains incarcerated.

Postscript

In 1983, the Court of Appeal overturned Bruce Lee's conviction for starting a fire in which 11 men died, after evidence came to light showing that the fire had been caused by a faulty boiler. As a result, this brought the number of deaths for which Lee was responsible down from 26 to 15. It is hard not to wonder whether Lee, the man who had claimed that his ambition was to 'break the Guinness World Record' for serial killers, was conflicted about this finding.

LINKS TO THEORY AND RESEARCH

As with many subjects of forensic interest, firesetting is an area where legal and clinical perspectives overlap, albeit under different labels and via distinct vocabularies. 'Arson' is a legal term that describes those crimes which are committed whenever a person maliciously and deliberately sets a fire with the intention of causing damage. The arsonist is one who commits an act of arson (Gavin, 2019). Arson is among the easiest of crimes to commit – the arsonist does not need to interact with any other person. Indeed, the arsonist does not need as much as a weapon, and it is easy to commit an act of arson on impulse (Burton, McNiel, & Binder, 2012).

The term 'firesetting', in contrast, derives from the clinical sphere, where it is the preferred term for describing the intentional setting of fires. In this context, it does not require the person setting a fire to have a malicious intent to cause damage (Gavin, 2019). A person burning leaves in the garden can be a firesetter without being an arsonist.[2] Firesetting is not necessarily a manifestation of underlying psychopathology, but pyromania is such a manifestation. It involves the repeated and deliberate setting of fires. 'In short, firesetting is a behaviour, arson is a crime, and pyromania is a psychiatric diagnosis' (Burton et al., 2012, p. 355).

Burton, McNiel and Binder (2012) argue that forensic experts can make a useful contribution to the legal system by educating non-clinicians on the difference between firesetting, arson and pyromania. These distinctions are a key point that the reader should take from this chapter.

Bruce Lee was convicted of arson following his trial and was, by his own admission, a firesetter. The Bruce Lee/Peter Dinsdale case raises important theoretical questions pertaining to psychopathology and our understanding of those who commit the crime of arson. These questions include the significance of pyromania, our understanding of serial killing and psychopathology, the relevance of sex in firesetting, a consideration of whether psychodynamic theorising adds to our understanding of firesetting, and the usefulness of profiling in identifying arsonists.

Psychopathology

Pyromania

The American Psychiatric Association's DSM-5 defines pyromania as a disorder that is characterised by firesetting which is repetitive, purposive and deliberate. Pyromaniac fire-setting behaviour is not related to any external rewards and should be accompanied by affective arousal or tension before the act of firesetting. To satisfy a diagnosis of pyromania, firesetting behaviour should be accompanied by gratification, pleasure or relief, and the firesetter should have a fascination with, interest in, curiosity about or attraction to fire and its situational contexts. The firesetting should not be explicable via any other diagnosis or behaviour (e.g. drug use) (American Psychiatric Association, 2013).

It should be noted that recorded instances of pyromania in the firesetting literature are rare. The most common diagnoses associated with firesetting seem to be conduct disorder and antisocial personality disorder (Gannon & Pina, 2010).

Conduct Disorder

Conduct disorder is characterized by behaviour that violates either the rights of others or major societal norms. These symptoms must be present for at least three months with one symptom having been present in the past six months. To be diagnosed with conduct disorder, the symptoms must cause significant

---

[2] Guilty author. Don't ask. Nobody was hurt and £20 covered the damage.

impairment in social, academic or occupational functioning. The disorder is typically diagnosed prior to adulthood. (American Psychiatric Association, 2013)

DSM-5 sets out a list of criteria and behaviours that must be met in order for a diagnosis of conduct disorder to be made. These include the person having perpetrated a forcible sex act on another, property destruction by arson, the person having run away from home at least twice, and having been truant before the age of 13. In addition, the person with conduct disorder will present with limited prosocial emotions. They will demonstrate a lack of remorse or guilt, a lack of empathy and callousness, and they will be unconcerned about performance and have shallow or deficient affect.

Antisocial Personality Disorder

Antisocial personality disorder is one of a range of personality disorders. Personality disorders can be understood as long-term patterns of behaviour and experience that deviate from the norms that are present in the culture of a given individual. Personality disorders are wide-ranging and diverse, but tend to first appear during adolescence and, once they have appeared, personality disorders tend to be stable over time (Field & Cartwright-Hatton, 2015). DSM-5 (American Psychiatric Association, 2013) sets out 10 personality disorders in three clusters:

- Cluster A, the odd-eccentric cluster, including paranoid, schizotypal and schizoid personality disorders;
- Cluster B, the dramatic-emotional cluster, including antisocial, borderline, histrionic, and narcissistic personality disorder; and
- Cluster C, the anxious-fearful cluster, including avoidant, dependant, and obsessive-compulsive personality disorder.

Bruce Lee is on record as saying that at least one of the fires that he started was because of a grudge that he held against the family occupying the house. Others, he says, were started simply because of the pleasure he derived from starting the fire (Gavin, 2019).

Working from second-hand sources it is obviously impossible to reach a definitive conclusion as to whether or not Dinsdale/Lee had an antisocial personality disorder or indeed whether he suffers from pyromania. However, it is clear that some aspects of his case fall into these general areas.

Another psychopathology that was raised in the course of the Lee case was psychopathy. The trial judge accepted Lee's plea of manslaughter on the grounds of diminished responsibility because the court accepted that Lee was suffering from a psychopathic personality disorder.

Psychopathy

It is important to note that psychopathy is not a diagnosis recognised by both the American Psychiatric Association's *Diagnostic and Statistical Manual of Mental*

Disorders or by the World Health Organisation's *International Classification of Diseases* (ICD) (Field & Cartwright-Hatton, 2015). However, the concept of psychopathy has been influential in terms of academic, forensic and clinical practice and, as such, it is important to consider psychopathy with regard to Bruce Lee, especially since psychopathic personality disorder was referred to in the case.

Psychopathy is a type of personality disorder marked by coldness, superficial charm and a ruthless callousness towards others. The idea of the psychopath has been around for a very long time. The concept adopted its modern guise in the writings of an American psychiatrist, Hervey M. Cleckley, whose *The Mask of Sanity* (1941) presented Cleckley's clinically rooted observation that, for some people – those we now call psychopaths – a mask of 'normality' hides an interiority that is dangerous and pathological.

Following Cleckley's 1941 work, the Canadian psychologist Robert Hare further developed the concept of psychopathy when he applied factor analysis to data derived from Cleckley's original criteria and developed a five factor model of psychopathy. The factors are: an inability to develop warm empathic relationships, an unstable lifestyle, the inability to accept responsibility for antisocial behaviour, an absence of intellectual and psychiatric problems and weak behavioural control. Hare went on to develop the Psychopathy Checklist (currently the PCL-R: Hare, 2003), a widely used assessment tool in clinical forensic practice (Hollin, 2013).

Glenn, Johnson and Raine (2013) report that one of the primary questions of the recent past facing those who study personality disorders is how the category of antisocial personality disorder relates to other constructs of psychopathology, including psychopathy. Glenn et al. offer the opinion that while, in some instances, there may be overlap between antisocial personality disorder and psychopathy, and some individuals diagnosed with antisocial personality disorder may have psychopathic traits, ultimately the underlying psychobiological processes may be distinct. While accepting that diagnoses cannot be made on the basis of secondary material such as that presented in this chapter, the facts as we know them of the Bruce Lee/Peter Dinsdale case certainly seem to bear out this point of view.

Psychodynamic Theory

Freud was one of the earliest thinkers to offer an explanation of firestarting, in his paper 'The acquisition of fire' (Freud, 1932). Over subsequent years, other psychodynamic theorists approached the subject and, perhaps unsurprisingly, sought an explanation that relates to sex. One view put forward is that firesetting is associated with either urethral or oral-fixated sex drives (Gannon & Pina, 2010). One of Freud's ideas is that urinating on fires (by males) is a manifestation of a homosexual urge (Gavin, 2019).

While there may be a sexual element to some of Bruce Lee's firesetting, relating to his unrequited interest in one of the sisters at the Selby Street attack, it should be noted that psychodynamic explanations are notoriously difficult to validate and sexual desire has been a recognised factor in very few firesetting cases (Gannon & Pina, 2010).

Social Learning Theory

Social learning theorists argue that there are two types of learning that are particularly relevant to moral behaviours and behaviours such as firestarting: direct leaning, whereby people are rewarded or punished for behaving in certain ways; and observational learning, where people learn from observing other people being rewarded or punished for behaving in certain ways (Westcott, 2006).

Understanding firesetting in terms of reward, as social learning theory suggests we should, is potentially very useful. Gannon and Pina (2010) report that firesetting is instantly rewarding, because fires are intensely exciting in and of themselves and because the sirens, fire engines, bustle and paraphernalia associated with fire are instantly stimulating and exhilarating. As Gannon and Pina (2010, p. 230) argue:

> social learning theory appears most likely to account for the etiology of revenge of anger-related firestarting ... thus poor childhood socialization characterized by exposure to negative developmental experiences (i.e. perceived failure), and role models may result in aggression, poor coping skills, and lack of assertiveness. These traits are associated characteristics of firesetters and so are likely to increase an individual's propensity to light fires in an attempt to gain positive environmental control.

This observation certainly seems to chime with the facts pertaining to Bruce Lee.

Social learning theory has been most useful in so far as it highlights the importance of developmental experiences in the aetiology of firesetting behaviours and it fits well with the evidence that is available regarding the developmental experiences of known firesetters. However, the theory is somewhat lacking in clinical utility as it cannot predict what factors will come together and produce firesetting behaviour and account for some people becoming firesetters, but not others (Gannon & Pina, 2010).

Functional Analysis Theory

Functional analysis theory was developed by Jackson, Glass and Hope (1987) in an attempt to understand recidivistic arson. The approach grew out of Jackson's clinical experiences of working with pathological firesetters in a maximum-security hospital. Functional analysis theory incorporates social learning principles and understands pathological firesetting to be an attempt by individuals to change their circumstances when other options have failed them.

Jackson et al. (1987) regard fascination and playing with fire as a 'normal' aspect of children's development. What matters in the development of pathological firesetting behaviour is how parents, peers and authority react. Antecedents (i.e. prior events and circumstances) and behavioural consequences interact to facilitate and maintain firesetting. Antecedent factors include psychosocial disadvantage, low self-esteem, previous experience of fire and triggering events that cause fear or frustration. Behavioural consequences serve to reinforce the firesetting behaviour. Such consequences can include everything from attention to excitement to relief from stress. Winder and Banyard (2012) even report cases of arsonists who have set fires in order to get back into prison because they experience prison as a place of safety.

Functional analysis theory (e.g. Gannon & Pina, 2010; Winder & Banyard, 2012) is useful because of its clinical utility and because it offers a theoretical coherence to understanding firestarting that builds on a solid developmental perspective (i.e. social learning theory).

Firesetting, Serial Killing and Moral Responsibility

Peter Dinsdale/Bruce Lee was Britain's most prolific serial killer at the time of his conviction. At the time of writing, almost 40 years later, Lee remains Britain's most prolific serial fatal arsonist, with responsibility for more than 30 fires (Gavin, 2019). It is interesting that firesetting is a feature in the histories of many serial killers (Miller, 2014). Why this might be the case is not clear.

The case of Bruce Lee raises important philosophical questions (see also Chapter 19 on Charles Whitman). If we accept that Bruce Lee felt compelled to set fires as a consequence of his personality disorder, what does that mean in terms of his culpability and responsibility? It does seem to be accepted that Lee lacked control over his impulse to set fires, hence his life sentence under the Mental Health Act.

If firesetting is the consequence of an uncontrollable impulse, and thus a medical condition (i.e. a personality disorder), what about free will (versus determinism) and moral responsibility? Deal (2010) argues that people should only be considered morally responsible when they choose their actions. Human beings are considered different from other animals because we are not slaves to our instincts or hard-wired responses. Humans act with intent and deliberation. Because we can decide to behave in certain ways, we are deemed to be responsible for our actions. This capacity to choose is generally understood as our having free will.

In contrast to free will, determinism is the view that the state of the world at any moment in time is determined by the previous state of the world. In my mind, this is a mechanical understanding of the universe and everything in it (including human beings): one turn of this cog means two turns of that cog, which in turn pushes this or pulls that. Put another way, because the laws of nature conspire, determinism suggests that everything that happens is unavoidable.[3] If this were the case, then serial killers, including Bruce Lee, could only act as they did, and it is hard to see how they are responsible for their actions.

---

[3] There's a great example of this in the film, *The Matrix* (1999): 'You hear that Mr Anderson? … That is the sound of inevitability.' If you're interested in philosophy, watch *The Matrix* trilogy.

However, even if you don't believe in free will (I do), there is still a way to square determinism with moral responsibility: compatibilism (Deal, 2010). Dennett (2003) argues that even though the laws of nature govern behaviour, we can still act with free will because that is how humans, as a species, have evolved. Biologically, I may have evolved to be susceptible to heart disease because of high cholesterol, but evolution has equipped me with the capacity to choose against eating chocolate for breakfast. In exactly the same way, serial killers can decide not to make the decisions that they do. All the powers of the universe did not compel Peter Dinsdale/Bruce Lee to set the fires that he did. Lee decided to light those fires and he is responsible for his actions.

CONCLUSION

Firesetting is an understudied area and we do not know much about why people deliberately set fires. Peter Dinsdale/Bruce Lee had a low IQ, which is often associated with firesetting, but the overwhelming majority of people with a low IQ are not firesetters. Lee was motivated by revenge, but it is not clear what this adds to our understanding of his firesetting. Problematic sexuality was another issue with Lee, but it is not unusual and seems overwhelmingly unrelated to firesetting and arson. Lee also ticked the developmental and impoverished boxes that are often associated with arson, but, in reality, what does that add to our understanding? There is clearly a significant gap in our knowledge. Unfortunately, after contemplating this case and associated theorising, we seem none the wiser, psychologically speaking, with regard to firestarting. As such, constructive, critical engagement with existing theory is arguably the best place to start in adding to our knowledge. Over to you.

REFLECTIVE QUESTIONS

1. Should psychopathy be included in the DSM and ICD manuals?
2. Does a psychiatric diagnosis mean that perpetrators of arson (and other crimes) are not responsible for their actions?
3. How might we best increase our knowledge about arson/firesetting?

FURTHER READING

Gannon, T. A., & Pina, A. (2010). Firesetting: Psychopathology, theory and treatment. *Aggression and Violent Behavior, 15*(3), 224–238. doi:10.1016/j.avb.2010.01.001

Jackson, H. F., Glass, C., & Hope, S. (1987). A functional analysis of recidivistic arson. *British Journal of Clinical Psychology, 26*(3), 175–185. doi:10.1111/j.2044-8260.1987.tb01345.x

17
THE MOTORCYCLE MURDER

LEARNING OBJECTIVES

By the end of this chapter you should be able to:

- Explain the difference between motorcyclists who are members of MC clubs and those who are members of MCC clubs
- Critically describe international law enforcement's understandings of MC clubs
- Discuss the importance of masculinity, honour and collective identity to MC members and how these feed into a potential for extreme violence

SYNOPSIS OF THE CASE

In Limerick, Ireland, at 3 pm on the afternoon of 20 June 2015, Alan 'Cookie' McNamara, aged 49, a member of the Caballeros MC (motorcycle club), drove to the clubhouse of the Road Tramps MC, where he shot Road Tramp Andrew O'Donoghue in the head, causing him fatal injuries. McNamara's grievance was that the day before three members of the Road Tramps motorcycle club had robbed him of his club patches in an altercation outside a pub. Andrew O'Donoghue had not been involved in the altercation.

BACKGROUND TO THE CRIME

Motorcycle Clubs

The distinction between types of motorcycle club is one which shows, at least when it comes to acronyms, that morphology (the study of how words are formed) matters. To the uninitiated, the acronyms MCC and MC could both signify 'motor-cycle club'. However, to those familiar with biker subculture, the distinction is a sharp one. MCCs are motorcycle clubs populated by enthusiasts. The Harley Own-ers Group, the Vintage Japanese Motorcycle Club, and the British Owners Club are all examples of MCCs. Owners of motorbikes meet up, ride out and organise shows.

Outlaw or 'one percenter' motorcycle clubs use the acronym MC. These are a completely different kettle of fish. To be a one percenter is literally a way of life. As one person with a knowledge of these clubs explains: 'If you belong to one of these clubs you got to be prepared to wake up to 30 bikers on your couch on a Sunday morning.' For one percenters, their club comes before everything – fam-ily, friends and employers. Examples of MC clubs include the Hell's Angels, the Outlaws, Bandido's and the Pagans.

The story of the 'one percent' moniker opens with the formation of the Ameri-can Motorcycle Association (AMA) in 1924. The AMA was set up to oversee motorcycle sport in the USA. It granted charters to a range of motorcycle clubs. Clubs with an AMA charter were considered to be legal and those without an AMA charter were considered 'outlaw'. In the years immediately following the Sec-ond World War the number of outlaw clubs increased as ex-servicemen organised clubs outside the AMA charter that rode motorbikes and drank together to 'let off steam'. Examples of these clubs included the 'Pissed Off Bastards of Blooming-ton', the 'Boozefighters' and the 'Market Street Commandos'.

In the summer of 1947, the AMA had organised a motorcycle race in the town of Hollister for the 4th of July weekend. The Los Angeles Boozefighters decided to attend and, over the holiday weekend, there was sufficient antisocial behaviour for Hollister's six local police officers to need to call in assistance from 40 additional Californian Highway Patrol policemen. The biker 'riots' at Hollister grabbed the attention of national media and were widely reported. In response, the AMA said that 99% of bikers were well behaved and that the rest were outlaws. Since then, MCs have been proud to be called the 1%.

Patches

Members of one percenter motorcycle clubs can be identified by the patches, gang insignia and tattoos that they wear. The right to wear gang insignia or patches is hard earned and jealously guarded by the MCs, as is the title 'MC'. Anyone who wears MC-style patches or one percenter badges without being a full member of an MC club is taking a significant risk.

MC 'colours' consist of three distinct 'rockers' or patches that club members wear on sleeveless and collarless waistcoats. Wearing colours indicates full mem-bership of an MC, and wearers are 'fully patched' members of an outlaw club. The top rocker carries the club's name, the middle patch is always the club logo, and the bottom rocker indicates the chapter of the club to which a member belongs. MC and 1% patches are worn on the front by some clubs and on the back by others. These colours are integral to the identity, and the pride of the man who wears them. Colours are only worn by men as women are never full members of an MC. Colours demonstrate that the wearer has reached the pinnacle of bikerdom.

In order to become a fully-patched member, a person must first become a 'prospect', then a 'probationary' member before finally becoming a full member. The journey from prospect to full member can take months or years and involves the prospect undertaking a range of menial and other tasks for the club in order to prove themselves and earn the respect and trust required for full membership. Potential members must be voted through each stage by other club members before becoming a 'brother'. Within MCs, loyalty is everything.

The Hell's Angels are one of the best-known MCs. Based in California, they have hundreds of affiliate clubs across the world. Sonny Barger, founder of the Hell's Angels, wrote that the 'story of the Hell's Angels Motorcycle Club is the story of a very select brotherhood of men who will fight and die for each other, no matter what the cause … When a Hell's Angel fights a citizen or a rival club member, everybody rat-packs to his side' (Barger & Zimmerman, 2000, p. 148).

The Battle of Kilmeaden

The roots of Alan McNamara's commission of murder can be traced to a mêlée known as the Battle of Kilmeaden, which took place in southeast Ireland in the summer of 1990. One significant aspect of MC culture is that clubs are very territorial and they will resist, in the strongest terms, what they understand as the incursion of other MCs into what they perceive as their territory. The Kilmeaden biker rally was organised by the Waterford Freewheelers MC, an Irish one percenter club. During the course of the rally, a member of the Hell's Angels pulled a knife on a member of an English club, the Pagans MC. The Pagan is reported to have responded by spraying his attacker in the face with ammonia, which he was carrying in his jacket pocket.

In the battle that followed, members of the Hell's Angels lined up against a mix of Irish MCs, including the Devil's Disciples from Dublin and Limerick's Road Tramps. Combatants used helmets, knives and lumps of wood. In the carnage that ensued, dozens of MC members were left with serious injuries. In the wake of the 1990 combat in Kilmeaden, the indigenous Irish MCs – the Freewheelers, the Devil's Disciples, the Road Tramps and the Vikings – came together in a formal '1% Alliance' with the purpose of keeping the international MCs out.

Hierarchy of MC Clubs

MC clubs can be divided into four categories: support clubs, which rely on the larger club for protection; satellite clubs, which serve as a source of recruits for larger clubs; regional clubs, with limited membership and territory; and the large MCs like the Hell's Angels, the Outlaws and the Bandidos. The Bandidos is one of the biggest international outlaw MCs and is ranked by the FBI as second in size only to the Hell's Angels. In recent years, these gangs have been expanding in Europe. In 2015, at the time of Andrew O'Donoghue's murder, Alan McNamara was a member of the Caballeros MC, a Bandidos' support club, with prospect status.

DESCRIPTION OF THE CASE

The events that led to the murder of Andrew O'Donoghue were set in train shortly after 10 pm on 19 June 2015, in the village of Doon, County Limerick. Alan McNamara, who would shoot Andrew O'Donoghue dead the following day, had driven into the village of Doon, on his motorbike, with his wife Mary. McNamara, a former member of the Road Tramps MC, was wearing his Caballero colours on the day. McNamara was later to describe this wearing of Caballero colours in Road Tramp territory as a 'red rag to a bull'. The McNamaras went into a pub in the village and, as they left the premises, they were approached by three members of the Road Tramps, Seamus Duggan (aged 51), James McCormack (41) and Raymond Neilon (50). James McCormack questioned McNamara about wearing his Caballero MC colours in what the Road Tramps considered to be their home patch. McCormack and Neilon then punched McNamara and stripped him of his Caballero colours while Duggan restrained McNamara's wife Mary. McNamara was left on the ground, with his clothing in a state of disarray.

Following the assault on McNamara, McCormack returned to the Road Tramps' clubhouse where he handed over McNamara's Caballero colours to the Road Tramp's Club President. Duggan, McCormack and Neilon subsequently pleaded guilty to the robbery of McNamara's jacket and had the Probation Act applied to them, meaning that they were released to the supervision of a probation officer. In his statement to the Gardai (Irish police), McCormack said that the Caballeros MC had set up in 'our area' and that they 'wouldn't be happy until they had taken over our club. … [The] word was they had become a Bandidos supporter club, who are like Hell's Angels. I was worried they would support the Bandidos. … I took the jacket off (McNamara) to insult him.' Speaking to the court in Duggan, McCormack and Neilon's trial for robbery, Detective Chris Coleman said that 'the taking of one's motorcycle colours is considered a significant insult. It is one of the major insults you can pay a fellow biker' (Raleigh, 2017, n.p.).

The following day, 20 June 2015, McNamara was in a state of high vexation in reaction to having had his colours removed. That morning he received a call from his stepson, Robert Cusack, saying that Cusack and two other Caballeros were in a car following a Road Tramp. The Road Tramp being followed was Seamus Duggan and there was a high-speed chase for a little over 20 kilometres. While being chased, Duggan phoned Road Tramp associates and it was decided that the best course of action was for Duggan to drive to the Road Tramps' clubhouse where club members would be waiting to open the gates and allow him in. One of those waiting on the gate was Andrew O'Donoghue. Meanwhile, on receiving the call from his stepson, Alan McNamara loaded a shotgun, got into his car and drove to the Road Tramps' clubhouse. Pulling up outside the clubhouse, McNamara got out of his car with the loaded gun. Andrew O'Donoghue tried to close the gate as McNamara approached, but was shot before he could do so. At this point, the car carrying the three men involved in the car chase passed by, and the gun used to murder Andrew O'Donoghue was handed to the car's occupants. The gun was later retrieved from the rear of McNamara's house.

In instructing the jury at McNamara's murder trial, the judge told the seven men and four women that they needed to examine the accused's state of mind at the time and ask 'what did he honestly believe?' The jury were instructed to think about both the manner of the shooting and the events leading up to it. Why had the accused come to be at the Road Tramps' clubhouse with a loaded shotgun? Was there a basis to McNamara's defence that he feared there was a threat to either himself or his family? The judge explained that homicide is not murder if committed in reasonable self-defence of oneself or others. The jury were also told that if the accused believed that he was using necessary force, but that the force was greater than a reasonable person would deem necessary, then he would be guilty of manslaughter rather than murder. Following two hours and 43 minutes of deliberation, the jury reached a unanimous verdict that Alan McNamara was guilty of murder. He received the mandatory life sentence for his crime.

Postscript to the Crime

In October 2016, the Bandidos initiated a new chapter in Limerick. Newspaper reports indicate that the Caballero club was 'granted' full membership as a result of McNamara's actions. At the time of the Irish Bandido chapter's initiation, the Bandidos posted a photo of McNamara on their blog with the words 'A tribute to Bandido Cookie who really showed what the patch and colors [sic] mean to him, when he took the matters in his own hands'. It is reported that McNamara is now a lifetime member of the club.

LINKS TO THEORY AND RESEARCH

In their *National Gang Report 2015*, the FBI define Outlaw Motorcycle Gangs as 'ongoing organizations, associations, or groups of three or more persons with a common interest or activity characterized by the commission of, or involvement in, a pattern of criminal conduct. Members must possess and be able to operate a motorcycle to achieve and maintain membership within the group' (Federal Bureau of Investigation/National Gang Intelligence Center, 2016, p. 22). The FBI regard outlaw motorcycle gangs, including the Hell's Angels MC, the Bandidos and the Outlaws, which are all specifically referred to in the National Gang Report, as 'sophisticated criminals'. The report cites the possession of weapons, threats and intimidation, assault and drug trafficking as the most common criminal activities committed by MCs. The FBI report also states that MCs have adopted a public stance of claiming that they are merely motorcycle riders who belong to a club, and that any criminal activities of individual members are not directed by the gang.

On this side of the Atlantic, Europol, the European Union's law enforcement agency, state that the 'main threat to public safety from outlaw motorcycle gangs stems from their propensity for extreme forms of violence. This includes the use of firearms and explosive devices such as grenades. In general, the use of intimidation and violence is intrinsic to the subculture of outlaw motorcycle gangs and serves to exert control over group members, rival gangs and others, such as victims of extortion' (Europol, n.d.). It is clear that the law enforcement perspective of both the US and the European agencies is that extreme violence is a core facet of MC behaviour.

There is currently a lack of academic information on violence and fatal violence involving outlaw motorcycle gangs (Bain & Lauchs, 2017; Rahman & Lynes, 2018). I am aware of only two significant academic texts which tackle the subject of British MCs and their use of violence in the last couple of decades (Rahman & Lynes, 2018; Silverstone & Crane, 2017), and no academic papers on outlaw MCs in an Irish context.

Silverstone and Crane (2017) argue that there are two core biker 'types'. One is the 'conservative' type. These are rebellious and antisocial individuals who hold to the traditional one percenter lifestyle and wish to live by their own rules. The second is the 'radical' type. These bikers want to attain the wealth that reflects the power and status of the club. According to Silverstone and Crane, the level of criminality associated with a given MC is a function of the balance in power between the conservative types and the radical types, or 'purists'.

Europol suggest that the main driver of MC expansion is the desire to increase their role in particular criminal markets, for example along the trafficking routes for drugs, weapons and human beings (Europol, 2012). Silverstone and Crane (2017) challenge this assertion and argue instead that the evidence, such as it is, shows that MCs are expanding in Europe because of their popularity and individual clubs' desire to out-do each other. They argue that in the UK, the people who gravitate to the MCs are of the 'conservative' rather than the 'radical' type (Silverstone & Crane, 2017, p. 80). Bikers want to be members of an outlaw club because of the values traditionally associated with such membership. Silverstone and Crane suggest that UK MCs are not involved in organised crime, and that a significant proportion of the violence which surfaces from time to time is a function of rival MCs long-standing animosity towards each other rather than a function of criminal competition. It seems likely that similar dynamics are at play with MCs in Ireland.

Where Silverstone and Crane (2017) do agree with Europol is that 'Merely establishing a chapter on the "turf" of another OMCG [outlaw motorcycle group] is interpreted as an act of provocation and is likely to result in violent confrontations and retaliation' (Europol, 2012). This was certainly the case in so far as it led to the assault on Alan McNamara, and the stripping of his colours, by the three Road Tramps on 19 June 2015. One of those convicted of removing McNamara's colours said as much to the police when he was arrested: the Caballeros had 'set up in our area' and 'wouldn't be happy until they had taken over our club'.

Honour

The propensity for violence is one of the major factors that distinguishes 'patched' bikers from mainstream bikers (Rahman & Lynes, 2018). Bosmia, Quinn, Peterson, Griessenauer and Tubbs (2014) report that if an MC member perceives disrespect from anyone, the outcome can be deadly. Writing for emergency department medical staff who may have to interact with injured MC members, Bosmia et al. report that MC members have an overarching requirement for face-saving and respect in all encounters. They also suggest that an MC member will not hesitate to injure or kill someone if he believes that a person has disrespected either the MC member himself or his club. Rather presciently, Bosmia et al. (2014) also point out that particular caution should be exercised when dealing with prospect or probationary members, as they are likely to be more prone to acts of aggression than full patch members in order to prove themselves worthy of full membership. Alan McNamara and his club, the Caballeros, were prospects for the Bandidos MC at the time of Andrew O'Donoghue's murder. According to reports, full membership of the Bandidos MC was granted to the Limerick Caballeros following the murder.

Masculinity

It is noteworthy that only men are fully patched members of MCs. In the MC subculture, club members have a 'hyper-masculine view of the world and their position in it' (Davies Robinson & Bain, 2017). The criminological literature on masculinities and violence has picked up on the notion of threatened masculinities and 'masculine honour'. The latter encompasses the cultural factors and influencers which might explain why some men enact hyper-aggressive forms of masculinity. Hallsworth and Silverstone (2009) analysed the importance of honour with regard to deadly gun-crime in Britain. They found that the way masculinity was constructed by their research participants, who were members of street gangs (Hallsworth & Silverstone, 2009, p.360), made it an imperative to retaliate violently when provoked by others. They also found that the honour, responsibilities and patterns of action related to masculinity meant that there were norms of never reporting to the police, always being loyal to one's area and one's associates, and the absolute importance of responding to physical or verbal attacks with equal or superior force. All of these findings apply to the case of MCs generally and the murder of Andrew O'Donoghue in particular.

Collective Identity

In their interestingly titled article, 'Ride to die: Masculine honour and collective identity in the motorcycle underworld', Rahman and Lynes (2018) explored the importance of masculine honour in the murder of Hell's Angel Gerry Tobin, in England in 2008, by seven members of the Outlaws MC. Gerry Tobin's murder has parallels, in terms of collective identities, with other crimes and, importantly, with the murder of Andrew O'Donoghue.

In 2001, a group of Hell's Angels were on the motorway heading for London when a dark-coloured car that had been following their three-bike convoy, pulled alongside them and shot one of them in the leg. In another incident, in the US in 2006, a Hell's Angel named Roger Mariani was murdered, also while riding his bike. Both of these incidents had been noted by two patched members of the South Warwickshire Chapter of the Outlaws MC – Simon Turner and Sean Creighton. In 2007, the president of the Outlaws MC in the US gave members the 'green light' to retaliate following the murder of an Outlaws' member outside a strip club in Georgia. Soon afterwards, Turner and Creighton set about planning and executing the murder of a Hell's Angel in retaliation.

As Gerry Tobin, a mechanic in one of the large London Harley-Davidson dealers, was making his way back to London following the 2008 Bulldog Bash, organised by the Hell's Angels, he was shot dead by the Outlaws MC members, including Turner and Creighton, from a car that pulled alongside him. He died instantly. Rahman and Lynes (2018) conclude that Gerry Tobin was murdered for no other reason than that he was a Hell's Angel. His murder was entirely a function of collective identity. The Outlaw MC hit team wanted to kill one of 'them'. Rahman and Lynes (2018, pp. 246–247) suggest that for the Hell's Angels MC and the Outlaws MC 'the sense of "oneness" or "we-ness" is exhibited no better than through acts of collective violent practice. … The seven members of the Outlaws MC who executed the murder of Gerry, merely saw him as an "object" that would enable them to defend and advance their "masculine honour".'

As in the Tobin case, Andrew O'Donoghue was murdered for no other reason than that he was a member of the Road Tramps MC. At the time of the crime, McNamara, with a gun in his hands, simply wanted to shoot a Road Tramp – any Road Tramp.

CONCLUSION

At present, there is a lack of scholarly work on motorcycle gangs within the UK and Ireland (Rahman & Lynes, 2018). The murder of Andrew O'Donoghue was one exceedingly violent crime, committed by a killer apparently motivated by identity-related drives. Without group-based understanding, the crime is difficult, perhaps impossible, to understand. But it is a useful and interesting case to consider for many reasons, not least because it allows us to consider a crime where 'they' is a consideration salient to the point where a homicide is committed.

One avenue of enquiry, or 'lens' that might usefully be brought to a consideration of this murder is that of collective identity, that is, the identities that people have as a function of the groups they belong to. The perspective of social identity in particular can be useful in understanding the collective psychology of these types of murder.

REFLECTIVE QUESTIONS

1. One percenter motorcycle clubs constitute secret societies with a reputation for violence that makes direct contact challenging (Quinn & Forsyth, 2009). As such, how might these clubs best be researched from an academic point of view?
2. Is there a useful distinction to be made between men who are outlaw bikers but are not organised criminals and those who are?

FURTHER READING

Bain, A., & Lauchs, M. (2017). *Understanding the Outlaw Motorcycle Gangs: International Perspectives*. Durham, NC: Carolina Academic Press.

This is one of the few academic texts available on the subject of MCs. It has an international perspective and is well worth a read.

18
RESERVE POLICE BATTALION 101

LEARNING OBJECTIVES

By the end of this chapter you should be able to:

- Define genocide
- Argue about the importance of situational and individual factors in our under-standing of genocide
- Link a discussion of genocide to relevant psychological theory and research

SYNOPSIS OF THE CASE

Stanley Milgram's obedience studies have been, and continue to be, widely taught in psychology. In part, this is because they raise a challenging question: what can explain the willingness of 'ordinary people' to do exceptional violence when ordered or asked to do so?

Reserve Police Battalion 101 was a unit of the German Order Police [Ordnung-spolizei or Orpo] that carried out a central role in the implementation of the 'Final Solution' in Eastern Europe during the Second World War. The participation of the Battalion 101 in the holocaust is especially striking because of their 'ordinariness'. Following the war, most of these middle-aged policemen returned to 'normal' civilian life. This chapter will use their case to reflect on classic and contemporary psychological explanations of genocide, ranging from the early work of Milgram (1963, 1974), Tajfel (1978, 1979, 1982) and Tajfel and Turner (1979, 1986) to more recent research conducted by Haslam and Reicher (2007).

DESCRIPTION OF THE CASE

Most people living in the Western world today have heard the names of Auschwitz, Treblinka, Sobibor, Belsen and Dachau. The roll-call of Nazi murder in Europe is terrifying in its magnitude. What is even more terrifying is the 'ordinariness' of the vast majority of those involved in the perpetration of the most colossal, wide-ranging and far-reaching episode of genocide in human history. The Holocaust, or the Shoah, is the descriptor most often applied to the systematic annihilation of some 6 million Jewish people in Europe between 1941 and 1945. Two-thirds of Europe's Jewish population died in the cataclysm.

The Holocaust is almost too huge to grasp. One useful way to attempt to comprehend this crime, and the horror of it, is to break the criminality down into manageable parts. The stories of identifiable, and imaginable, entities, such as the individual battalions and their personnel, is a good place to start. I am incapable of imagining the richness and complexity of the 6 million lives snuffed out because of their Jewishness. I can, however, imagine one relatively small town in southeast Poland during mid-July 1942. The town is called Józefów.

When German Reserve Police Battalion 101, from Hamburg, came to Józefów in 1942 there were about 1,800 Jewish people in residence there. The policemen were tasked with rounding these people up, separating out the men of working age, who were to be sent to nearby work camps, and shooting everyone else on the spot. Mothers, children, the elderly and the infirm, all were to be executed.

The men of Reserve Police Battalion 101 were predominantly middle-aged and from the Hamburg area. There were a few Luxembourgers in the battalion, but they were, and would have been seen, as outsiders. Hamburg was, anecdotally at least, one of the least Nazified cities in the Third Reich. Most of the men in Reserve Police Battalion 101 came from ordinary, working-class backgrounds. At the time of their arrival in Poland, the Battalion was commanded by Major Wilhelm Trapp, a 53-year-old career policeman and veteran of the First World War, who had been awarded an Iron Cross First Class for bravery in that war. Reserve Police Battalion 101 comprised 11 officers, five administrative officials and 486 other ranks. These men were organised into three companies of three platoons which were in turn divided into four squads, with each squad commanded by either a corporal or a sergeant.

On 12 July 1942, the majority of Reserve Police Battalion 101 assembled in Bilgoraj, where Major Trapp met with Captain Wohlauf and Lieutenant Gnade, leaders of the first and second companies. First Lieutenant Hagan, Trapp's adjutant, met the other officers in the battalion. The officers were informed that on the following day, 13 July, they were to shoot all Jews who were not male and not fit for work. One of the officers, 38-year-old Lieutenant Heinz Buchmann, refused to take part in the massacre. Buchmann is reported to have said that he 'would in no case participate in such an action, in which defenceless women and children are shot' and asked for another assignment. Trapp's adjutant arranged for Buchmann to be in charge of the escort taking the men who were intended for work, and thus not earmarked for execution, to Lublin. The rank and file of Reserve Police Battalion 101 were not informed on 12 July that they were to perpetrate a massacre on the following day. However, there was some inkling as to what was in store for the battalion. The men were issued with extra ammunition and there was talk of 'Judenaktion'.

At 2 am on 13 July 1942, trucks carrying the men of Battalion 101 rolled into Józefów. On disembarkation from their transports, the men were addressed by their commander, who outlined the genocidal task planned for the day ahead. Amazingly, Trapp told the assembled men that any man who did not feel that they were up to the murder ahead could step out. Some 10–12 men did so. Those who stepped forward were told to turn in their rifles and await further instructions from the Major. None of the men who declined to take part were subsequently punished by the military authorities as a result of their refusal. Two platoons from the Third Company surrounded Józefów. Their orders were to shoot anyone who tried to escape. The rest of the battalion were instructed to round up Józefów's Jews and take them to the marketplace. Anyone incapable of walking there was to be shot on the spot.

Once the people were assembled in the marketplace, the 'work Jews' were to be selected. The 'work Jews' were to be accompanied out of the village by an escort of men from the First Company. The remainder of First Company were to go the forest adjacent to Józefów in order to form firing squads. Those who were to be murdered were loaded onto waiting trucks by men of the Second and Third Companies and driven in relays to the forest. Once the Józefów operation got underway, Battalion Commander Trapp appears to have been overcome with distress. He is reported to have spent the day in a state of agitation and to have stayed clear of the execution site because he could not bear to see it.

Much screaming and the sound of gunfire accompanied the first part of the operation – the rounding-up. Several people were shot dead immediately, before the Jewish populace were assembled in the square. At this stage, as the round-up was ending, the men of First Company were taken to one side and given instruction by the battalion doctor in how to shoot in order to instantly kill their victims. Fixed bayonets were to be placed in a spot on the people's backs as an aiming guide and rifle triggers were to be pulled. The first firing squads were taken by truck to Józefów's forest where the men climbed off their vehicles and awaited their victims.

When the first truck transporting Jewish people arrived, it contained about 35–40 individuals. These people were paired off, face to face, with the policeman who was designated to murder them. The group then marched further into the forest. People were made to lie down in a row, the policemen lined up behind their victims, put their bayonets on people's backbones, above their shoulder blades, as the battalion doctor had shown them. Then, on command, everyone lying on the ground was shot.

The basic process was repeated all day long and well into the night. Józefów's executioners were not practised and this was a messy, brutal and bloody affair. Not all victims died with the first salvo. As the day progressed, the psychological strain showed on some of the policemen, and they were unable to continue with the murder. In order to keep going, some of the policemen adopted strategies that seem beyond belief to the outside eye. One of the policemen, a 35-year-old former metalworker from Bremerhaven, shot only children. The policeman did so, according to his own account, because he reasoned that the children could not live without their mothers. In this policeman's eyes, he was 'releasing' the children. Christopher Browning, in his book about Reserve Police Battalion 101, entitled *Ordinary Men* (2001), notes that the policeman's use of the word release, *erlösen*, is significant – *erlösen*, when used in a religious sense, means 'to redeem'. Thus, the person who releases, the *Erlöser*, is the redeemer, the saviour.

In the 17 hours that they spent in Józefów that summer day in 1942, Reserve Police Battalion 101 murdered about 1,500 people. It is estimated that about 80% of those called on to commit murder continued to do so until 'the job was done'. A question that continues to burn almost 80 years after these atrocities is how did a group of middle-aged German policemen become mass murderers?

Postscript

By the end of the Second World War, Reserve Police Battalion 101 were responsible for the direct execution of approximately 38,000 Jewish people. The Battalion was responsible for deporting an estimated 45,200 more Jewish people to the Treblinka death camp. Unimaginable.

LINKS TO THEORY AND RESEARCH

The Holocaust is a difficult subject. Perhaps the most difficult subject. It is a sea of suffering that presents with unfathomable depths. To paraphrase a sentiment from Christopher Browning's superb book, in our explaining of things, we do not necessarily excuse them, and if we understand things, we do not of necessity forgive them (Browning, 2001). I think it is important that we attempt to understand what happened in the Shoah in order to honour its victims and maintain their memory so that we can strive to ensure that it never happens again.

Defining Genocide

The United Nations (1948) defines genocide as:

> any of the following acts committed with intent to destroy, in whole or in part, a national, ethnical, racial or religious group, as such:

(a) Killing members of the group;

(b) Causing serious bodily or mental harm to members of the group;

(c) Deliberately inflicting on the group conditions of life calculated to bring about its physical destruction in whole or in part;

(d) Imposing measures intended to prevent births within the group;

(e) Forcibly transferring children of the group to another group.

A Polish lawyer, Raphäel Lemkin, introduced the word 'genocide' in 1944. Lemkin's book, *Axis Rule in Occupied Europe* (1944) deployed the term, in part, as a response to the systematic murder of Jewish people during the war, and also in recognition of the various instances across recorded history where one group has attempted to destroy another. The term is a composite of the Greek *genos*, meaning race or tribe, and the Latin *cide*, meaning killing (United Nations, n.d.). The crime of genocide was first recognised under international law by the United Nations in 1946. The crime was codified by the 1948 *Convention on the Prevention and Punishment of the Crime of Genocide* (the Genocide Convention).

In considering genocide, we need to be mindful that the perpetration of genocide is not restricted to those who are obviously 'monsters'. This point was powerfully brought home to me when, about 20 years ago, during a pleasant summer afternoon spent in the vineyards of Southern Germany, I passed some time talking to an old man who was very good company and enthralled me with tales of 'the old days'. My brother in law, whose family are from the area, knew the old man well. It turned out that the old man had been a member of the SS during the war, had been a perpetrator of unspeakable atrocities and had spent many years after the war in prison for his war crimes. He was living proof that not all devils wear horns, and apparently benign people are capable of awful things.

Max Hastings (2019, p. 237) reports a conversation between a US sergeant in Vietnam and his commanding officer, which took place when Hastings was a young journalist covering the war in that country: 'Before you leave here sir, you're going to learn that one of the most brutal things in the world is your average nineteen year old American boy.' It is important to recognise that genocide is not restricted to long-dead monsters who stare out from behind the glass of faded black and white photographs. In our own time, we have witnessed genocide in Rwanda, Bosnia and, most recently, against the Rohingya in Myanmar.

The Holocaust casts an important and complex shadow in psychology. Is the answer as to why people participate in genocide to be found in individual or social psychology? Perhaps a combination of both? 'Ultimately, the holocaust took place because at the most basic level individual human beings killed other human beings in large numbers over an extended period of time' (Browning, 2001, p. xv). The question that psychology must attempt to answer is why? Since the Second World War, considerable effort has been expended on attempts to answer this question and, of necessity, this chapter can only deliver a flavour of these. I strongly encourage you to follow the leads presented below, join the debate and search for your own answers.

Authoritarian Personalities

Knowledge in social psychology (and indeed knowledge generally) is always situated in the context of wider social and political events and processes. Following the Second World War, and particularly because of the Holocaust, psychology became focused on prejudice. 'Psychologists wanted to understand how irrational antipathies based on faulty generalisations – to adopt Gordon Allport's (1954, p. 9) famous definition of the prejudiced mind – might contribute to racial hatred, violence and even genocide' (Dixon, 2007, p. 147).

Adorno, Frankel-Brunswik, Levinson and Sanford (1950), in their study of the 'authoritarian personality', argued, based on psychodynamic theory, that there are people with a conscious respect for authority that masks a repressed resentment for that very authority. The authoritarian personality is seen as adhering rigidly to conventional values, submitting readily to authority, displaying aggression towards outgroups, a tendency to stereotype, and a preoccupation with power and toughness. Because of their repressed resentment for authority, 'authoritarian personalities' displace their repressed anger onto scapegoat groups. In the case of the Holocaust and Reserve Police Battalion 101, this repressed anger has been displaced onto 'the Jews'. Authoritarian personalities are understood as harbouring a repressed and generalised hatred of those who are 'different'.

Browning (2001, p. 166) cites Zygmunt Bauman as summing up the authoritarian personality approach as follows: 'Nazism was cruel because Nazis were cruel; and the Nazis were cruel because cruel people tended to become Nazis.' It is hard to disagree with Bauman and Browning. A major flaw of the Adorno et al. approach to the authoritarian personality is that it does not account for social influence, or the apparent fact that 'ordinary' people are capable of genocide.

Evolving Perspectives

As a consequence of two distinct events, 1961 was a watershed year in terms of how we, as human beings, understand our own capacity for evil. The first event was the trial in a Jerusalem court of the notorious Adolf Eichmann, the man who arranged the transport on which Holocaust victims were conveyed to their deaths. The second event was an obedience study conducted at Yale University in New Haven, Connecticut.

Eichmann and the Banality of Evil

Adolf Eichmann had personally arranged the murder of millions of Jewish people in Europe. In doing so, Eichmann shared some common ground with the men of Reserve Police Battalion 101 in that he was a uniformed member of the Nazi machine that orchestrated the Holocaust. There was also commonality in so far as Eichmann saw himself as a man who was merely 'following orders'. After the war, Eichmann had escaped from US custody and emigrated to Argentina where, in 1960, Israeli agents captured him and brought him back to Israel to stand trial for war crimes and crimes against humanity. Eichmann was convicted in 1961 and hung in 1962. Why this is relevant to the discussion in this chapter is that Eichmann, on the basis of his trial, came across as being entirely 'normal'.

Hannah Arendt, a social philosopher and a Jewish woman, who had herself fled Nazi Germany, published one of the most important books of the twentieth century, *Eichmann in Jerusalem: A Report on the Banality of Evil*, based on what she witnessed at the Eichmann trial (Arendt, 1963). As Arendt stated (1963, p. 276): 'The trouble with Eichmann was precisely that so many were like him, and that the many were neither perverted nor sadistic, that they were, and still are, terribly and terrifyingly normal.' Arendt also reported that psychiatrists had certified Eichmann as 'normal' and that one of them 'had found that his whole psychological outlook, his attitude to his wife and children, mother and father, brothers, sisters, and friends, was "not only normal but most desirable"' (Arendt, 1963, pp. 25–26).

Arendt's most famous observation, arising from the Eichmann trial was that Eichmann and his crimes illustrated the 'fearsome, word and thought defying banality of evil' (Arendt, 1963, p. 252). In this phrase, Arendt changed the world. Previously, those who had committed genocide and war crimes were regarded as aberrant and pathological. In identifying the 'banality of evil', Arendt challenged the consensus, and she challenged us: perhaps the people who commit these acts are just like you and me?

Milgram and the Obedience Studies

Stanley Milgram was an American, of Jewish heritage, whose parents hailed from Eastern Europe (Reicher & Haslam, 2012). As a child during the war, and coming of age in its immediate aftermath, Milgram came to psychology at a time when North American interests were focused on understanding how Hitler had managed to garner the support of the German nation in his pursuit of an aggressive war. People generally, and academia in particular, wanted to know why the German military had carried out orders that were genocidal (Hollway, 2007a).

In a series of research studies that were conducted through the 1960s Milgram examined whether participants would continue to give people increasingly powerful electric shocks that were potentially harmful (and/or lethal) if they were ordered to do so by someone in authority. The classic account of these studies is *Obedience to Authority* (Milgram, 1974). Milgram was interested in triads, where one party commands another to do harm to a third (Hollway, 2007a). Milgram's studies rested on the premise that people are socialised to respect the authority of the state (Hogg & Vaughan, 2018). According to Milgram (1974, p. 6): 'Arendt's conception of the banality of evil comes closer to the truth that one might dare imagine. The ordinary person who shocked the victim did so out of a sense of obligation – a conception of his duties as a subject – and not from any peculiarly aggressive tendencies.'

Browning (2001) explicitly considers the relevance of the Milgram experiments with regard to the Józefów massacre and reports that many of Milgram's insights seem to apply. For instance, both Milgram and the Józefów massacre evidence the key importance of conformity and the mutual reinforcement of authority (Browning, 2001, p. 175). Also, as with Milgram, the policemen at Józefów in closest proximity to the killing were the most likely to recoil and discontinue because physical distance seems to have correlated negatively with feelings of responsibility towards those being harmed. There is certainly a strong sense of obligation expressed in the testimony of the men who took part in the Józefów massacre.

Zimbardo and the Lucifer Effect

Philip Zimbardo, a contemporary of Stanley Milgram, is another prominent American social psychologist whose career, in the wake of the Holocaust, focused on addressing the question of why it is that 'ordinary' people can behave in extraordinarily brutal and abusive ways towards others. Zimbardo's research first came to international attention following the (in)famous Stanford Prison Experiment (SPE) in 1971, in which a mock prison was established in the basement of the Psychology Department at Stanford University. The prison was staffed by 'Guards', who quickly became tyrannical and abusive in their behaviour towards 'prisoners' (Zimbardo, 1971). Zimbardo argued that this tyrannical behaviour was a consequence of the guard role to which some of his participants were allocated. In his work on the SPE, and subsequently in his book *The Lucifer Effect* (Zimbardo, 2007), Zimbardo radically shifted the conversation away from dispositional explanations of tyranny to a situational understanding, whereby people's behaviour is understood in terms of the social context in which they find themselves. In invoking Lucifer, Zimbardo is using the idea of 'fallen angel' as a metaphor for 'ordinary' people who fall into the commission of evil acts because of the circumstances in which they find themselves. According to Zimbardo, we are all capable of evil acts – if situational forces conspire to make it so. To paraphrase the core message of *The Lucifer Effect*, there are no bad apples, just bad barrels.

Zimbardo (2007, p. 285) referenced the atrocities committed by Reserve Police Battalion 101 in Poland and, as in the Stanford Prison Experiment, he attributed the policemen's behaviour to the roles that they occupied. In doing so, Zimbardo drew parallels between the psychology underlying the genocidal behaviour of those involved in the Józefów massacre and of those US military police who were involved in the abuse perpetrated in Iraq's Abu Graib prison after the Iraq war. According to Zimbardo, these actions were a consequence of the situation in which the perpetrators found themselves and their roles within that situation. Browning (2001, p. 168) endorses Zimbardo's emphasis on the situation, stating that 'Zimbardo's spectrum of guard behaviour bears an uncanny resemblance to the groupings that emerged within Reserve Police Battalion 101'. In light of Zimbardo's research, it is clear that any one of us is capable of reacting in a similar way in a similar situation.

Henri Tajfel and Social Identity Theory

Another towering figure in social psychology whose work has a bearing in this discussion is Henri Tajfel. Tajfel, a Jewish man from Poland, had been studying chemistry at the Sorbonne in Paris when the Second World War erupted. He enlisted in the French army, was captured by the Nazis, but survived the war as a prisoner by concealing his Jewish identity. Tajfel saw from his own life experience that the groups that people belong to can mean the difference between life and death.

After the war, Tajfel came to Britain where he studied psychology and became one of the twentieth century's most important thinkers in social psychology. He developed social identity theory (SIT), along with his PhD student John Turner (Tajfel & Turner, 1986). Tajfel argued that how we understand ourselves is a function of the groups that we belong to, and when a given group identity is salient (i.e. active), we behave in line with the norms, behaviours and stereotypes of that group. Furthermore, we divide the world into 'us' and 'them' on the basis of self-categorisation processes. 'They' become depersonalised and interchangeable placeholders of their category. From this social identity perspective, the people who were murdered at Józefów were no longer seen as individuals with their own personalities, but rather as depersonalised and interchangeable exemplars of the category 'Jew'.

Steve Reicher and Alex Haslam: Developing Social Identity Theory

British social psychologists Steve Reicher and Alex Haslam have taken the seminal work of Tajfel and Turner (1986) and applied it to a critical consideration of the research conducted by both Stanley Milgram and Philip Zimbardo. Beginning with Milgram, Reicher and Haslam (2012) questioned the accepted wisdom with regard to how the Milgram studies should be understood. Rather than obedience being the key factor, Reicher and Haslam argued that it is social identity theory that best explained the research participants' behaviour. According to Reicher and Haslam's interpretation, it was the participants' identity as guards or prisoners that dictated their behaviour: 'People are seeking out justifications for acting one way rather than another from people they trust and identify with' (Reicher & Haslam, 2012, p. 122).

Reicher and Haslam's (2012) interpretation of the Milgram study is illuminating in understanding the massacre at Józefów. It is plausible that the men of Police Reserve Battalion 101 behaved as they did because they identified with each other and their role. For them, Jews were simply the enemy, even if they were babes in arms. 'The Dehumanization of the Other contributed immeasurably to the psychological distancing that facilitated killing' (Browning, 2001, p. 162). This is a startlingly shocking thought.

Regarding Zimbardo's work, Reicher and Haslam (2012) endorse his efforts to pull away from the dispositional understandings of tyranny that preceded his work with the Stanford Prison Experiment. However, in contrast to Zimbardo's extreme situationalism, Reicher and Haslam argue for the integration of context (e.g. Zimbardo's situationalism) and traits (e.g. Adorno's dispositional factors (Adorno, Frankel-Brunswik, Levinson, & Sanford, 1950)). According to Reicher and Haslam (2012, p. 139), 'it appears that the interaction of person and context which leads to tyranny (and also to resistance) is dynamic such that, on the one hand, group contexts transform individuals but, on the other, individuals transform contexts, primarily through their capacity to represent, lead and mobilize groups'.

We can see this tension between group memberships manifest in the split between those who did and those who did not participate in the mass shootings in Józefów in 1942. Lieutenant Buchmann, in particular, was one individual who refused to participate and left us with a record of his reasons for not doing so. Buchmann (Browning, 2001, p. 75) explained: 'I was somewhat older then and moreover a reserve officer, so it was not particularly important to me to be promoted or otherwise to advance, because I had my prosperous business back home. The company chiefs … on the other hand, were young men and career policemen who wanted to become something.' This statement reveals several salient social identities: Buchmann saw himself as older, a businessman and a reserve officer, and these social identities led him to appraise the situation at Józefów differently from those who identified as career policemen and 'wanted to become something'.

CONCLUSION

It would be comforting to believe that we have moved on from a state where people commit atrocities and genocide. Sadly, the evidence does not support this view. As such, we should accept that in order to change the world, we must first understand it. The social identity perspective is one that holds the promise of fruitful future research in this area. However, there are many other useful perspectives which have yet to be harnessed. Understanding the processes that led to the horrors of the Holocaust should help us to ensure that such atrocities are brought to an end.

Browning (2001, p. 189) closes his history of Reserve Police Battalion 101 with a haunting paragraph:

Everywhere society conditions people to respect and defer to authority, and indeed [we] could scarcely function otherwise. Everywhere people seek career advancement. In every modern society, the complexity of life and the resulting bureaucratization and specialization attenuate the sense of personal responsibility of those implementing official policy. Within virtually every social collective, the peer group exerts tremendous pressures on behaviour and sets moral norms. If the men of Reserve Police Battalion 101 could become killers under such circumstances, what group of men cannot?

Good question.

REFLECTIVE QUESTIONS

1. What do you think you would have done if you were a member of Reserve Police Battalion 101?
2. Was Milgram correct that the men of Reserve Police Battalion 101 committed genocide simply because they were socialised to be obedient?
3. What is the role of personality in genocide?
4. How important are the groups we belong to?

FURTHER READING

Browning, C. R. (2001). *Ordinary Men: Reserve Police Battalion 101 and the Final Solution in Poland*. London: Penguin.

Zimbardo, P. (2007). *The Lucifer Effect: Understanding How Good People Turn Evil*. New York: Random House.

A useful website is: www.un.org/en/genocideprevention/genocide.shtml

An interesting website is: www.bbcprisonstudy.org/

19

CHARLES WHITMAN: MASS KILLING

LEARNING OBJECTIVES

By the end of this chapter you should be able to:

- Define mass murder
- Discuss the relationship between domestic violence and mass murder
- Discuss personality disorder in relation to Charles Whitman
- Appreciate what social psychology offers to the understanding of the Whitman mass killings

SYNOPSIS OF THE CASE

On 1 August 1966, in Austin, Texas, while still a student, Charles J. Whitman murdered his wife and mother. He then shot and killed 14 people and wounded 33 others. He was eventually shot dead by the police.

DESCRIPTION OF THE CASE

Charles J. Whitman was the youngest Eagle Scout in the history of the USA, a Marine Corps sharp shooter and a scholar. He also perpetrated uxoricide, matricide and a mass shooting. In March 1966, about four months before his mass killing spree, Whitman met University of Texas psychiatrist, Dr Maurice Heatly, who recorded in his clinical notes that Whitman had said he was 'thinking about going up on the Tower with a deer rifle and start shooting people'. The psychiatrist noted that although Whitman was 'oozing with hostility', 'there was something about him that suggested and expressed the all-American boy' (Lavergne, 1997, pp. 70–71). More than half a century after the killings, Charles Whitman remains an enigma.

Early Development

Charles J. Whitman was born in Florida during the summer of 1941, a first child. His parents owned and ran a successful plumbing business, and were relatively wealthy. He had two younger brothers, Patrick born in 1945 and John born in 1949. Charles was a healthy child, regarded by neighbours as normal and fun. His mother, a devout Catholic, regularly brought her children to mass, and Charles attended Catholic school, played the piano exceptionally well and seemed to the world like a perfectly 'normal' child.

When he was 8 years old, Whitman became a Cub Scout, but had to drop out of the organisation a short time later because of a lack of Cub Scout leaders. When he was 11, he joined the Boy Scouts, where he became an Eagle Scout by the age of 12 years and three months, the youngest boy to do so. Eagle Scout is the highest rank in scouting and his achievement of this rank was an unusual and distinguished feat. As a consequence, Charles received national recognition. Much like his excellence at the piano, it is believed that Charles' father, C. A. Whitman, was the dynamo behind his achievement.

But Whitman was a bright boy in his own right. An IQ test administered in 1947 delivered a score of 138.9. Whitman was also keen on making money. As a teenager, he had a large paper round, which was big enough to fund the purchase of a Harley-Davidson motorcycle in 1955. Whitman pitched for the baseball team and managed the football team. A good looking and athletic boy, he certainly gave the appearance of being an 'All American Boy'.

However, a closer look at Whitman's childhood reveals aspects that were significantly less 'motherhood and apple pie' than scouting, working and playing the piano. Charles J. Whitman grew up in a household where violence was the norm. Whitman's father openly admitted his domestic abuse: 'I did on many occasions beat my wife, but I loved her … I have to admit it, because of my temper, I knocked her around' (Lavergne, 1997, p. 2). Whitman senior also believed that his use of fists and belt to discipline his sons was evidence of a moderate approach to parenting. Given the events that were to unfold, it is also notable that Charles J. Whitman's father was a gun fanatic and that, as a child, Charles was always around guns. There was one infamous photograph of him as a toddler holding two rifles. By the time he had reached adolescence, Charlie could 'plug the eye out of a squirrel' (Lavergne, 1997, p. 9).

The Marines Corps

When he was 18 years of age, Whitman rebelled against his strict, overbearing father and, in an act of defiance, joined the Marine Corps. Following basic training, Whitman was sent to Guantanamo Bay, Cuba. At the time, this was one of the world's most tense trouble spots and it is believed that this posting put a strain on Whitman. As a young marine, he approached his job diligently, earned a sharpshooter's badge, a Good Conduct medal and the Marine Corps' Expeditionary Medal. His commanding officers were impressed by the young Marine's demeanour and it looked as if Whitman had a bright career ahead of him.

Marriage

Things were looking bright for Whitman on the personal front too. In Needville, Texas, on 17 August 1962, Charles J. Whitman married 19-year-old student Kathy Leissner. Whitman had met Kathy at the University of Texas, where he was enrolled as a Marine Corps scholar and officer candidate, majoring in mechanical engineering, and she was studying to become a teacher.

Failed Student

By the spring semester of 1963, clouds were appearing on the horizon of Whitman's life. Insufficient engagement with his studies had led Whitman to be recalled to active service by the Marine Corps. He was posted to Camp Lejeune in North Carolina, and separated from his new wife, who remained at her studies in Texas. By now, the heady days of Eagle Scout stardom were long behind him and Whitman was struggling with authority. In November 1963 Whitman was court-martialled for gambling, usury and possessing a non-military pistol. By this stage, he hated the Marine Corps and wanted out. Following some intense lobbying, the Marine Corps released Whitman with an honourable discharge in December 1964.

In 1965, Whitman re-enrolled at the University of Texas, this time as a student of architectural engineering. At the same time, he took up the first in a series of part-time jobs. His wife Kathy graduated in the summer of 1965 and embarked on a teaching career, which she supplemented with a series of part-time jobs, becoming, in effect, the main income earner in their home and supporting her husband financially.

Life for Charles was not going well. By the end of 1965, Whitman was directing serious resentment towards his father and had become pre-occupied with surpassing him. Whitman was also putting on weight, racked with insecurity and beating his wife. He admitted assaulting his wife on two occasions, and Kathy confided to her parents that she was in fear of Whitman's temper and that she was worried that he could end up killing her.

Meanwhile, in Florida, Charles Whitman's parents were in the final throes of a marriage that was falling apart and things were about to get a whole lot worse in the world of Charles Whitman. In early 1966, Whitman's mother left his father and moved to Texas to be near her eldest son, Charles. Whitman was depressed and this was not helped by the presence of his newly arrived mother and incessant phone calls from his father seeking his son's assistance to reconnect with his ex-wife. By now, Whitman also felt that something was happening to him and that he didn't feel himself. On 29 March 1966, Whitman visited a University of Texas GP, who prescribed Valium and referred him to a staff psychiatrist, Dr Maurice Heatly.

Following Whitman's consultation with Dr Heatly, the psychiatrist surmised that the main reason for Whitman's visit was distress over his parents' separation. During the meeting, Whitman admitted to having twice assaulted his own wife and talked of the turmoil with and resentment of his father. The psychiatrist noted that Charles exuded hostility and recorded his threat to shoot people from the Tower. Dr Heatly was used to hearing the Tower come up in consultations, it being a dominant feature of the University of Texas landscape. He concluded that Whitman was not a danger to himself or others and invited him to visit again a week later, or to make contact as necessary. This was the first and last meeting between the psychiatrist and Whitman.

Charles was taking significant amounts of Dexedrine (amphetamine) during this period, and in early 1966 was using drugs in order to stay awake. Evidence given to the Texas Legislature subsequently identified him as a serious drug abuser. It may be that this abuse was a contributing factor to the frequent headaches that Whitman reported experiencing.

It was extremely hot in Texas on 31 July 1966. Austin experienced a record high of almost 40 degrees Celsius. Kathy Whitman worked a split shift at her job in the South-western Bell Telephone Company and her mother-in-law, Margaret Whitman, worked until 9.15 pm at her job in Wyatt's cafeteria. That afternoon Whitman had resolved to murder them both, recording on a typed page: 'It was after much thought that I decided to kill my wife Kathy, tonight after I pick her up from work at the telephone company' (Lavergne, 1997, p. 96). Whitman also set out how 'I've been having fears and violent impulses. I've had some tremendous headaches. I am prepared to die. After my death, I wish an autopsy on me to be performed to see if there's any mental disorders' (*Time*, 1966, n.p.).

In the early hours of 1 August 1966, Whitman murdered his mother at her apartment, probably by strangulation. He also stabbed his mother with a large hunting knife and hit her hand hard enough to almost crush her fingers. This hand wound was inflicted post-mortem, and it has been suggested that the purpose of the injury was to prevent Whitman's father from retrieving her wedding ring. Before leaving, Whitman wrote a note admitting the murder. He said that he had killed his mother Margaret 'to relieve her suffering' and that he 'loved the woman with all my heart'. Whitman also made reference in the note to the 'intense hatred I feel for my father' (Lavergne, 1997, p. 103). Whitman then returned to his own house, where his wife was asleep. He used the same hunting knife to murder Kathy as she slept, stabbing her in the heart and probably killing her instantly.

With Kathy dead, Whitman spent a considerable period of time perusing and annotating, with the time and date, diary entries he had made about his wife over the years. He then wrote four more notes. As with the notes left with his mother's body, Whitman attempted to apportion blame to his father. He wrote one note was for the police, one for each of his two brothers and one note to his father.

At 5.45 am Whitman phoned his dead wife's supervisor and said that Kathy would not be at work that day because of illness. It was imperative to his plan that the bodies of his wife and mother not be found until he had set about his grim task on the Texas University Tower. At 7 am Whitman left his home and drove to a rental company where he rented a two-wheeled hand cart. Later in the morning, he bought some additional weapons and ammunition before returning to the shed at his house to collect his arsenal. Loading all the weapons and the hand cart into his car, Whitman left home for the University of Texas at about 11 am. His wife had been dead for eight hours at this point.

Whitman drove to the University of Texas Clock Tower and, dressed as a maintenance man in one-piece overalls, made his way to the 27th floor in order to secure access to the viewing deck of the tower. Once there, Whitman attacked Edna Townsley, a 47-year-old receptionist who was employed as a supervisor of the observation deck, when her back was turned. He smashed the back of her skull with his rifle butt before hiding her unconscious body behind a couch. Edna never regained consciousness. Next to die were 19-year-old Mike Gabour and his aunt Marguerite Lamport. They had arrived, with other members of their family, at the viewing deck just as Whitman was setting up for his attack. Whitman blasted them at close range and then barricaded himself onto the viewing platform.

At 11.48 am Whitman started shooting. For the following 96 minutes, he used his telescopically-sighted sniper rifle to rain death and injury on an unsuspecting populace moving about the University of Texas campus in the glorious sunshine. First on the ground to die was the unborn baby of eight months' pregnant Claire Wilson. Claire was 18 years old. Seeing that she was pregnant, Whitman had purposely aimed for her abdomen. When Claire fell to the ground, her boyfriend, Thomas Eckman, bent down to help her. Whitman shot him too, fatally, through the neck. Before the spree was over, and Whitman lay dead at the hands of the police, 17 people would be mortally wounded and 30 more would be injured.

Author Gary Lavergne suggests that the Whitman case is the point when America discovered mass murder and how vulnerable we all are to the destructive power of a determined and armed individual. Sadly, it seems that history continues to support Lavergne's thesis.

Autopsy

Following his death, an autopsy was conducted on the body of Charles Whitman. Examiners found a tumour (measuring $2 \times 1.5 \times 1$ cm) in the hypothalamus region of his brain. The coroner also found that Whitman's skull was unusually thin.

LINKS TO THEORY AND RESEARCH

Mass Killing

Multiple homicide is an event where an individual, or 'body', kills a large number of people either in a single event or over a longer period (Brookman, 2005). The category of multiple homicide includes mass killings (the focus of this chapter), spree killings (discussed below) and serial killing (considered in the next chapter). Mass killing can be defined as multiple killings that are perpetrated in a single episode and in the same general geographic location. Spree killings are generally understood to take place over a longer time span than mass killings (up to 30 days) (Holmes & Holmes, 2010) and often spree killings are regarded as occurring in more than one place (Brookman, 2005).

So was Charles Whitman a mass killer or a spree killer? Because of the distinct locations of his crimes – the mother's apartment, his own home, the University of Texas campus – and the fact that the murders took place over an extended period of time, they are arguably spree killings. However, Coleman and Norris (2000, p. 89) argue that the concept of spree killing is 'an unnecessary complication'. I agree. There is no consensus with regard to the differences between mass homicides and spree homicides (Brookman, 2005). Rather, it is more effective to think of mass homicide as including crimes that are commonly referred to as spree killings.

Typologies of Mass Murderers

Brookman (2005) presents a typology of mass murder that classifies mass killers into four distinct types. The first type is the 'pseudo-commando', a mass killer who is fascinated with guns and weaponry. This category certainly seems to fit Charles J. Whitman's crime. A second type is the 'disciple', who kills under the guidance of a charismatic leader. The third type is the 'family annihilator' (see Chapter 21 on Alan Hawe). The final type is the 'disgruntled employee'.

Pseudo-commandos tend to attack either as individuals or in pairs. They usually attack in daylight and their behaviour evidences planning and the gathering of weapons. These types of mass killers do not usually plan for escape and are prepared to die in the execution of their murderous acts or by suicide (Gavin, 2019). Whitman may have been able to escape from the Clock Tower, but he chose not to do so.

Mass murderers are likely to manifest with severe psychiatric problems, including severe depression, schizophrenia or psychosis. It is often the case that the killings are committed with the intention of relieving the psychological distress the killer is experiencing (Walters & Hickey, 2015). Gavin (2019) highlights the strong feelings of anger and persecution that lie behind mass killings, and how these feelings make the murders seem like an act of 'revenge' to the perpetrator. Once again, these observations seem to fit with what we know about Whitman and the hatred he carried towards his father. The evidence points to an overwhelming desire on Whitman's part to take his revenge on his father.

However, a feature of the perpetrators of mass killings is that they rarely survive their attacks, so in their attempt to understand mass killing, researchers can only surmise the killer's motives.

Suicide by Cop

Suicide by cop happens when an individual acts in a way designed to provoke a deadly response from the police or others who have the right to engage with them (e.g. military personnel or security personnel). People who commit suicide by cop kill, or attempt to kill, other people with the express aim of attracting police attention so that their murderous act ultimately results in their own death. In some cases, the murderer's 'prize' is suicide via a death sentence and execution (Gavin, 2019). It is clear that Whitman had decided that his shooting spree would end in his death. It is a clear example of suicide by cop.

Domestic Violence

One factor that seems to come up again and again in the backgrounds of many of those who perpetrate violence, from terrorists to mass murderers, is the presence of or a history of domestic violence and intimate partner violence. One of the (many) shocking aspects of the background to the Whitman murders is the frank, almost blasé manner in which the killer's father spoke openly about the violence he perpetrated on this wife, even though he stated he loved her (Lavergne, 1997). Charles J. Whitman grew up in a household where violence was the norm, especially violence against his mother. Misogyny was evident, even when expressed within the context of a 'loving' relationship. While Whitman's crime has not, to my knowledge, been widely thought of as a gendered crime, I think that it should be.

In an excellent book, Smith (2019) considers the role of domestic violence in turning men into terrorists. Smith argues that a history of domestic violence is one of the greatest risk factors for the commission of terrorist attacks. The gap between terrorist attack and Charles Whitman's mass murders does not appear to be a very large one, and there is little doubt but that this crime was in large part about the commission of violence against women. There is also no doubt that Whitman grew up in a home where domestic violence was normalised and that Whitman perpetrated domestic violence upon his own wife. Think about it for a moment. Whitman murdered his mother and wife because he 'loved' them. That's a very strange kind of love. His first victim in the tower was a middle-aged woman whose skull he smashed. He then shot a pregnant woman in the abdomen. These acts are clearly misogynistic. Smith (2019, p. 47) writes about how the normalisation of domestic abuse (such as that in the lived experience of the young Whitman) creates 'a pool of angry men with an unusually low threshold for other forms of violence'. My view is that this crime was a gendered crime and that in order to understand this crime, and these types of crime, the role of domestic violence in mass killings needs to be recognised. Domestic violence will be considered in more depth in Chapter 21 on Alan Hawe, but for now, the key point must be that the intergenerational transmission of domestic violence should be both a focus of research and a societal priority (Gavin, 2019).

Tumour

In one of his notes, Whitman referred to having suffered 'some tremendous headaches', experiencing 'fears and violent impulses', and he even requested an autopsy because he suspected some mental disorder.. Lavergne (1997) noted that many who knew Whitman were comforted by this note and saw it as evidence that he knew that something was amiss with his brain and that it was not Charles J. Whitman who committed the mass murder; it was the tumour in his brain. This interpretation has been widely challenged (e.g. Stearns, 2008) and most physicians and criminologists who have considered this case have concluded that the explanation for Whitman's behaviour does not rest with the tumour. The tumour is 'innocent' (Lavergne, 1997, p. 268).

Heat and Crime/Violence

Another factor that has been considered is heat. While Whitman clearly planned his murders well in advance of their execution, it is noteworthy that Austin was in the middle of an extreme heatwave when Whitman exploded with violence in his mother's apartment, his wife's bedroom and on the University of Texas campus. 'As the ambient temperature rises, there are increases in domestic violence (Cohn, 1993), violent suicide (Maes, DeMeyer, Thompson, Peeters, & Cosyns, 1994), and collective violence (Carlsmith & Anderson, 1979)' (Hogg & Vaughan, 2018, p. 490). Obviously, the heat in Texas on 1 August 1966 was no more to blame for the murders than Whitman's tumour. However, the social psychological literature does make a clear link between violent crime and temperature. In the Whitman case, we have murderous domestic violence, murderous violence and suicide by cop. Was it a coincidence that the events described in this chapter occurred during a heatwave?

Psychiatry

Given that a psychiatrist saw Whitman in his clinic relatively close in time to the murders, it is worth returning to the role of psychiatry. Dr Heatly found no evidence of psychosis in his meeting with Whitman (Lavergne, 1997). Furthermore, Heatly said that he could not account for what happened on a 'pure and uncomplicated psychiatric basis' (Lavergne, 1997, p. 235). Because Whitman told Heatly that he was thinking about shooting people from the Tower, the question might be raised as to why Dr Heatly did not go to the police or have Whitman committed. That is not reasonable. As Lavergne reports, having a violent fantasy is not a crime. Nor is having a violent fantasy uncommon.

Narcissism

We should accept Dr Heatly's view that what happened in this case is not explicable in terms of psychosis. It does not necessarily follow that toxic personality factors were not at play. Arntfield and Danesi (2017) examined the available text of Whitman's notes and concluded that in these documents:

> there is the recurring use of the first person pronoun ('I' and 'my'), in contrast to serial killer manifestos where the emphasis is instead on other people, usually the victims. This self-focus clearly indicates that the mass murderer

is fixated on his own situation as a key one – his letdowns, frustrations, and so on … the mass murderer's writing evidences a specific level of entitlement that puts his own needs on a higher level … manifesting a disordered pattern of thinking. (Arntfield & Danesi, 2017, pp. 156–157).

The American Psychiatric Association (2013) classify this disordered pattern of thinking as narcissistic personality disorder. Narcissistic personality disorder is always toxic and dangerous; it takes hold of the perpetrator to the point where he explodes emotionally, and needs to eliminate anyone perceived as standing in his way in order to right perceived wrongs (Arntfield & Danesi, 2017). Angry, vengeful, aggressive and cruel, and treating the lives of others as inferior and trivial, the narcissist label certainly seems to fit Charles J. Whitman.

Other Issues

Two other issues that were raised by Lavergne (1997) are Whitman's drug abuse and the question of whether TV violence played a role in the Whitman mass murders. Bandura, Ross and Ross (1961), in their Bobo Doll studies, alongside Bandura and Walters' (1963) book *Social Learning and Personality Development*, had put social learning theory on the map, and the idea that aggression could be acquired was being widely discussed at the time of the Whitman murders in 1966. The findings of Bandura and colleagues that learning takes place as a consequence of modelling and imitation is robust and useful. In the Whitman case it emerges in the sphere of domestic violence and the intergenerational transmission of violent behaviours.

With regards to Whitman's drug abuse, while it is the case that serial killers do have a high lifetime prevalence of drug abuse (Hill, Habermann, Berner, & Briken, 2007), drugs and alcohol serve to facilitate rather than drive homicidal behaviours (Gavin, 2019).

CONCLUSION

A myriad of toxic variables came together and manifested in Charles J. Whitman on that August day in 1966. Narcissism, socially learnt domestic violence, misogyny, frustration, depression, anger and easy access to high-powered weapons were certainly among these factors. Although it is statistically a rare crime, there have been too many mass killings since Charles Whitman's crime. Dealing with mass killing requires a twin-track approach – one short-term strategy and one a long-term approach. The short-term strategy is relatively straightforward: gun control, making it harder for people to access firearms, especially semi-automatic weapons with an ever-greater capacity to kill. The long-term strategy is more difficult: the need to address domestic violence. The intergenerational transmission of domestic violence is a persisting issue in our society, which acts as a breeding ground for all sorts of other criminal violence. The cycle needs to be broken and dealing with this problem begins by understanding it. More research is needed.

REFLECTIVE QUESTIONS

1. Do you agree with the suggestion that domestic violence may have played a significant role in the mass killings of Charles J. Whitman?
2. Is it credible to invoke ambient temperature, as social psychology seems to suggest we should, in our attempts to understand Whitman's crimes?
3. Might Whitman's brain tumour have played a role in his behaviour?

FURTHER READING

Time Magazine (1966). Nation: The madman in the tower. *Time Magazine*, 12 August. Available at: http://content.time.com/time/subscriber/article/0,33009,842584-1,00.html

Washington Post (2016). The loaded legacy of the UT Tower shooting. *Washington Post*, 31 July. An article marking the 50th anniversary of the Whitman shooting. Also available at: www.washingtonpost.com/sf/local/2016/07/31/the-loaded-legacy-of-the-ut-tower-shooting/?utm_term=.0af6e1faeff8

Lavergne, G. M. (1997). *A Sniper in the Tower: The Charles Whitman Murders*. Denton, TX: University of North Texas Press.

Smith, J. (2019). *Home-Grown: How Domestic Violence Turns Men into Terrorists*. London: Riverrun.

20

STEPHEN GRIFFITHS: THE BRADFORD MURDERS

LEARNING OBJECTIVES

By the end of this chapter you should be able to:

- Define serial murder
- Discuss some theories of serial killing
- Debate the relevance of criminal narrative to the case of Stephen Griffiths

SYNOPSIS OF THE CASE

Stephen Griffiths was undertaking a PhD in criminology when he murdered three women in Bradford. Canter (1994, p. 299) states that 'through his actions the criminal tells us about how he has chosen to live his life. The challenge is to reveal his destructive life story; to uncover the plot in which crime appears to play such a significant part…'. Canter argues that criminals are limited people and that their limited narratives share a common factor – the victim is regarded as less than human. The Stephen Griffiths case is used to reflect on Canter's view of the importance of the criminal narrative.

DESCRIPTION OF THE CASE

Stephen Griffiths, the self-styled 'crossbow cannibal', was born in West Yorkshire in 1969. There are many deeply unpleasant characters discussed in these pages, but Stephen Griffiths is surely among the most repulsive.

The Victims

One curious aspect about media and academic treatment of serial killers is that the spotlight tends to fall on the killers rather than their victims. Stephen Griffiths murdered three vulnerable women.

The first woman to fall victim to Stephen Griffiths was Susan Rushworth. Also known as Sue and Susie, Susan was a 43-year-old mother of three. She had a good relationship with her children but had had her struggles with heroin addiction over the years. At the time of her murder, Susan had been off drugs for about five weeks and seemed to be in the process of pulling her life together. Susan disappeared from Bradford on 22 June 2009.

Shelley Armitage disappeared from Bradford on 26 April 2010. Shelley, aged 31, had bought a puppy, from whom she could not bear to be separated, just prior to her disappearance. Shelley grew up in a good family in Bradford and had dreams of becoming a model. Staff in the Catholic school that she attended recall a quiet and pleasant girl. From the age of about 16 Shelley had struggled with drug and alcohol addiction.

Suzanne Blamires disappeared from Bradford on 21 May 2010. She was 36 years old. In her earlier life, Suzanne had travelled widely and had begun training to become a nurse. She had a happy childhood and a loving family. Like Shelley and Susan, Suzanne also struggled with addiction.

Another factor that linked Susan, Shelley and Suzanne was that they had all been driven into prostitution in order to feed their drug addictions. All three women 'worked' in Bradford's red-light district.

Bradford's Red-Light District

Bradford's red-light district has been described in the newspapers as 'a magnet for vulnerable women and violent, predatory men'. It is hard to quibble with this assessment. The 'Yorkshire Ripper', Peter Sutcliffe, who loomed large in the imagination of Stephen Griffiths, had begun his murderous serial killing in the area. Another predatory killer who had murdered in Bradford's red-light district was Kenneth Valentine. Valentine sexually assaulted and killed Leeds woman Janet Willoughby in a 1991 attack for which he was convicted of manslaughter. Janet was not involved in prostitution. Valentine's second victim was Caroline Creevy. Caroline was a 25-year-old woman who paid Valentine £5 a session for the use of a room in his Bradford flat so she could have sex with her clients. Caroline had resorted to prostitution in order to feed her drug habit. Valentine's flat was in Soho Mills, a converted factory on Thornton Road. In 1996 Valentine raped and murdered Caroline Creevy after she rejected his advances. When Valentine was arrested for murder in November 1996, police discovered a third woman locked in his bedroom. It is likely that Valentine intended to murder her too. Following Valentine's arrest for murder in 1996, Soho Mills was renamed Holmfield Court. One resident who was in place before and after the renaming was Stephen Griffiths.

Stephen Griffiths

Stephen Griffiths is a very odd and unpleasant man. His parents separated when he was a child and he grew up with his family in Yorkshire. As a boy, Griffiths won a scholarship to public school and was an impressive student, gaining good A-levels and subsequently a first-class degree in psychology. Griffiths committed his first crime at the age of 17 when, unprovoked, he attacked a supermarket manager with a knife. Following his arrest, Griffiths said that he saw himself becoming a murderer. Psychiatrists warned at the time that Griffiths was fantasising about becoming a serial killer. In 1991, Griffiths was diagnosed as a 'schizoid psychopath'. In 1992, he was sentenced to two years in prison for holding a knife to a girl's throat.

Friends report Griffiths as having a strong interest in animals. He had a peculiar habit of taking his lizards for walks on a lead. There are reports of Griffiths feeding live rats to lizards and relishing, in front of witnesses, the rat's grizzly demise. He is also said to have eaten live baby mice, which he washed down with a glass of water. Griffiths does not seem to have been inhibited in his discussions about, or perpetration of, animal torture. Nor does he seem to have shied away from sharing his fantasies of cannibalism. It was hardly an accident that Griffiths located himself in the heart of Bradford's red-light district. Here he could observe vulnerable people coming and going as he tortured his pets, studied murder and fantasised about killing.

Griffiths was studying for a PhD in criminology at the time of his arrest aged 40. The subject of his PhD was, perhaps unsurprisingly, murder. *The Guardian* newspaper reported that Griffiths had

> developed an outlandish persona [on social media sites], portraying himself as 'Ven Pariah' and a 'misanthrope who brought hate into heaven'. He appeared in a photograph naked from the chest upward and quoted the Bible (Ezekiel 25:17): 'The path of the righteous man is beset on all sides.' The quote acquired notoriety when it was used in a gory execution scene in Quentin Tarantino's film *Pulp Fiction*. (Carter, 2010)

The Murders, Capture and Conviction

On 24 May 2010, Stephen Griffiths was arrested for the murder of Suzanne Blamires. Earlier that day one of the caretakers who worked at Holmfield Court, where Griffiths had lived in his third-floor flat for some 15 years, had contacted the police. While going through CCTV video recorded over the weekend, the caretaker found shocking images of Suzanne Blamires. Suzanne could be seen, in the video, following a man into his flat. Almost immediately, she is seen fleeing from the flat, being chased by a man armed with a crossbow, who brought her to the ground. The man is seen shooting Suzanne in the back of the head with a crossbow bolt before dragging her dead body back into the flat. The man then returns to the CCTV camera that recorded these images and, with his crossbow in one hand, points the middle finger of his other hand at the camera. The man is instantly recognisable as Stephen Griffiths. It subsequently transpired that Suzanne was Griffiths' third victim. On arrest, Griffiths said to the police 'I'm Osama bin Laden' and on arrival at the police station he boasted 'I've killed a lot more than Suzanne Blamires – I've killed loads'.

Later that day, as police went through Griffiths' computer, they found images of a woman, naked and tied up, in his bath. 'My Sex Slave' was spray-painted on her back. Police were able to identify this woman as Shelley Armitage.

While in police custody, Griffiths confessed to the killing of Shelley Armitage and Susan Rushworth. All of Griffiths' victims were dismembered and there is evidence that he committed cannibalism. Judge Mr Justice Openshaw, who heard the case against Stephen Griffiths, said that 'The circumstances of these murders are so wicked and monstrous they leave me in no doubt the defendant should be kept in prison for the rest of his life'. Suzanne Blamires' body was found in a river, at Shipley; along with part of Shelley Armitage's. West Yorkshire Police believe that it is extremely unlikely that Susan Rushworth's body will ever be found.

LINKS TO THEORY AND RESEARCH

Defining Serial Murder

There are many definitions of serial murder. One influential definition is 'The unlawful killing of two or more victims by the same offender(s), in separate events' (National Center for the Analysis of Violent Crime (NCAVC) United States of America, 2008). A more familiar definition is 'the killing of three or more people over a period of more than 30 days, with a significant cooling-off period between the killings' (Holmes & Holmes, 2010, p. 5). Gavin (2019) describes this definition as one of the most influential and it is probably the definition that Stephen Griffiths would have been familiar with too.

Serial murder is distinct from mass killing because of the cooling-off period required by the definition of serial killing (Holmes & Holmes, 2010). This cooling-off period is puzzling for many, myself included. How is it possible to navigate everyday life, without apparent rage or psychosis, and at the same time fantasise about, and perpetrate, the most heinous of crimes? Serial killers tend to target victims weaker than themselves, and their victims tend to be members of vulnerable groups. Those murdered by Stephen Griffiths were certainly extremely vulnerable. Because of the perceived vulnerability of their victims, much academic analysis suggests that the people targeted by serial killers present some sort of symbolic meaning to their killer (Gavin, 2019). One argument that will be made in this chapter is that criminal narrative, the stories that perpetrators weave about themselves, is useful in attempting to understand the minds of monsters.

Myths About Serial Murder

Before proceeding further, it is worth addressing some of the misconceptions and myths that are commonly attributed to serial murder. These myths were identified at a 2005 conference on serial murder that was hosted by the National Center for the Analysis of Violent Crime (NCAVC), Quantico, Virginia (National Center for the Analysis of Violent Crime (NCAVC) United States of America, 2008).

Myth #1: Serial Killers Are Dysfunctional Loners

Stephen Griffiths was a dysfunctional loner. However, most serial killers are not social misfits who live alone. Most do not appear to be monsters and most do not appear strange. Harold Shipman, possibly the most prolific serial killer ever, with more than 200 victims, is an excellent example of a serial killer who hid in plain sight and, as a practising doctor, held a position of respectability within his community. Serial murderers often have families, homes and responsible jobs.

Myth #2: Serial Killers Are All White Males

Stephen Griffiths is a white male, but it is important to recognise that serial killers come from all racial groups. The FBI report on serial murder that followed the 2005 conference on the same subject (National Center for the Analysis of Violent Crime (NCAVC) United States of America, 2008) indicates that the racial diversification of serial killers in the USA generally mirrors that of the overall population.

Myth #3: Serial Killers Are Only Motivated by Sex

While there was a sexual aspect to Stephen Griffiths' murders, it would be a mistake to think that all serial murders are sexually-based. There is a plethora of motivations for serial murders, including anger, thrill-seeking, financial gain and attention-seeking.

Myth #4: Serial Killers Cannot Stop Killing

It is not the case that serial killers cannot stop killing. There are many examples of serial killers who stop murdering years before they are caught. For example, Dennis Rader murdered his last victim in 1991, although he was not caught until 14 years later in 2005.

Myth #5: All Serial Killers Are Insane or Are Evil Geniuses

Insanity is a legal rather than a psychiatric category. While it is the case that some serial killers, including Griffiths, are likely to be psychopaths, it is not the case that they are insane in the eyes of the law. Indeed, insanity would be the exception rather than the norm. Stephen Griffiths was a good student, and had the capacity to complete a PhD, but he is not a genius.

Theories of Serial Murder

Popular Attitudes to Serial Killing

Before looking at academic theories, it is worth pausing to consider how we (in the broadest sense) think about serial killing. The book *Serial Killers: Philosophy for Everyone* (Waller, 2010) presents an unusual take on serial murder which serves to illustrate the somewhat odd attitude we, as a society, have towards serial killers. 'Jack the Ripper' has fascinated an enthralled audience for more than 100 years. Books on Ted Bundy, Peter Sutcliffe and others fly off the shelves. Dietrich and Fox Hall (2010) consider the allure of serial killers. They argue that what we find alluring is the idea of the serial killer. In part, we are curious and simply want to understand, but we are also attracted to dangerous things and, in an abstract sense, we are drawn to the idea of things that could potentially kill us. In the case of serial killers, their appeal rests on a concrete requirement for there to be a safe distance between them and us. 'For most of us, sitting down with a real serial killer would not be an artistic, philosophical experience, but rather a terrifying, repulsive one' (Dietrich & Fox Hall, 2010, p. 102).

Understanding Serial Murder

Holmes and Holmes (2010) categorise theories of serial murder into three groups: biological theories, psychological theories and sociological theories. This is a useful starting point. Another useful approach is narrative theory (Canter & Youngs, 2009), which is also considered here.

The notion that criminals are a biologically distinct group within humanity is an old one. According to Lombroso's (1911) idea of '*homo criminalis*', human biology is at the root of criminal behaviour. Criminals are understood to be defective throwbacks. Killers, according to Lombroso, act as they do as a consequence of inherent biological defects. In an important sense, the present-day idea of the psychopath is similar to Lombroso's idea of 'the criminal man'. Like *homo criminalis*, contemporary psychopathy researchers understand criminality as being rooted in defective individual biology. 'Psychopathy researchers frequently argue that the manifest behavioural signs of psychopathy are merely rough approximations of the more fundamental and true biological signs' (Jalava, 2006, p. 427). Was Stephen Griffiths a psychopath? There is a problematic circularity that applies to psychopathy – psychopaths are people who commit callous acts with little regard for others and people who commit acts that are callous and have little regard for others are often psychopaths.

Gavin (2019) cites criminologist David Wilson, who regards Griffiths as a misogynist with a narcissistic personality disorder (NPD). Griffiths set his sights on murdering three people in order that he be recognised as a serial killer.

Narcissistic personality disorder 'has primarily been identified by striking external features, such as superiority, attention seeking and a critical or condescending attitude' (Ronningstam, 2020, p. 80). Importantly, the disorder is marked by a complete lack of empathy towards others (Comer, 2012). From a forensic perspective, NPD is one of the most difficult personality disorders to treat because those with NPD are unwilling to acknowledge that they have any weaknesses, they don't incorporate feedback, and they do not appreciate that their behaviour impacts others (Comer, 2012). David Wilson's assessment of Stephen Griffiths as presenting with NPD is accurate.

One important biological factor that has been invoked in the consideration of serial murder is head trauma. Allely, Minnis, Thompson, Wilson and Gillberg (2014), for example, found that head trauma is a feature that many serial killers share. In their systematic review, Allely et al. discovered that a significant proportion of serial killers may have been impacted neuro-developmentally through head injury. In their review of 239 serial killers, more than a fifth (n = 51; 21.34%) had experienced either a definite or suspected head injury. However, there are millions of people who survive head injury and never commit violence against anyone. There is nothing to suggest that Stephen Griffiths had experienced either neurological problems or head trauma (Gavin, 2019).

Psychological explanations of serial murder can go further than explanations based on the medical or psychiatric model in seeking to understand the crimes of serial killers. Gavin (2019), for example, invokes psychodynamic theory, developmental psychology and evolutionary psychology. Freud believed that the superego, that is an individual's social consciousness, played a vital role in controlling antisocial behaviour. Holmes and Holmes (2010) report that psychodynamic theorists, including those who followed Freud, argue that criminal behaviour is rooted in conflict between the id (the instinctual, pleasure seeking, part of the psyche that includes sex and other drivers) and the super ego (the largely unconscious and internalised moral and ethical rules and regulations of a society). Brookman (2005) cites the work of a prison psychiatrist (Gilligan, 2000) as a modern example of how psychodynamic theorising can be applied to the understanding of murder.

Gilligan (2000) describes some preconditions that can result in men becoming killers. First is the killer's experience of shame. Second is the killer's appraisal that there are no non-violent means by which their shame can be reduced. The third, important precondition is that the killer lacks the emotional capacity to inhibit violent impulses.

There are, however, significant issues with applying the psychoanalytical approach to understanding crime. Psychoanalytical understanding builds on a complex model of internal, often unconscious, psychological conflict which is impossible to observe. The psychoanalytical approach is also criticised because of the strong emphasis it places on early childhood experience and, consequently, the approach often ignores adult experiences and situational factors (Brookman,

2005). In the case of Stephen Griffiths, this would seem to be important because, in so far as we can tell, he had a 'normal' childhood.

In a developmental frame, Leary, Southard, Hill and Ashman (2017) examined the cases of 280 serial killers and found that bed-wetting, firesetting and torturing animals were common aspects in the developmental backgrounds of serial killers. This combination of behaviours, known as the MacDonald Triad, was first identified in the early 1960s, but care must be taken in how we interpret the finding. Gavin (2019) reports that the prevalence of the MacDonald Triad in a population of children who have grown to be 'normal' adults is yet to be assessed.

From the perspective of evolutionary psychology, Buss (2005, p. 219) argues that 'serial killers murder because they seek vengeance for status denied'. Buss is convinced that social status is what drives many serial murderers. It does seem that Stephen Griffiths was actively seeking recognition. However, rather like psychodynamic theory, evolutionary approaches tend to be more heavily weighted in terms of theory than in empirical evidence, because hypothesis testing is extraordinarily difficult to conceive in evolutionary terms.

Applying social psychological and/or sociological theories to serial murder leads to a focus on context. Social identity theory (Tajfel & Turner, 1979) is one approach that may be especially useful as it offers conceptual tools relating to how individuals divide the world in terms of 'us' and 'them', and how 'they' are capable of depersonalising others. Stephen Griffiths had no respect for his victims. Indeed, he did not treat them as fellow human beings at all. It is difficult not to draw the conclusion that he did not see them as people. Holmes and Holmes (2010) report how serial killers dehumanise their victims in order to reduce them to the level of objects. Depersonalising them in this way allows the perpetrator to rationalise their murderous behaviour. To the best of my knowledge, social identity theory has not been applied to an analysis of serial murder, but the approach may provide a useful theory for future research.

Criminal Narrative

Criminal narrative is the term used to account for how criminals make sense of their own story, how they position themselves in their own personal worldview; it is the story they create to account for their criminal behaviour. We have noted earlier in this chapter that Stephen Griffiths may have embarked on his series of killings expressly because he fantasised about being categorised as a serial killer (Gavin, 2019). To do so, he knew he had to murder three or more people. This observation begs the question: what narrative did Griffiths create for himself? We know that Griffiths respected Peter Sutcliffe ('the Yorkshire Ripper') and other serial murderers. He referred to these men as misanthropes and regarded them as heroes. It is perhaps telling that Griffiths also referred to himself as a misanthrope and a pariah. It is also interesting that he quoted from the 1994 movie *Pulp Fiction*. This is a critically acclaimed crime movie with graphic content, a very catchy soundtrack, and unconventional structure. In a very literal sense, these observations raise the question: what story was he creating for himself?

Canter and Youngs (2009, p. 329) argue that the central challenge 'in explaining the cause of serial killing comes from recognition that the development and creation of a serial killer is a process rather than a simple cause–effect mechanism (Canter, 1994). In this regard, the narrative framework offers a potentially fruitful way forward. … It may be that this way of construing what happens during one's life, as much as the events themselves, distinguishes those individuals who become violent criminals from those who do not.' They outline how criminal narratives are about embedding self-identity in a social matrix and how some criminals may revel in the story they can tell of their criminality.

This certainly rings true in the case of Stephen Griffiths, and can help us to understand what he was trying to do when he killed three victims, why he returned and gestured so provocatively at the CCTV camera, choosing to reveal his identity, why he told the police officers interviewing him that he had 'killed loads', and why he identified himself as the 'crossbow cannibal'. Through his actions and his words, Griffiths may have been attempting to tell a story to himself, and to the world at large. In that story, he is the hero in precisely the same way as Peter Sutcliffe was a hero to him. Pathetic as this appears to the outside viewer, there is a discernible inner logic for what otherwise appears to be incoherent. Could it be that understanding Stephen Griffiths as the narrator and chief actor in the unfolding story of his life is key to making sense of his actions? A narrative perspective certainly seems to offer a way of making sense of what seems like a bizarre desire to become a serial killer.

Canter and Youngs (2009) propose that one of four mythic themes can dominate the personal narratives of individual criminals. These themes are irony, adventure, tragedy and quest. These themes are shorthand summaries that allow us to begin thinking in ways that will facilitate engagement with the much more nuanced and complex narratives that drive the unfolding stories that manifest as criminal behaviour. At first blush, Canter and Youngs' quest theme seems to capture the essence of Stephen Griffiths' drive for recognition as a serial killer.

CONCLUSION

It may be, as Gavin (2019, p. 135) succinctly suggests, that 'Stephen Griffiths is simply a highly unfortunate product of the world's fascination with murder'. In order to understand Griffiths, and others who commit serial murder, significantly more work is needed. A model with good explanatory power would include elements that consider the individual's biography (i.e. their life story and formative experiences), psychology (e.g. development, 'personality' and mental illness) and their social environment (e.g. the groups that people belong to, and the stories that they weave for themselves and others). Only time will tell.

REFLECTIVE QUESTIONS

1. Why do you think media attention falls on serial killers rather than their victims?
2. Are serial killers a biologically distinct group within society?
3. Is psychopathy a useful concept in understanding all cases of serial murder?
4. Do the concepts of 'social identity theory' and 'criminal narrative' help us to understand the behaviour of Stephen Griffiths?

FURTHER READING

www.theguardian.com/uk/2011/mar/05/crossbow-cannibal-stephen-griffiths

www.fbi.gov/stats-services/publications/serial-murder

Holmes, R. M., & Holmes, S. T. (2010). *Serial Murder* (3rd edition). Thousand Oaks, CA: Sage.

21
ALAN HAWE: MURDER-SUICIDE

LEARNING OBJECTIVES

By the end of this chapter you should be able to:

- Describe what is meant by familicide with reference to a relevant case
- Discuss how familicide is linked to domestic and interpartner violence
- Apply relevant psychological theory to a discussion of murder-suicide

SYNOPSIS OF THE CASE

The circumstances surrounding Alan Hawe's murder of his family and suicide at his home in Cavan, Ireland, during August 2016, seem to share many characteristics found in other murder-suicides. Hawe, a deputy school principal, appears to have been deeply worried that some 'dark secret' of his was about to be exposed. In any event, he murdered his wife and three children in the most brutal and distressing of fashions. This chapter will set out some of the psychological factors important to understanding cases of familicide, murder suicide and domestic violence. It will also (briefly) consider how the media report on cases such as this.

DESCRIPTION OF THE CASE

> Until August 2016, Hawe was considered by most, to be a respectable, clean living, deeply religious husband and father with a steady career as the deputy head teacher at Castlerahan National School, near his home in Co Cavan. That respectability was a façade perfected over years, his work-a-day life pitted with passive aggression, lies and pretence. (Beattie, 2019)

In the early hours of 29 August 2016, the Hawe family were at home in County Cavan, Ireland. Clodagh Hawe, a 39-year-old teacher and mother of three, was sitting down, having a cup of tea, and browsing potential holiday destinations on her laptop. Her three boys, Liam, 13, Niall, 11, and 6-year-old Ryan were upstairs in bed. Alan Hawe, the 40-year-old deputy principal of a local primary school, husband to Clodagh and father of Liam, Niall and Ryan, had earlier turned the settee Clodagh was sitting on so that its back was facing the sitting-room door. On that dreadful night, Hawe came through the door with an axe in his hand. Hawe approached his wife from behind, hit her in the head with the axe and then stabbed her in the back with a knife. The attack was of such ferocity that Clodagh's hand was almost severed as she raised it in an attempt to defend herself.

It is believed that after murdering his wife, Hawe went to the kitchen and penned a murder-suicide note, which he placed in a sealed envelope on the kitchen table. With Clodagh dead, and his note written, Hawe was not yet finished. He took another kitchen knife and walked up the stairs to murder his sleeping children. The older boys, Liam and Niall, shared a room, and the youngest child, Ryan, had a room to himself. Hawe killed Liam, the eldest, strongest, boy first. He did so purposively and in such a way that Liam could not make any noise that might arouse the other children. Then he murdered Niall and Ryan last. Like Clodagh, Liam and Niall had defensive wounds on their hands. The knife used to kill the boys was left on Ryan's pillow and the boys' quilts were thrown on top of their bodies.

Having murdered his family in the most brutal manner one could imagine, Hawe went back to the kitchen, where he wrote a second note on the outside of the envelope in which he had sealed the first. Hawe also placed a note on the back door asking for the police to be called. He then hanged himself from the banister rail in the hall.

On the morning of 29 August 2016, Clodagh's mother, Mary Coll, was worried when Clodagh had not arrived, as expected, with two of her boys. Mary drove over to Clodagh's house to check that everything was alright. She was just about to put her key in the back door when she saw Alan Hawe's handwritten note asking for the police to be called. Mary rang 999 and went to a neighbour's house. '"I told them I think Alan has done something terrible, that Alan had killed them all," Mrs Coll said' (*Belfast Telegraph*, 2020).

The police officers who first entered the house found Clodagh lying face down in her pyjamas and dressing gown on a couch in the sitting room. Alan

Hawe's body was found next in the hall. They then went upstairs where they found the bodies of the dead children. A police officer who was on the scene broke down in tears as she later recounted the events of that morning to a coroner's inquest. The police also found a number of jewellery boxes stacked neatly on the bed of the main bedroom and the notes, all of which were written by Hawe.

Initial reporting in the media was the cause of some controversy in the immediate wake of the murders. For example, on 31 August 2016, two days after Alan Hawe had murdered his family and committed suicide, the *Irish Independent* newspaper ran the headline 'Alan was an accomplished athlete and founding member of handball club' over a story in which Hawe was described as a 'proud man' who would be 'sorely missed'. The article set out Hawe's athletic prowess and made no mention of his victims except in terms of his family name and the 'Ballyjamesduff tragedy'. There was something of a backlash against what was perceived as a sympathetic reporting of an extreme act of domestic violence, with *The Guardian* running the headline 'Reporting of man who killed his family too sympathetic, say women's groups' on 2 September 2016.

In the months after the murders, a coroner's inquest found that Alan Hawe had severe mental illness at the time of the killings. Professor Harry Kennedy, a forensic psychiatrist, prepared a report for the coroner based on Alan Hawes' medical records and suicide note, and concluded that Hawe had progressed from a long-standing depressive illness to a severe depressive episode with psychotic symptoms. Professor Kennedy is also reported as adding that his opinion was confined by the fact that information pertaining to Alan Hawe was limited. The coroner decided against releasing the content of Hawe's suicide notes, although this was shared with the jury of the coroner's inquiry.

Media Reports Regarding the Suicide Notes

In the weeks and months following the murder of Clodagh Hawe and her boys, there was significant media interest in the content of the suicide notes that Alan Hawe had left. There was speculation that Hawe had been caught accessing pornography and masturbating at the school where he worked and that, with the school year about to start, he was facing an imminent 'fall from grace'. The school subsequently denied reports that Hawe was facing disciplinary procedures and that he had accessed pornographic material on school premises.

On 27 February 2019, the *Irish Mirror* newspaper published what it reports were some contents of the suicide notes. According to this report, Hawe wrote that 'All the good stuff we did I was really into it. But I think there was some sort of psychosis that made me enjoy that yet in the next moment I was the complete opposite' and 'I'm sorry for how I murdered them all but I simply had no other way'. Hawe is also reported to have written in one of the notes that 'it was easier for them [i.e. his family] to die' than to have to live with the truth of what he was doing.

LINKS TO THEORY AND RESEARCH

'Murder-suicide does not really present definitional challenges – the person has clearly died by suicide – but [it] raises another question: Why murder someone first?' (Joiner, 2005, p. 149). The facts pertaining to this case are, in one sense, clear – Alan Hawe murdered his family in the most horrific way and then committed suicide. But, as noted by Joiner (2005), the burning question is why? The suggestions presented in this chapter are, of necessity, speculative. As Wilson (2012) points out, there can be no single grand theory of murder. Instead, what we have is a complex interaction between 'faulty' individuals and circumstances that are conducive to murder.

In order to usefully contemplate what we know about the case of Alan Hawe, suicide will be briefly examined and several theoretical lenses will be brought to bear on the murders. Violence (both instrumental and expressive) will be discussed in the broader context of intimate partner violence and domestic violence. Psychological perspectives will also be applied to our consideration of those terrible events that took place in Cavan in the early autumn of 2016. The discourse and reporting that accompanied the events will also be scrutinised.

Suicide

Suicide is a significant public health issue (e.g. Knox, Conwell, & Caine, 2004). In the UK, there were 6,507 cases of suicide recorded by the Office for National Statistics (ONS) in 2018. Three-quarters of those who died by suicide in 2018 were men. The largest proportion of these men were middle-aged and, more than half of those men died by hanging (Office for National Statistics, 2019b).

Joiner (2005) suggests that marriage can act as a buffer against suicide because of the belongingness that is associated with being in a marital relationship. In contrast, thwarted belongingness can act as a risk for death by suicide. Muldoon et al. (2019) report that negative responses to trauma are more apparent where trauma serves to undermine valued social identities. On the basis of the evidence that we have, it seems that Alan Hawe believed that at least two of his valued social identities were threatened – his identity as a husband and his identity as a 'pillar of the community'. We know that when a person's sense of their social self is compromised, this compromise is intimately entwined with an experience of trauma (Haslam, Jetten, Cruwys, Dingle, & Haslam, 2018). These observations about identity and the trauma associated with threatened identity loss may be helpful in understanding why Alan Hawe killed himself. What the observations about suicide do not help with is understanding why Alan Hawe murdered his family.

Aggression

'Trying to understand why humans aggress against their own kind, and the factors that make them behave with viciousness and brutality towards one another in ways and degrees unparalleled in other animals, has led to much speculation since ancient times' (Hogg & Vaughan, 2018, p. 472). There are a range of definitions of aggression in the psychological literature. One useful definition is that offered by Carlson et al., who defined aggression as 'the attempt to harm' (Carlson et al., 1989, cited in Hogg & Vaughan, 2018, p. 472). Harm was certainly the intent of Alan Hawe when he used extreme violence to murder his family with an axe and knives, weapons that are both brutal and intimate. Hawe's intent was to harm to the fullest extent possible – murder.

Violence

Criminal assault is a form of aggression and a crime of violence is committed when a perpetrator uses illegitimate force against a victim (Takarangi & Flowe, 2012). When thinking about violence in academic terms, we can separate out two distinct strands of violence: instrumental violence and expressive violence.

Instrumental violence is used to gain a specified end (Wilson, 2012). For example, one might employ instrumental violence to facilitate a robbery. There is a rationality associated with this type of violence because it is perpetrated in the pursuit of an objective, a gain to the perpetrator.

Expressive violence, on the other hand, lacks rationality. The objective of expressive violence is to inflict harm; the focus is not gain, but anger. Wilson (2012) suggests that expressive violence is intertwined with the emotive expression of personal identity. Wilson also points out that we should not presume that there is a neat separation between these two categories of violence and that the boundaries between them are regularly blurred.

Intimate Partner Violence

Intimate partner violence (IPV) describes the physical, psychological and sexual violence committed in an intimate relationship (past or present). Violence against women is an international problem of significant proportions. A survey, based on interviews with 42,000 women conducted by the European Union in 2014, found that one in three women had experienced some form of sexual or physical violence since the age of 15 (Shreeves & Prpic, 2019). Slightly more than one in five women had experienced physical and/or sexual violence from either a current or a previous partner, and almost half (43%) of the women had experienced some type of behaviour that can be understood as either psychologically abusive or controlling while they were in a relationship. Shockingly, Shreeves and Prpic (2019) report that half of all female murder victims in the EU were killed by an intimate partner, relative or family member. Shreeves and Prpic state that about seven women die every day in the EU as a consequence of domestic violence.

Tinney and Gerlock (2014) compiled a list of four contexts in which IPV has been studied: IPV with coercive control; IPV as reactive violence; IPV without coercive control; and IPV as pathological violence. The context of pathological violence, which may be influenced by psychological problems, might, on the face of things, and in light of the evidence given by forensic psychiatrist Professor

Harry Kennedy at the coroner's inquest into the Hawe murders, seems to 'fit'. However, 'it is important to note that violence embedded within any of these contexts can be dangerous and lethal. Determining context is not an attempt to minimize the level of risk and danger of IPV' (Tinney & Gerlock, 2014, p. 402).

There is an element of 'normality' associated, at a societal level, with attitudes to domestic violence, and violence against women, that collectively, we must address better. One recent paper (Naughton, O'Donnell, Greenwood, & Muldoon, 2015), for example, reports an instance where a member of the judiciary made reference to 'ordinary decent domestic violence'. That is not good enough.

Family Violence

The definition of family violence is wider than that of intimate partner violence. Family violence includes any assault, intimidation, battery, sexual assault, or any other criminal offence that causes personal injury or death to another who is living in the same single dwelling unit (Tinney & Gerlock, 2014). It is clearly the case that Alan Hawe committed an act of extreme, lethal, family violence when he murdered his sons and his wife. Tinney and Gerlock (2014, p. 290) cite the American Psychological Association's view that 'at the heart of family violence is usually the perpetrator's misuse of power, control, and authority'. Such was clearly the case with Alan Hawe. It is noteworthy that in cases where family violence is perpetrated, one form of violence, or dysfunction, is generally accompanied by other forms (Tinney & Gerlock, 2014).

Familicide

Websdale (2010, p. 1) defines familicide as 'the deliberate killing within a relatively short period of time of a current or former spouse or intimate partner and one or more of their children, perhaps followed by the suicide of the perpetrator. The word familicide therefore refers to a killing event, a strange and disturbing, albeit relatively rare, episode that punctuates social life in the modern era.'

Familicide is the ultimate form of family violence (Tinney & Gerlock, 2014), and it is, thankfully, relatively rare, accounting for less than 2% of all homicide. One side-effect of the rarity, however, is that familicide is a somewhat neglected area of research (Tinney & Gerlock, 2014). Brookman (2005, p. 196) reports that a particular feature of familicide that dominates many of these cases is a breakdown of the marital relationship. The killings seem to be linked to the father's perceptions of himself as a failure and his 'general feelings of 'hopelessness', 'helplessness', 'powerlessness' and 'uselessness'. It does appear that Alan Hawe was foreseeing the breakdown of his marriage, and the content of media reports regarding Hawe's state of mind seem consistent with Brookman's observations.

In their consideration of child victims of homicide, Alder and Polk make the point that we can only speculate about the possible rationales and emotions that lead to familicide, but it may be that familicide is the 'ultimate statement of power and control' (Alder & Polk, 2001, p. 166). There is evidence to suggest that in Alan Hawe's case, issues of power and control might have been tied up with a perception that the family's future was about to be 'ruined and beyond redemption' (Hollin, 2013, p. 134). This egocentricity, and the fact that any imminent 'ruin' was nothing to do with Clodagh Hawe or her boys, is one of the facets of this particular case that serves to magnify the tragedy and add to the apparent incomprehensibility of it.

Psychoanalytic Psychology

The psychoanalytic approach most relevant to the Hawe case/domestic violence is Freud's theory of the innate death instinct (Thanatos) and its opposite, the innate life instinct (Eros), which are discussed in more detail in Chapter 6 (Freud, 1920/1990). In Freud's view, Thanatos is like the sexual urge in so far as it builds up naturally from bodily tension, and must be expressed. Whereas initially it is directed inwardly, towards self-destruction, it can manifest later as aggression towards others. It may be that Alan Hawe simply erupted in a one-time expression of murderous aggression. However, such an explanation circles back to the question: 'Why are some people more aggressive than others?' Also, importantly, it also raises the question, if Thanatos is innate, why does it only affect some?

There are other psychodynamic perspectives that are arguably of relevance to abuse and domestic violence. These include object relations theory, which is the idea that adult relationships are a function of relationship patterns learnt in childhood, and attachment theory, which posits that those with an insecure attachment style are more prone to the commission and intergenerational transfer of abusive and violent norms (Gavin, 2019).

Gavin (2019) argues that, because psychodynamic approaches concentrate on processes that are internal to the individual and do not take account of contextual factors, the psychodynamic approach may not be the best placed to facilitate an understanding of aggression and violence in intimate relationships. With regards to the suicidal aspect of the Hawe case, it is worth considering Joiner's view (2005, p. 35): 'The first half of the twentieth century was dominated by psychoanalysis, and, to be blunt, it is difficult to think of a lasting contribution to the understanding of suicide from this perspective.'

Social Learning Theory

Bandura's social learning theory (Bandura, 1977; Bandura & Walters, 1963) is a social psychological theory that has been developed specifically with a consideration of aggression in mind (see Bandura, Ross, & Ross, 1963). In contrast to the individualistic orientation of the psychodynamic perspective outlined above, social learning theory is all about the context. The idea is that people learn by experience. This learning experience can either be direct – learned from one's own experience – or indirect – learned by observing others.

Bandura argues that, in order to understand aggression, three aspects are crucial: how aggressive behaviour is acquired; how the aggression is instigated (i.e. those environmental conditions that have previously precipitated violence); and how aggressive behaviour has been positively reinforced (i.e. those conditions that maintain the aggression). In the Hawe case, it is the maintenance of aggression that is the most interesting aspect. What, if any, were the aggressive behaviours in the previous history of Alan Hawe that had been positively reinforced? What, if any, aggressive behaviour had he encountered that gave him a sense of pride or achievement from behaving in that way? These are important questions because understanding the genesis of these (thankfully rare) incidents of extreme domestic violence is the first step in dealing with them.

Social learning theory is often brought to bear in the consideration of violent crimes. It is not easy to see what social learning theory adds to understanding when applied to the specifics of this case.

Psychiatry

Professor Harry Kennedy, a forensic psychiatrist, reported that Hawe had progressed from a long-standing depressive illness to a severe depressive episode with psychotic symptoms. According to DSM-5, for a diagnosis of depressive episode at least five of the symptoms below must be present during the same two-week period (and at least one of the symptoms must be depressed mood or the diminished interest or the loss of pleasure):

Depressed mood;
Diminished interest or loss of pleasure in almost all activities (anhedonia);
Significant weight change or appetite disturbance;
Sleep disturbance (insomnia or hypersomnia);
Psychomotor agitation or retardation;
Fatigue or loss of energy;
Feelings of worthlessness;
Diminished ability to think or concentrate;
Indecisiveness;
Recurrent thoughts of death, recurrent suicidal ideation without a specific plan, or a suicide attempt or specific plan for committing suicide.

In relation to psychosis, when people experience psychotic symptoms they lose contact with reality and experience things like delusions – strange ideas that do not relate to reality. People experiencing psychotic symptoms may also perceive things that are not really there (hallucinations). This is the medical context in which Professor Kennedy believed Alan Hawe committed his crimes, with the proviso that his opinion was confined by the fact that information pertaining to Alan Hawe was limited.

Discourse and Reporting

One striking feature of the Hawe murder-suicide is the way that it was covered in the media. Quinn, Prendergast and Galvin (2019) report that 42% of print media articles on the story on 30 August 2016 tended to omit Clodagh Hawe, and on the following day 36% of articles did so. These authors also state that social media was heavily critical that the mainstream media coverage of Alan Hawe was too sympathetic. They argue that there was:

> a distinct tendency to represent Hawe in more sympathetic terms (SAH) (foregrounding possible reasons and mitigating factors for his actions) compared with fewer articles framing explicit criticisms of his actions (CAH) (for example, foregrounding male-oriented patterns of domestic violence in past murder-suicides). (Quinn et al., 2019, p. 320)

In addition, they state that the reporting bias in the Hawe case

> relates strongly to the imposition of a patriarchal frame, or perspective on news coverage, whereby the male is central to the narrative, while the female is secondary, or conceptualised primarily in terms of her relationship to the male agent. More than 34% of newspaper reports refer to Clodagh Hawe as 'his wife', 'a mother of three', as opposed to describing other characteristics. Meanwhile, Alan Hawe is categorised as a father, husband, son, community and family man in over a quarter of news stories coded, as opposed to the author of a murder-suicide with five victims. (Quinn et al., 2019, p. 321)

It is hard to disagree. The Hawe case was a gendered crime where extreme domestic violence left four innocent people dead. Language is important. Alan Hawe was the abuser, perpetrator and murderer of his family. Newspaper reports suggesting that he was a 'proud man' who would be 'sorely missed' completely miss the point.

CONCLUSION

Hogg and Vaughan (2018, p. 505) argue that while there are no simple answers to domestic violence, there are some factors that are recognised as playing a role. Perpetrators of violence are often in a generational cycle of abuse; the proximity of family members makes them more likely to be sources of annoyance and targets of annoyance; stresses, including illnesses (e.g. depression) are associated with domestic violence; our patriarchal society gives power to men and makes it possible for unhealthy styles of interaction to dominate; and male alcohol abuse is a correlate of domestic violence. Notwithstanding the relevance of these factors, the sad reality is that more men, like Alan Hawe, will commit familicide. This was a gendered crime. We need to better understand this crime in order to better deal with it in future. Investigating domestic violence and IPV is an appropriate place to start.

REFLECTIVE QUESTIONS

1. Do you agree that the Hawe case was a gendered crime?
2. Is my linking of domestic violence to these crimes warranted? Why, or why not?
3. Is the psychiatric understanding of a long-standing depressive illness that progressed to a severe depressive episode with psychotic symptoms sufficient for understanding this crime?

FURTHER READING

www.rte.ie/search/query/Alan%20Hawe/

www.theguardian.com/world/2016/sep/02/reporting-alan-hawe-murder-suicide-family-sympathetic-say-womens-groups-wife-children

European Parliament briefing paper on violence against women: www.europarl.europa.eu/RegData/etudes/BRIE/2018/630296/EPRS_BRI(2018)630296_EN.pdf

Hogg, M. A., & Vaughan, G. M. (2018). Chapter 12: Aggression. In *Social Psychology*. (8th edition). Harlow: Pearson.

REFERENCES

Adjorlolo, S., & Chan, H. C. (2014). The controversy of defining serial murder: Revisited. *Aggression and Violent Behavior, 19*(5), 486–491. doi:10.1016/j.avb.2014.07.003

Adorno, T. W., Frenkel-Brunswik, E., Levinson, D. J., & Sanford, R. N. (1950). *The Authoritarian Personality*. New York: Harper.

Aiken, M. (2016). *The Cyber Effect: A Pioneering Cyberpsychologist Explains How Human Behaviour Changes Online*. London: Hachette UK.

Alder, C., & Polk, K. (2001). *Child Victims of Homicide*. Cambridge: Cambridge University Press.

Allely, C. S., Minnis, H., Thompson, L., Wilson, P., & Gillberg, C. (2014). Neurodevelopmental and psychosocial risk factors in serial killers and mass murderers. *Aggression and Violent Behavior, 19*(3), 288–301. doi:10.1016/j.avb.2014.04.004

Allport, G. W. (1954). *The Nature of Prejudice*. Boston, MA: Addison Wesley.

Amador, X. F., & Paul-Odouard, R. (2000). Defending the Unabomber: Anosognosia in schizophrenia. *Psychiatric Quarterly, 71*(4), 363–371.

Ameratunga, R., Klonin, H., Vaughan, J., Merry, A., & Cusack, J. (2019). Criminalisation of unintentional error in healthcare in the UK: A perspective from New Zealand. *British Medical Journal, 365*, l706. doi:10.1136/bmj.l706

American Psychiatric Association. (1952). *Diagnostic and Statistical Manual of Mental Disorders* (DSM-I). Arlington, VA: American Psychiatric Association.

American Psychiatric Association. (1968). *Diagnostic and Statistical Manual of Mental Disorders* (DSM-II). Arlington, VA: American Psychiatric Association.

American Psychiatric Association. (1980). *Diagnostic and Statistical Manual of Mental Disorders* (DSM-III). Arlington, VA: American Psychiatric Association.

American Psychiatric Association. (2013). *Diagnostic and Statistical Manual of Mental Disorders* (DSM-5®). Arlington, VA: American Psychiatric Association.

Anderson, T. L., & Kavanaugh, P. R. (2009). Theft and shoplifting. In J. M. Miller (Ed.), *21st Century Criminology: A Reference Handbook* (pp. 541–548). Thousand Oaks, CA: Sage.

Arendt, H. (1963). *Eichmann in Jerusalem: A Report on the Banality of Evil*. London: Penguin UK.

Arlinghaus, K. R., Foreyt, J. P., & Johnston, C. A. (2016). The issue of aversion in lifestyle treatments. *American Journal of Lifestyle Medicine, 11*(2), 119–121. doi:10.1177/1559827616680554

Arntfield, M., & Danesi, M. (2017). *Murder in Plain English: From Manifestos to Memes – Looking at Murder through the Words of Killers*. London: Prometheus Books.

Atran, S. (2010). *Talking to the Enemy: Faith, Brotherhood, and the (Un)Making of Terrorists*. New York: Ecco.

Baele, S. J. (2014). Are terrorists 'insane'? A critical analysis of mental health categories in lone terrorists' trials. *Critical Studies on Terrorism*, 7(2), 257–276. doi:10.1080/17539153.2014.902695

Bain, A., & Lauchs, M. (2017). Introduction. In A. Bain & M. Lauchs (Eds.), *Understanding the Outlaw Motorcycle Gangs: International Perspectives*. Durham, NC: Carolina Academic Press.

Bandura, A. (1977). *Social Learning Theory*. Toronto: Prentice-Hall of Canada.

Bandura, A., Ross, D., & Ross, S. A. (1961). Transmission of aggression through imitation of aggressive models. *The Journal of Abnormal and Social Psychology*, 63(3), 575–582. doi:10.1037/h0045925

Bandura, A., Ross, D., & Ross, S. A. (1963). Imitation of film-mediated aggressive models. *The Journal of Abnormal and Social Psychology*, 66(1), 3–11. doi:10.1037/h0048687

Bandura, A., & Walters, R. H. (1963). *Social Learning and Personality Development*. New York: Holt, Rinehart & Winston.

Barger, R., & Zimmerman, K. (2000). *Hell's Angel: The Life and Times of Sonny Barger and the Hell's Angels Motorcycle Club*. London: HarperCollins UK.

Baumgartner, M. P. (1984). Social control from below. In D. J. Black (Ed.), *Toward a General Theory of Social Control: Fundamentals* (pp. 303–45). London: Academic Press.

BBC (2018). The psychology of stealing office supplies. *BBC*, 24 May. Retrieved from: www.bbc.com/capital/story/20180524-the-psychology-of-stealing-office-supplies

Beattie, J. (2019). Alan Hawe was a cross-dressing porn addict with an even darker secret that drove him to kill. *Belsfast Live*, 26 February. Retrieved from: www.belfastlive.co.uk/news/uk-world-news/alan-hawe-cross-dressing-porn-15886411

Belfast Telegraph (2020). Mother recalls feeling of foreboding at inquest into Hawe family deaths. *Belfast Telegraph*, 1 September.

Bennett, T., & Wright, R. (1984). *Burglars on Burglary: Prevention and the Offender*. Aldershot, UK: Gower.

Berkowitz, M. (2012). The Madoff paradox: American Jewish sage, savior, and thief. *Journal of American Studies*, 46(1), 189–202. doi:10.1017/s0021875811001423

Bielby, C. D. (2010). Remembering the Red Army Faction. *Memory Studies*, 3(2), 137–150. doi:10.1177/1750698009355676

Black, D. (2004). The Geometry of Terrorism. *Sociological Theory*, 22(1), 14–25. doi:10.1111/j.1467-9558.2004.00201.x

Blackburn, R. (1993). *The Psychology of Criminal Conduct: Theory, Research and Practice*. Hoboken, NJ: John Wiley & Sons.

Bosmia, A. N., Quinn, J. F., Peterson, T. B., Griessenauer, C. J., & Tubbs, R. (2014). Outlaw motorcycle gangs: Aspects of the one-percenter culture for emergency department personnel to consider. *Western Journal of Emergency Medicine*, 15(4), 523–528. doi:10.5811/westjem.2014.2.17919

Brenkert, G. G. (2009). Innovation, rule breaking and the ethics of entrepreneurship. *Journal of Business Venturing*, 24(5), 448–464. doi:10.1016/j.jbusvent.2008.04.004

Brookman, F. (2005). *Understanding Homicide*. Thousand Oaks, CA: Sage.

Brown, A. D. (2005). Making sense of the collapse of Barings Bank. *Human Relations*, 58(12), 1579–1604. doi:10.1177/0018726705061433

Brown, F. (1930). An historical and clinical study of criminality with special reference to theft. *Journal of the American Institute of Criminal Law and Criminology, 21*(3), 400. doi:10.2307/1134343

Brown, S. J., & Steenbeek, O. W. (2001). Doubling: Nick Leeson's trading strategy. *Pacific-Basin Finance Journal, 9*(2), 83–99. doi:10.1016/s0927-538x(01)00004-x

Browning, C. R. (2001). *Ordinary Men: Reserve Police Battalion 101 and the Final Solution in Poland.* London: Penguin.

Brownmiller, S. (1975). *Against Our Will: Men, Women, and Rape.* New York: Simon & Schuster.

Bureau of Justice Statistics (BJS). (2018). *Criminal Victimization 2017.* Washington, DC: Bureau of Justice Statistics. Retrieved from: www.bjs.gov/content/pub/pdf/cv17_sum.pdf

Burt, M. R. (1980). Cultural myths and supports for rape. *Journal of Personality and Social Psychology, 38*(2), 217–230. doi:10.1037/0022-3514.38.2.217

Burton, F. (1978). *The Politics of Legitimacy: Struggles in a Belfast Community.* Abingdon, UK: Taylor & Francis.

Burton, P. R., McNiel, D. E., & Binder, R. L. (2012). Firesetting, arson, pyromania, and the forensic mental health expert. *Journal of the American Academy of Psychiatry Law, 40*(3), 355–65.

Buss, D. M. (2005). *The Murderer Next Door: Why the Mind is Designed to Kill.* Harmondsworth: Penguin.

Cairns, E. (1987). *Caught in Crossfire: Children and the Northern Ireland Conflict.* Syracuse, NY: Syracuse University Press.

Campbell, J. H., & DeNevi, D. (2004). *Profilers: Leading Investigators Take You Inside the Criminal Mind.* New York: Pyr Books.

Carlsmith, J. M., & Anderson, C.A. (1979). Ambient temperature and the occurrence of collective violence: A new analysis. *Journal of Personality and Social Psychology, 37,* 337–344.

Carlson, M., Marcus-Newhall, A., & Miller, N. (1989). Evidence for a general construct of aggression. *Personality and Social Psychology Bulletin, 15*(3), 377–389. doi:10.1177/0146167289153008

Canter, D. (1994). *Criminal Shadows.* London: HarperCollins Publishers.

Canter, D. V., & Alison, L. J. (2000). Profiling property crimes. In *Profiling Property Crimes* (pp. 1–31). Farnham, UK: Ashgate.

Canter, D. V., & Youngs, D. (2009). *Investigative Psychology: Offender Profiling and the Analysis of Criminal Action.* Hoboken, NJ: John Wiley & Sons.

Carter, H. (2010). Stephen Griffiths: The self-styled demon who drew inspiration from serial killers. *The Guardian,* 21 December.

Chaliand, G., & Blin, A. (2016). *The History of Terrorism: From Antiquity to ISIS.* Oakland, CA: University of California Press.

Change Institute, The. (2008). *Study on the best practices in cooperation between authorities and civil society with a view to the prevention and response to violent radicalisation.* Retrieved from website: https://ec.europa.eu/home-affairs/sites/homeaffairs/files/doc_centre/terrorism/docs/ecvr_best_practice_core_report_en.pdf

Chase, A. (2003). *A Mind for Murder: The Education of the Unabomber and the Origins of Modern Terrorism.* New York: W. W. Norton & Co.

Chel'loob, M. (2019). Suicide: The last frontier in being a good Muslim: Islamic attitudes from anti-suicide to pro-suicide. *The Heythrop Journal, 60*(3), 436–446. doi: 10.1111/heyj.12306

Cherry, F. (1995). *Stubborn Particulars of Social Psychology: Essays on the Research Process*. London & New York: Routledge.

Clark, C. (2014). Psychopathy. *Medico-Legal Journal*, *82*(4), 132–143. doi.org/10.1177/0025817214559167

Clarkson, W. (2016). *Sexy Beasts: The True Story of the 'Diamond Geezers' and the Record-Breaking $100 Million Hatton Garden Heist*. New York: Hachette Books.

Cleckley, H. (1941). *The Mask of Sanity: An Attempt to Reinterpret the So-Called Psychopathic Personality*. St Louis, MO: The C. V. Mosby Company.

Clines, F. X. (1986). Britain breaks Syrian ties; cites proof of terror role; El Al suspect is convicted; U.S. recalls envoy. *The New York Times*, 25 October.

Cohn, E. G. (1993). The prediction of police calls for service: The influence of weather and temporal variables on rape and domestic violence. *Journal of Environmental Psychology*, *13*(1), 71–83. doi:10.1016/s0272-4944(05)80216-6

Coleman, C., & Norris, C. (2000). *Introducing Criminology*. London: Willan.

Comer, R. J. (2012). *Abnormal Psychology* (8th Edition). Basingstoke: Macmillan.

Conklin, J. E. (1972). *Robbery and the Criminal Justice System*. Philadelphia, PA: Lippincott Williams & Wilkins.

Cook, K. (2014). *Kitty Genovese: The Murder, the Bystanders, the Crime that Changed America*. New York: W. W. Norton & Co.

Cottam, M. L., Dietz-Uhler, B., Mastors, E., & Preston, T. (2010). *Introduction to Political Psychology* (2nd edition). New York & London: Psychology Press.

Cressey, D. R. (1953). *Other People's Money: A Study in the Social Psychology of Embezzlement*. Glancoe, IL: Free Press.

Damasio, A. (2010). *Self Comes to Mind: Constructing the Conscious Brain*. New York: Random House.

Darby, M. (1998). In Ponzi we trust. *Smithsonian Magazine*, December. Retrieved from: www.smithsonianmag.com/history/in-ponzi-we-trust-64016168/

Darley, J. M., & Latané, B. (1968). Bystander intervention in emergencies: Diffusion of responsibility. *Journal of Personality and Social Psychology*, *8*(4, Part. 1), 377–383. doi:10.1037/h0025589

Davies Robinson, A., & Bain, A. (2017). Bikes, Bros, and Hoes: Sex and the OMCG. In A. Bain & M. Lauchs (Eds.), *Understanding the Outlaw Motorcycle Gangs: International Perspectives* (pp. 29–45). Durham, NC: Carolina Academic Press.

Daykin, A., & Hamilton, L. (2012). Arson. In B. Winder & P. Banyard (Eds.), *A Psychologist's Casebook of Crime: From Arson to Voyeurism* (pp. 6–23). Basingstoke: Palgrave Macmillan.

Deal, W. E. (2010). The Serial Killer was (Cognitively) Framed. In S. Waller (Ed.), *Serial Killers – Philosophy for Everyone: Being and Killing*. Hoboken, NJ: John Wiley & Sons.

DeMatteo, D., Fairfax-Columbo, J., & Scully, M. (2017). Psychopathy. In A. Wenzel (Ed.), *The SAGE Encyclopedia of Abnormal and Clinical Psychology*. Thousand Oaks, CA: Sage.

Dennett, D. C. (2003). *Freedom Evolves*. Harmondsworth: Penguin.

Dháibhéid, C. N. (2017). *Terrorist Histories: Individuals and Political Violence since the 19th Century*. London: Routledge.

Dickerson, P. (2012). *Social Psychology: Traditional and Critical Perspectives*. London: Pearson.

Dietrich, E., & Fox Hall, T. (2010). The allure of the serial killer. In S. Waller (Ed.), *Serial Killers – Philosophy for Everyone: Being and Killing*. Hoboken, NJ: John Wiley & Sons.

Dixon, J. (2007). Prejudice, conflict and conflict reduction. In W. Hollway, H. Lucey, & A. Phoenix (Eds.), *Social Psychology Matters*. Milton Keynes, UK: McGraw-Hill Education.

Dixon, L., & Bowen, E. (2018). Interpersonal violence and stalking. In G. M. Davies & A. R. Beech (Eds.), *Forensic Psychology: Crime, Justice, Law, Interventions*. Hoboken, NJ: John Wiley & Sons.

Dodd, N. J. (2000). The psychology of fraud. In D. V. Canter & L. J. Alison (Eds.), *Profiling Property Crimes* (pp. 209–232). Farnham, UK: Ashgate.

Douglas, J., Burgess, A. W., Burgess, A. G., & Ressler, R. K. (2006). *Crime Classification Manual: A Standard System for Investigating and Classifying Violent Crimes* (2nd edition). Hoboken, NJ: John Wiley & Sons.

Dovidio, J. F. (1984). Helping behavior and altruism: An empirical and conceptual overview. *Advances in Experimental Social Psychology*, *17*, 361–427. doi:10.1016/s0065-2601(08)60123-9

Dozier, C. L., Iwata, B. A., & Worsdell, A. S. (2011). Assessment and treatment of foot–shoe fetish displayed by a man with autism. *Journal of Applied Behavior Analysis*, *44*(1), 133–137. doi:10.1901/jaba.2011.44-133

Drescher, J. (2015). Out of DSM: Depathologizing homosexuality. *Behavioral Sciences*, *5*(4), 565–575. doi:10.3390/bs5040565

Drummond, H. (2003). Did Nick Leeson have an accomplice? The role of information technology in the collapse of Barings Bank. *Journal of Information Technology*, *18*(2), 93–101. doi:10.1080/0268396032000101153

Ellemers, N., Van Knippenberg, A., & Wilke, H. A. (1990). The influence of permeability of group boundaries and stability of group status on strategies of individual mobility and social change. *British Journal of Social Psychology*, *29*(3), 233–246. https://doi.org/10.1111/j.2044-8309.1990.tb00902.x

Europol. (2012). *Fear of turf war between outlaw motorcycle gangs in Europe. The Hague: Europol*. Retrieved from www.europol.europa.eu/newsroom/news/fear-of-turf-war-between-outlaw-motorcycle-gangs-in-europe

Europol. (n.d.). *Outlaw motorcycle gangs*. The Hague: Europol. Retrieved from: www.europol.europa.eu/crime-areas-and-trends/crime-areas/outlaw-motorcycle-gangs

Eysenck, H. J. (1965). *Fact and Fiction in Psychology*. London: Penguin.

Fajmonova, V., Moskalenko, S., & McCauley, C. (2017). Tracking radical opinion in polls of US Muslims. *Perspectives on Terrorism*, *11*(2), 36–48.

Faure, G. O. (2003). Negotiating with terrorists: The hostage case. *International Negotiation*, *8*(3), 469–494. doi:10.1163/1571806031310752

Fay, S. (1996). *The Collapse of Barings*. New York: W. W. Norton & Co.

Federal Bureau of Investigation. (2014). *Offense definitions*. Washington, DC: Federal Bureau of Investigation. Retrieved from: https://ucr.fbi.gov/crime-in-the-u.s/2014/crime-in-the-u.s.-2014/resource-pages/offense-definitions

Federal Bureau of Investigation/National Gang Intelligence Center. (2016). *National Gang Report 2015*. Washington, DC: Federal Bureau of Investigation/National Gang Intelligence Center. Retrieved from: www.fbi.gov/file-repository/stats-services-publications-national-gang-report-2015.pdf/view

Ferguson, N., & Binks, E. (2015). Understanding radicalization and engagement in terrorism through religious conversion motifs. *Journal of Strategic Security, 8*(1–2), 16–26. doi:10.5038/1944-0472.8.1.1430

Ferguson, N., & McKeown, S. (2016). Social identity theory and intergroup conflict in Northern Ireland. In S. McKeown, R. Haji, & N. Ferguson (Eds.), *Understanding Peace and Conflict through Social Identity Theory: Contemporary Global Perspectives* (pp. 215–227). London: Springer.

Field, M., & Cartwright-Hatton, S. (2015). *Essential Abnormal and Clinical Psychology.* Thousand Oaks, CA: Sage.

Finlay, A. (1999). 'Whatever you say, say nothing': An ethnographic encounter in Northern Ireland and its sequel. *Sociological Research Online, 4*(3), 139–153. doi:10.5153/sro.296

First, M. B. (2014). DSM-5 and Paraphilic Disorders. *The Journal of the American Academy of Psychiatry and the Law, 42*(2).

Fisher, N. L., & Pina, A. (2013). An overview of the literature on female-perpetrated adult male sexual victimization. *Aggression and Violent Behavior, 18*(1), 54–61. doi:10.1016/j.avb.2012.10.001

Fletcher, G. P. (1995). *With Justice for Some: Victims' Rights in Criminal Trials.* New York: Perseus Books.

Flombaum, J. I., & Santos, L. R. (2005). Rhesus monkeys attribute perceptions to others. *Current Biology, 15*(5), 447–452. doi:10.1016/j.cub.2004.12.076

Freud, S. (1920/1990). *Beyond the Pleasure Principle (1920).* New York: W. W. Norton & Company.

Freud, S. (1932). The acquisition of fire. *The Psychoanalytic Quarterly, 1*(2), 210–215. doi:10.1080/21674086.1932.11925143

Frunza, M. (2016). Nick Leeson. In *Introduction to the Theories and Varieties of Modern Crime in Financial Markets* (pp. xxiii–xxxix). Cambridge, MA: Academic Press.

Furnham, A., Richards, S. C., & Paulhus, D. L. (2013). The dark triad of personality: A 10 Year review. *Social and Personality Psychology Compass, 7*(3), 199–216. doi:10.1111/spc3.12018

Gage, B. (2011). Terrorism and the American experience: A state of the field. *Journal of American History, 98*(1), 73–94. doi:10.1093/jahist/jar106

Gambetta, D. (2006). *Making Sense of Suicide Missions.* New York & Oxford: Oxford University Press.

Gannon, T. A., & Pina, A. (2010). Firesetting: Psychopathology, theory and treatment. *Aggression and Violent Behavior, 15*(3), 224–238. doi:10.1016/j.avb.2010.01.001

Gardham, D. (2011). Terrorist who tried to kill pregnant fiancee must be considered for parole, court says. *The Daily Telegraph,* 1 April.

Gavin, H. (2014). *Criminological and Forensic Psychology.* London & Thousand Oaks, CA: Sage.

Gavin, H. (2019). *Criminological and Forensic Psychology* (2nd edition). London: Sage.

Gelles, D., & Tett, G. (2011). From behind bars, Madoff spins his story. *Financial Times,* 8 April. Retrieved from: www.ft.com/content/a29d2b4a-60b7-11e0-a182-00144feab49a

Gergen, K. J. (2001). Psychological science in a postmodern context. *American Psychologist, 56*(10), 803–813. doi:10.1037/0003-066x.56.10.803

Gergen, K. J. (2015). *An Invitation to Social Construction.* Thousand Oaks, CA: Sage.

Giami, A. (2015). Between DSM and ICD: Paraphilias and the transformation of sexual norms. *Archives of Sexual Behavior, 44*(5), 1127–1138. doi:10.1007/s10508-015-0549-6

Gill, P. (2007). A multi-dimensional approach to suicide bombing. *International Journal of Conflict and Violence*, *1*(2), 142–159.

Gilligan, J. (2000). *Violence: Reflections on Our Deadliest Epidemic*. London: Jessica Kingsley.

Glenn, A. L., Johnson, A. K., & Raine, A. (2013). Antisocial Personality Disorder: A current review. *Current Psychiatry Reports*. doi: 10.1007/s11920-013-0427-7

Gonzalez, F. J. (2010). Perversion. *The International Journal of Psychoanalysis*, *91*(2).

Goodwin, L. (2008). Burglary. In D. Canter (Ed.), *Criminal Psychology: Topics in Applied Psychology*. Oxford & New York: Oxford University Press.

Gough, B., Robinson, S., Kremer, J., & Mitchell, R. (1992). The social psychology of intergroup conflict: An appraisal of Northern Ireland research. *Canadian Psychology/ Psychologie canadienne*, *33*(3), 645–651. doi:10.1037/h0078722

Gottfredson, M. R., & Hirschi, T. (1990). *A General Theory of Crime*. Stanford, CA: Stanford University Press.

Grant, J. E., & Chamberlain, S. R. (2018). Symptom severity and its clinical correlates in kleptomania. *Annals of Clinical Psychiatry*, *30*(2), 97–101.

Green, P., & Ward, T. (2017). Understanding state crime. In A. Liebling, S. Maruna, & L. McAra (Eds.), *The Oxford Handbook of Criminology*. Oxford & New York: Oxford University Press.

Green, S. P. (2007). *Lying, Cheating, and Stealing: A Moral Theory of White-Collar Crime*. Oxford & New York: Oxford University Press.

Greener, I. (2006). Nick Leeson and the collapse of Barings Bank: Socio-technical networks and the 'rogue trader'. *Organization*, *13*(3), 421–441. doi:10.1177/1350508406063491

Greenwood, C. (2016). Barrister's admiration for the Hatton Garden gang: Lawyer who represented man cleared of involvement says heist was 'extraordinary' and 'very well planned. *Daily Mail*, 17 January 2016. Available at https://www.dailymail.co.uk/news/ article-3404148/Barrister-s-admiration-Hatton-Garden-gang-Lawyer-represented-man-cleared-involvement-says-heist-extraordinary-planned.html (accessed 29 January 2021).

Gunn, J. (2006). Abuse of psychiatry. *Criminal Behaviour and Mental Health*, *16*(2), 77–86. doi:10.1002/cbm.624

Hallsworth, S., & Silverstone, D. (2009). 'That's life innit': A British perspective on guns, crime and social order. *Criminology & Criminal Justice*, *9*(3), 359–377. doi:10.1177/1748895809336386

Hamden, R. H. (2019). *The Psychology of Terrorists: Profiling and Counterterrorism*. London: CRC Press.

Hamilton-Giacritsis, C., & Sleath, E. (2018). Effects of interpersonal crime on victims. In G. M. Davies & A. R. Beech (Eds.), *Forensic Psychology: Crime, Justice, Law, Interventions*. Hoboken, NJ: John Wiley & Sons.

Hare, R. D. (2003). *Hare Psychopathy Checklist – Revised: PCL-R. Technical Manual*. London: Pearson Clinical.

Hare, R. D. (2006). Psychopathy: A clinical and forensic overview. *Psychiatric Clinics of North America*, *29*(3), 709–724. doi:10.1016/j.psc.2006.04.007

Hare, R. D., & Cox, D. N. (1978). Clinical and empirical conceptions of psychopathy, and the selection of subjects for research. In R. D. Hare & D. Schalling (Eds.), *Psychopathic Behaviour: Approaches to Research*. Hoboken, NJ: John Wiley & Sons.

Harkins, L., Ware, J., & Mann, R. (2018). Treating dangerous offenders. In G. M. Davies & A. R. Beech (Eds.), *Forensic Psychology: Crime, Justice, Law, Interventions*. Hoboken, NJ: John Wiley & Sons.

Harmon, V., Mujkic, E., Kaukinen, C., & Weir, H. (2018). Causes and explanations of suicide terrorism: A systematic review. *Homeland Security Affairs*, 14.

Harris, R. (1986 [1972]). *Prejudice and Tolerance in Ulster: A Study of Neighbours and 'Strangers' in a Border Community*. Manchester, UK: Manchester University Press.

Haslam, C., Jetten, J., Cruwys, T., Dingle, G., & Haslam, A. (2018). *The New Psychology of Health: Unlocking the Social Cure*. London: Routledge.

Haslam, S. A., & Reicher, S. (2007). Beyond the banality of evil: Three dynamics of an interactionist social psychology of tyranny. *Personality and Social Psychology Bulletin*, 33(5), 615–622. doi:10.1177/0146167206298570

Haslam, S. A., Reicher, S. D., & Platow, M. J. (2011). *The New Psychology of Leadership: Identity, Influence and Power*. London: Psychology Press.

Hastings, M. (2019). *Vietnam*. New York. Harper Perennial.

Heider, F. (1958). *The Psychology of Interpersonal Relations*. New York: Wiley.

Henriques, D. B. (2011). *The Wizard of Lies: Bernie Madoff and the Death of Trust*. Basingstoke: Macmillan.

Henriques, D. B. (2018). A case study of a con man: Bernie Madoff and the timeless lessons of history's biggest Ponzi scheme. *Social Research: An International Quarterly*, 85(4), 745–766.

Hepburn, A. (2011). *An Introduction to Critical Social Psychology*. Thousand Oaks, CA: Sage.

Hill, A., Habermann, N., Berner, W., & Briken, P. (2007). Psychiatric disorders in single and multiple sexual murderers. *Psychopathology*, 40(1), 22–28. doi:10.1159/000096386

Hockey, D. (2016). Burglary crime scene rationality of a select group of non-apprehend burglars. *SAGE Open*, 6(2), 215824401664058. doi:10.1177/2158244016640589

Hogg, M. A. (2016). Social identity theory. In S. McKeown, R. Haji, & N. Ferguson (Eds.), *Understanding Peace and Conflict through Social Identity Theory: Contemporary Global Perspectives* (pp. 215–227). London: Springer.

Hogg, M. A., & Vaughan, G. M. (2008). *Social Psychology* (5th edition). Harlow: Pearson.

Hogg, M. A., & Vaughan, G. M. (2018). *Social Psychology* (8th edition). Harlow: Pearson Higher Education.

Hollin, C. R. (2013). *Psychology and Crime: An Introduction to Criminological Psychology* (2nd edition). London: Routledge.

Hollway, W. (2007a). Methods and knowledge in social psychology. In W. Hollway, H. Lucey, & A. Phoenix (Eds.), *Social Psychology Matters* (pp. 65–92). Milton Keynes, UK: McGraw-Hill Education.

Hollway, W. (2007b). Conclusion: Social psychology matters. In W. Hollway, H. Lucey, & A. Phoenix (Eds.), *Social Psychology Matters* (pp. 200–206). Milton Keynes, UK: McGraw-Hill Education.

Holmes, D. A. (2010). *Abnormal, Clinical and Forensic Psychology*. Upper Saddle River, NJ: Prentice Hall Business Publishing.

Holmes, R. M., & Holmes, S. T. (2010). *Serial Murder* (3rd edition). Thousand Oaks, CA: Sage.

Holmes, S. T., & Holmes, R. M. (2009). *Sex Crimes: Patterns and Behavior*. Thousand Oaks, CA: Sage.

Horgan, J. (2005). *Terrorism and Political Violence: The Psychology of Terrorism*. London: Routledge. doi:10.4324/9780203496961

Howitt, D. (2011). *Introduction to Forensic and Criminal Psychology*. London: Pearson Education.

Hudson, R. (2018). *Who Becomes a Terrorist and Why? The Psychology and Sociology of Terrorism*. New York: Skyhorse Publishing.

Hunter, J. A., Stringer, M., & Watson, R. P. (1991). Intergroup violence and intergroup attributions. *British Journal of Social Psychology*, *30*(3), 261–266. doi:10.1111/j.2044-8309.1991.tb00943.x

Ibrahim, A. (2019). ISIS's church attacks break Mohammed's own pledges. *Foreign Policy*, 8 May. Retrieved from: https://foreignpolicy.com/2019/05/08/isiss-church-attacks-break-mohammeds-own-pledges/

Innes, M., & Levi, M. (2017). Making and managing terrorism and counter-terrorism: The view from criminology. In A. Liebling, S. Maruna, & L. McAra (Eds.), *The Oxford Handbook of Criminology*. Oxford & New York: Oxford University Press.

Jackson, H. F., Glass, C., & Hope, S. (1987). A functional analysis of recidivistic arson. *British Journal of Clinical Psychology*, *26*(3), 175–185. doi:10.1111/j.2044-8260.1987.tb01345.x

Jacobs, F. (1964). Circularity and responsibility. *Philosophy*, *39*(149), 268–274. doi:10.1017/s0031819100055649

Jahoda, G., & Harrison, S. (1975). Belfast children: Some effects of a conflict environment. *The Irish Journal of Psychology*, *3*(1), 1–19. doi:10.1080/03033910.1975.10557616

Jalava, J. (2006). The modern degenerate. *Theory & Psychology*, *16*(3), 416–432. doi:10.1177/0959354306064286

Joiner, T. E. (2005). *Why People Die by Suicide*. Cambridge, MA: Harvard University Press.

Jonason, P. K., & Webster, G. D. (2012). A protean approach to social influence: Dark Triad personalities and social influence tactics. *Personality and Individual Differences*, *52*(4), 521–526. doi:10.1016/j.paid.2011.11.023

Jonason, P. K., Wee, S., & Li, N. P. (2015). Competition, autonomy, and prestige: Mechanisms through which the Dark Triad predict job satisfaction. *Personality and Individual Differences*, *72*, 112–116. doi:10.1016/j.paid.2014.08.026

Kahneman, D. (2011). *Thinking, Fast and Slow*. London: Penguin UK.

Kassin, S. M. (2017). The killing of Kitty Genovese: What else does this case tell us? *Perspectives on Psychological Science*, *12*(3), 374–381. doi:10.1177/1745691616679465

Kim, B., Benekos, P. J., & Merlo, A. V. (2016). Sex offender recidivism revisited: Review of recent meta-analyses on the effects of sex offender treatment. *Trauma, Violence, & Abuse*, *17*(1), 105–117. doi:10.1177/1524838014566719

Knox, K. L., Conwell, Y., & Caine, E. D. (2004). If suicide is a public health problem, what are we doing to prevent it? *American Journal of Public Health*, *94*(1), 37–45. doi:10.2105/ajph.94.1.37

Kryvoi, Y. (2018). Economic crimes in international investment law. *International and Comparative Law Quarterly*, *67*(03), 577–605. doi:10.1017/s0020589318000131

La Macchia, S. T., & Louis, W. R. (2016). Crowd behaviour and collective action. In S. McKeown, R. Haji, & N. Ferguson (Eds.), *Understanding Peace and Conflict through Social Identity Theory: Contemporary Global Perspectives* (pp. 89–104). London: Springer.

Larouzée, J., & Guarnieri, F. (2015). *From theory to practice: Itinerary of Reasons' Swiss Cheese Model. ESREL 2015*, European Safety and Reliability Association (ESRA), September, Zurich, Switzerland, pp. 817–824. doi:10.1201/b19094-110

Lavergne, G. M. (1997). *A Sniper in the Tower: The Charles Whitman Murders*. Denton, TX: University of North Texas Press.

Law, R. D. (2016). *Terrorism: A History*. Hoboken, NJ: John Wiley & Sons.

Leader-Elliott, I., & Naffine, N. (2000). Wittgenstein, rape law and the language games of consent. *Monash University Law Review, 26*(1), 48–73.

Leary, T., Southard, L., Hill, J., & Ashman, J. (2017). The Macdonald Triad revisited: An empirical assessment of relationships between triadic elements and parental abuse in serial killers. *North American Journal of Psychology, 19*(3), 627–640.

Le Bon, G. (1995/1895). *The Crowd: A Study of the Popular Mind*. London: Transaction.

Lemkin, R. (1944). *Axis Rule in Occupied Europe*. Washington: Carnegie Endowment for International Peace.

Levin, R. J., & van Berlo, W. (2004). Sexual arousal and orgasm in subjects who experience forced or non-consensual sexual stimulation – a review. *Journal of Clinical Forensic Medicine, 11*(2), 82–88. doi:10.1016/j.jcfm.2003.10.008

Levy, D., Ziegler, D., & Koch, S. (2014). Risk assessment profiling procedure (RAPP) for air cargo security. *Journal of Air Transport Studies, 5*(1).

Lieberman, M. D. (2013). *Social: Why Our Brains are Wired to Connect*. Oxford & New York: Oxford University Press.

Liebling, A., Maruna, S., & McAra, L. (Eds.) (2017). *The Oxford Handbook of Criminology*. Oxford & New York: Oxford University Press.

Liu, J., Francis, B., & Soothill, K. (2008). Kidnapping offenders: Their risk of escalation to repeat offending and other serious crime. *Journal of Forensic Psychiatry & Psychology, 19*(2), 164–179. doi:10.1080/14789940701619178

Lombroso, C. (1911). *Criminal Man*. New York: G. P. Putnam & Sons.

Lorenz, K. (1966). *On Aggression*. London: Psychology Press.

Lurigio, A. J. (2015). Crime narratives, dramatizations, and the legacy of the Kitty Genovese murder. *Criminal Justice and Behavior, 42*(7), 782–789. doi:10.1177/0093854814562954

Maes, M., De Meyer, F., Thompson, P., Peeters, D., & Cosyns, P. (1994). Synchronized annual rhythms in violent suicide rate, ambient temperature and the light-dark span. *Acta Psychiatrica Scandinavica, 90*(5), 391–396. doi:10.1111/j.1600-0447.1994.tb01612.x

Magid, A. K. (2009). The Unabomber revisited: Reexamining the use of mental disorder diagnoses as evidence of the mental condition of criminal defendants. *Indiana Law Journal, 84*(5).

Manning, P. (2018). Madoff's Ponzi investment fraud: A social capital analysis. *Journal of Financial Crime, 25*(2): 320–336. doi:10.1108/jfc-06-2017-0057

Manning, P., Stokes, P. J., Visser, M., Rowland, C., & Tarba, S. Y. (2018). Dark open innovation in a criminal organizational context: The case of Madoff's Ponzi fraud. *Management Decision, 56*(6), 1445–1462. doi:10.1108/md-05-2017-0535

Manningham-Buller, E. (2011). *BBC Reith Lectures, Securing Freedom. Lecture One: Terror*. https://www.bbc.co.uk/programmes/b0145x77

Marthinsen, J. E. (2018). Doubling strategies. In R. W. Kolb (Ed.), *The SAGE Encyclopedia of Business Ethics and Society* (pp. 970–974). Thousand Oaks, CA: Sage.

Maruna, S. (1999). Desistance and development: The psychosocial process of going straight. *The British Criminology Conference: Selected Proceedings, 2*, 1–25.

Masuda, A., Donati, L., Schaefer, W., & Hill, M. L. (2016). Terrorism as an act-in-context: A contextual behavioral science account. In M. Taylor, J. Roach, K. & Pease (Eds.), *Evolutionary Psychology and Terrorism* (pp. 124–128). Abingdon: Routledge.

McCauley, C. (2018). Explaining homegrown western jihadists: The importance of western foreign policy. *International Journal of Conflict and Violence, 12*.

McCauley, C., & Moskalenko, S. (2008). Mechanisms of political radicalization: Pathways toward terrorism. *Terrorism and Political Violence, 20*(3), 415–433. doi:10.1080/09546550802073367

McCluskey, J. D. (2009). Robbery. In J. M. Miller (Ed.), *21st Century Criminology: A Reference Handbook* (pp. 507–514). Thousand Oaks, CA: Sage.

Meloy, J. R., & Gill, P. (2016). The lone-actor terrorist and the TRAP-18. *Journal of Threat Assessment and Management, 3*(1), 37–52. doi:10.1037/tam0000061

Melton, H. C. (2000). Stalking: A review of the literature and direction for the future. *Criminal Justice Review, 25*(2), 246–262. doi:10.1177/073401680002500206

Merry, S., & Harsent, L. (2000). Intruders, pilferers, raiders and invaders: The interpersonal dimension of burglary. In D. V. Canter & L. J. Alison (Eds.), *Profiling Property Crimes*. Farnham, UK: Ashgate.

Mews, A., Di Bella, L., & Purver, M. (2017). *Impact Evaluation of the Prison-Based Core Sex Offender Treatment Programme*. Retrieved from Ministry of Justice Analytical Series website: https://assets.publishing.service.gov.uk/government/uploads/system/uploads/attachment_data/file/623876/sotp-report-web-.pdf

Milgram, S. (1963). Behavioral study of obedience. *The Journal of Abnormal and Social Psychology, 67*(4), 371–378. doi:10.1037/h0040525v

Milgram, S. (1974). *Obedience to Authority*. New York: Harper & Row.

Miller, L. (2014). Serial killers: I. Subtypes, patterns, and motives. *Aggression and Violent Behavior, 19*(1), 1–11. doi:10.1016/j.avb.2013.11.002

Millington, C. (2018). Were we terrorists? History, terrorism, and the French Resistance. *History Compass, 16*(2), e12440. doi:10.1111/hic3.12440

Moser, C. (2016). DSM-5 and the Paraphilic Disorders: Conceptual issues. *Archives of Sexual Behavior, 45*(8), 2181–2186. doi:10.1007/s10508-016-0861-9

Muldoon, O. T. (2003). The psychological impact of protracted campaigns of political violence on societies. In A. Silke (Ed.), *Terrorists, Victims and Society: Psychological Perspectives on Terrorism and its Consequences* (pp. 161–174). Hoboken, NJ: John Wiley & Sons.

Muldoon, O. T., Haslam, S. A., Haslam, C., Cruwys, T., Kearns, M., & Jetten, J. (2019). The social psychology of responses to trauma: Social identity pathways associated with divergent traumatic responses. *European Review of Social Psychology, 30*(1), 311–348. doi:10.1080/10463283.2020.1711628

Muldoon, O. T., & Lowe, R. D. (2012). Social identity, groups, and post-traumatic stress disorder. *Political Psychology, 33*(2), 259–273. doi:10.1111/j.1467-9221.2012.00874.x

Muldoon, O. T., Mclaughlin, K., Rougier, N., & Trew, K. (2008). Adolescents' explanations for paramilitary involvement. *Journal of Peace Research, 45*(5), 681–695. doi:10.1177/0022343308094330

Murray, H. A. (1938). *Explorations in Personality: A Clinical and Experimental Study of Fifty Men of College Age*. New York: Oxford University Press.

Nadler, A. (2002). Inter-group helping relations as power relations: Maintaining or challenging social dominance between groups through helping. *Journal of Social Issues, 58*(3), 487–502. doi:10.1111/1540-4560.00272

National Center for the Analysis of Violent Crime (NCAVC) United States of America. (2008). *Serial Murder: Multi-disciplinary Perspectives for Investigators*. Edited by R. J. Morton. Quantico, VA: NCAVC.

Naughton, C. M., O'Donnell, A. T., Greenwood, R. M., & Muldoon, O. T. (2015). 'Ordinary decent domestic violence': A discursive analysis of family law judges' interviews. *Discourse & Society, 26*(3), 349–365. doi:10.1177/0957926514564738

Nee, C., & Taylor, M. (2000). Examining burglars' target selection: Interview, experiment or ethnomethodology? *Psychology, Crime & Law, 6*(1), 45–59. doi:10.1080/10683160008410831

Nesser, P. (2004). *Jihad in Europe: A Survey of the Motivations for Sunni Islamist Terrorism in Post-Millenium Europe.* Kjeller: FFI Norweigan Defence Academy.

NFCC. (n.d.). *Arson.* Retrieved from https://www.nationalfirechiefs.org.uk/Arson (1 December 2020).

Noor-Mohamed, M. K. (2014). The definitional ambiguities of kidnapping and abduction, and its categorisation: The case for a more inclusive typology. *Howard Journal of Criminal Justice, 53*(1): 83–100.

O'Connor, J. J. (Director). (1989, June 13). Death of a terrorist [Television series episode]. In *Frontline.* Boston: PBS.

Odlaug, B. L., & Grant, J. E. (2010). Impulse-Control Disorders in a college sample: Results from the self-administered Minnesota Impulse Disorders Interview (MIDI). *The Primary Care Companion to the Journal of Clinical Psychiatry, 12*(2). doi:10.4088/pcc.09m00842whi

Office for National Statistics. (2018). *Statistical Bulletin Crime in England and Wales: Year Ending June 2018.* Retrieved from: www.ons.gov.uk/peoplepopulationandcommunity/crimeandjustice/bulletins/crimeinenglandandwales/yearendingjune2018

Office for National Statistics. (2019a). *Crime in England and Wales Statistical Bulletins,* 7 February. Retrieved from: www.ons.gov.uk/peoplepopulationandcommunity/crimeandjustice/bulletins/crimeinenlandandwales/previousReleases

Office for National Statistics. (2019b). *Suicides in the UK.* September. Retrieved from: www.ons.gov.uk/peoplepopulationandcommunity/birthsdeathsandmarriages/deaths/bulletins/suicidesintheunitedkingdom/2018registrations

Ostas, D. (2018). Fraud. In R. W. Kolb (Ed.), *The SAGE Encyclopedia of Business Ethics and Society* (pp. 1479–1482). Thousand Oaks, CA: Sage.

Overton, I. (2019). *The Price of Paradise.* London: Hachette (UK).

Paulhus, D. L, & Williams, K. M. (2002). The dark triad of personality: Narcissism, Machiavellianism, and psychopathy. *Journal of Research in Personality, 36,* 556–563.

Pelonero, C. (2014). *Kitty Genovese: A True Account of a Public Murder and Its Private Consequences.* New York: Simon & Schuster.

Perkins, C. (2003). *Weapon Use and Violent Crime National Crime Victimization Survey, 1993–2001.* Retrieved from Bureau of Justice Statistics website: www.bjs.gov/content/pub/ascii/wuvc01.txt

Pinker, S. (2011). *The Better Angels of Our Nature: Why Violence has Declined.* London: Penguin.

Pipes, D. (1989). Terrorism: The Syrian connection. *The National Interest, 15,* 15–28.

Porter, L. E. (2010). Robbery. In J. M. Brown & E. A. Campbell (Eds.), *The Cambridge Handbook of Forensic Psychology.* Cambridge: Cambridge University Press.

Putnam, R. D. (2001). *Bowling Alone: The Collapse and Revival of American Community.* New York: Simon & Schuster.

Quinn, J. F., & Forsyth, C. J. (2009). Leathers and Rolexs: The symbolism and values of the Motorcycle Club. *Deviant Behavior, 30*(3), 235–265. doi:10.1080/01639620802168700

Quinn, J. F., Prendergast, M., & Galvin, A. (2019). Her name was Clodagh: Twitter and the news discourse of murder suicide. *Critical Discourse Studies*, *16*(3), 312–329. doi:10.1080/17405904.2019.1568896

Ragan, P. W., & Martin, P. R. (2000). The psychobiology of sexual addiction. *Sexual Addiction & Compulsivity*, *7*(3), 161–175. doi:10.1080/10720160008400216

Rahman, M., & Lynes, A. (2018). Ride to die: Masculine honour and collective identity in the motorcycle underworld. *Journal of Criminological Research, Policy and Practice*, *4*(4), 238–252. doi:10.1108/jcrpp-05-2018-0017

Raleigh, D. (2017, April 6). Three bikers plead guilty to 'ultimate insult' after violent robbery of rival's club jacket. *Irish Examiner* [Cork].

Rand, D. G., Tomlin, D., Bear, A., Ludvig, E. A., & Cohen, J. D. (2017). Cyclical population dynamics of automatic versus controlled processing: An evolutionary pendulum. *Psychological Review*, *124*(5), 626–642. doi:10.1037/rev0000079

Raymond, M. J. (1956). Case of fetishism treated by aversion therapy. *British Medical Journal*, *2*(4997), 854–857. doi:10.1136/bmj.2.4997.854

Reason, J. (1990). *Human Error*. Cambridge: Cambridge University Press

Reason, J. (2000). Human error: Models and management. *British Medical Journal*, *320*(7237), 768–770. doi:10.1136/bmj.320.7237.768

Reay, B. (2018). Straight but not straight. *GLQ: A Journal of Lesbian and Gay Studies*, *24*(1), 159–161. doi:10.1215/10642684-4254567

Reicher, S. (1996). 'The Battle of Westminster': Developing the social identity model of crowd behaviour in order to explain the initiation and development of collective conflict. *European Journal of Social Psychology*, *26*(1), 115–134.

Reicher, S., & Haslam, S. A. (2012). Obedience: Revisiting Milgram's shock experiments. In J. R. Smith & S. A. Haslam (Eds.), *Social Psychology: Revisiting the Classic Studies* (pp. 106–125). London: Sage.

Reicher, S., Spears, R., & Haslam, S. A. (2010). The social identity approach in social psychology. In M. Wetherell & C. Talpede Mohanty (Eds.), *The SAGE Handbook of Identities*. London: Sage.

Reilly, B., Rickman, N., & Witt, R. (2012). Robbing banks: Crime does pay – but not very much. *Significance*, *9*(3), 17–21. doi:10.1111/j.1740-9713.2012.00570.x

Renard, T., & Coolsaet, R. (2018). Returnees: Who are they, why are they (not) coming back and how should we deal with them? Assessing policies on returning foreign terrorist fighters in Belgium, Germany and the Netherlands. *Egmont Papers 101*, Egmont Institute, Brussels. Retrieved from: www.egmontinstitute.be/returnees-assessing-policies-on-returning-foreign-terrorist-fighters-in-belgium-germany-and-the-netherlands/

Ridley, N., & Harrison, K. (2017). The law relating to financial crime in the United Kingdom. *Current Criminal Law* (online), *9*(4), 2–27.

Rolls, G. (2010). *Classic Case Studies in Psychology* (2nd edition). London: Hachette (UK).

Rolls, G. (2019). *Classic Case Studies in Psychology* (4th edition). Oxon, UK: Routledge.

Ronningstam, E. (2020). Internal processing in patients with pathological narcissism or narcissistic personality disorder: Implications for alliance building and therapeutic strategies. *Journal of Personality Disorders*, *34*(Supplement), 80–103. doi:10.1521/pedi.2020.34.supp.80

Routledge, C., & Arndt, J. (2008). Self-sacrifice as self-defence: Mortality salience increases efforts to affirm a symbolic immortal self at the expense of the physical self. *European Journal of Social Psychology*, *38*(3), 531–541. doi:10.1002/ejsp.442

Roy, O. (2017). *Jihad and Death: The Global Appeal of the Islamic State*. Oxford & New York: Oxford University Press.

Russell, S. S., & Swartout, E. C. (2016). Machiavellianism. In S. G. Rogelberg (Ed.), *The SAGE Encyclopedia of Industrial and Organizational Psychology*. London: Sage.

Sageman, M. (2014). The stagnation in terrorism research. *Terrorism and Political Violence, 26*(4), 565–580. doi:10.1080/09546553.2014.895649

Salkind, N. J. (2012). *Exploring Research*. Harlow, UK: Pearson Education.

Sammons, A., & Putwain, D. (2019). *Psychology and Crime* (2nd edition). London: Routledge.

Schouten, R. (2010). Terrorism and the behavioral sciences. *Harvard Review of Psychiatry, 18*(6), 369–378. doi:10.3109/10673229.2010.533005

Schuchter, A., & Levi, M. (2013). The Fraud Triangle revisited. *Security Journal, 29*(2), 107–121. doi:10.1057/sj.2013.1

Seal, M. (2009). Madoff's world. *Vanity Fair*, April. Retrieved from: www.vanityfair.com/news/2009/04/bernard-madoff-friends-family-profile

Shuy, R. W. (2014). *The Language of Murder Cases: Intentionality, Predisposition, and Voluntariness*. Oxford & New York: Oxford University Press.

Silke, A. (2003). *Terrorists, Victims and Society: Psychological Perspectives on Terrorism and its Consequences*. Hoboken, NJ: John Wiley & Sons.

Simon, B. (2004). *Identity in Modern Society: A Social Psychological Perspective*. Oxford: Blackwell.

Simon, J. D. (2008). The forgotten terrorists: Lessons from the history of terrorism. *Terrorism and Political Violence, 20*(2), 195–214. doi:10.1080/09546550801907599

Shapira, Z. (2002). *Organizational Decision Making*. Cambridge: Cambridge University Press.

Shreeves, R., & Prpic, M. (2019). *Violence against Women in the EU: State of Play*. Brussels: European Parliament. Retrieved from: www.europarl.europa.eu/RegData/etudes/BRIE/2018/630296/EPRS_BRI(2018)630296_EN.pdf

Silverstone, D., & Crane, P. (2017). Mapping and conceptualizing organized motorcycle gangs: The British, German and Spanish experience. In A. Bain & M. Lauchs (Eds.), *Understanding the Outlaw Motorcycle Gangs: International Perspectives* (pp. 67–86). Durham, NC: Carolina Academic Press.

Skiba, J. M. (2017). *Psychology of Fraud: Integrating Criminological Theory into Counter Fraud Efforts*. Bloomington, IN: iUniverse.

Sleath, E., & Bull, R. (2009). Male rape victim and perpetrator blaming. *Journal of Interpersonal Violence, 25*(6), 969–988. doi:10.1177/0886260509340534

Slootman, M., & Tillie, J. (2006). Processes of radicalisation: why some Amsterdam Muslims become radicals. *(Report) Institute for Migration and Ethnic Studies*, Universiteit van Amsterdam, Amsterdam, pp. 1–129.

Smith, J. (2019). *Home-Grown: How Domestic Violence Turns Men into Terrorists*. London: Riverrun.

Snider, L. (2008). Corporate economic crimes. In J. Minkes & L. Minkes (Eds.), *Corporate and White Collar Crime* (pp. 39–60). Thousand Oaks, CA: Sage.

Somaiya, R. (2010). Bernie behind bars: Madoff's plush new prison life. *Newsweek*, 6 July.

Stainton Rogers, W. (2011). *Social Psychology*. Milton Keynes, UK: McGraw-Hill Education.

Stearns, P. N. (2008). Texas and Virginia: A bloodied window into changes in American public life. *Journal of Social History*, *42*(2), 299–318. doi:10.1353/jsh.0.0130

Stein, M. (2000). The risk taker as shadow: A psychoanalytic view of the collapse of Barings Bank*. *Journal of Management Studies*, *37*(8), 1215–1230. doi:10.1111/1467-6486.00222

Stonham, P. (1996). Whatever happened at Barings? Part Two: Unauthorised trading and the failure of controls. *European Management Journal*, *14*(3), 269–278. doi:10.1016/0263-2373(96)00006-0

Sugarman, L. (2001). *Life-span Development: Frameworks, Accounts and Strategies*. Hove: Psychology Press.

Syed, M. H. (2002). *Islamic Terrorism, Myth or Reality*. Delhi: Kalpaz Publications.

Synnott, J., Canter, D., Youngs, D., & Ioannou, M. (2016). Variations in the journey from crime: Examples from tiger kidnapping. *Journal of Investigative Psychology and Offender Profiling*, *13*(3), 239–252. doi:10.1002/jip.1454

Szasz, T. (2007). *The Medicalization of Everyday Life: Selected Essays*. Syracuse, NY: Syracuse University Press.

Tajfel, H. (1972). La catégorisation sociale (English Trans.). In S. Moscoveci (Ed.), *Introduction à la psychologie sociale* (Vol. 1, pp. 272–302). Paris: Larousse.

Tajfel, H. (1978). *Differentiation between Social Groups: Studies in the Social Psychology of Intergroup Relations*. Cambridge, MA: Academic Press.

Tajfel, H. (1979). Individuals and groups in social psychology. *British Journal of Social and Clinical Psychology*, *18*(2), 183–190. doi:10.1111/j.2044-8260.1979.tb00324.x

Tajfel, H. (1982). *Social Identity and Intergroup Relations*. Cambridge: Cambridge University Press.

Tajfel, H., & Turner, J. (1979). An integrative theory of intergroup conflict. In W. G. Austin & S. Worchel (Ed.), *The Social Psychology of Intergroup Relations* (W. G. Austin, Trans.) (pp. 33–47). Monterey, CA: Brooks/Cole.

Tajfel, H., & Turner, J. (1986). The social identity theory of intergroup behaviour. In S. Worchel & W. G. Austin (Eds.), *The Psychology of Intergroup Relations* (pp. 7–24). Chicago, IL: Nelson-Hall: Publisher.

Takarangi, M. K., & Flowe, H. D. (2012). Violent crime: Robbery and assault. In B. Winder & P. Banyard (Eds.), *A Psychologist's Casebook of Crime: From Arson to Voyeurism*. Basingstoke: Palgrave Macmillan.

Taylor, M. (1991). *The Fanatics: A Behavioural Approach to Political Violence*. Lincoln, NE: Potomac Books.

Taylor, M. (2018). Terrorism. In G. M. Davies & A. R. Beech (Eds.), *Forensic Psychology: Crime, Justice, Law, Interventions* (pp. 335–363). Hoboken, NJ: John Wiley & Sons.

Time (1966). Nation: The madman in the tower. *Time*, 12 August 1966. Available at http://content.time.com/time/subscriber/article/0,33009,842584-1,00.html (accessed 29 January 2021).

Tinney, G., & Gerlock, A. A. (2014). Intimate partner violence, military personnel, veterans, and their families. *Family Court Review*, *52*(3), 400–416. doi:10.1111/fcre.12100

Tjaden, P., & Thoennes, N. (2000). Prevalence and consequences of male-to-female and female-to-male intimate partner violence as measured by the National Violence Against Women Survey. *Violence Against Women*, *6*(2), 142–161. doi:10.1177/10778010022181769

Tory, P. (2010). The beauty, sex in chains and me. *British Journalism Review, 21*(4), 61–67. doi:10.1177/0956474810393611

Turner, J. C., & Oakes, P. J. (1986). The significance of the social identity concept for social psychology with reference to individualism, interactionism and social influence. *British Journal of Social Psychology, 25*(3), 237–252. doi:10.1111/j.2044-8309.1986.tb00732.x

Tversky, A., & Kahneman, D. (1986). Rational choice and the framing of decisions. *The Journal of Business, 59*(S4), 251–278. doi:10.1086/296365

United Nations. (1948, December 9). *Convention on the Prevention and Punishment of the Crime of Genocide*. New York: United Nations. Retrieved from: www.un.org/en/genocideprevention/documents/atrocity-crimes/Doc.1_Convention%20on%20the%20Prevention%20and%20Punishment%20of%20the%20Crime%20of%20Genocide.pdf

United Nations. (n.d.). *United Nations Office on Genocide Prevention and the Responsibility to Protect*. New York: United Nations. Retrieved from: www.un.org/en/genocideprevention/genocide.shtml

United Nations Security Council. (2004). *Resolution 1566 (2004)*. Retrieved from https://www.un.org/ruleoflaw/files/n0454282.pdf

United Nations (2005). *Fact Sheet 5: Economic and Financial Crimes: Challenges to Sustainable Development*. Vienna: United Nations Office on Drugs and Crime.

US Department of State Archive. (n.d.). *Glossary*. Retrieved from https://2001-2009.state.gov/s/ct/info/c16718.htm

Vella-Zarb, R. A., Cohen, J. N., McCabe, R. E., & Rowa, K. (2017). Differentiating sexual thoughts in obsessive-compulsive disorder from paraphilias and nonparaphilic sexual disorders. *Cognitive and Behavioral Practice, 24*(3), 342–352. doi:10.1016/j.cbpra.2016.06.007

Wakefield, J. R., Bowe, M., Kellezi, B., McNamara, N., & Stevenson, C. (2019). When groups help and when groups harm: Origins, developments, and future directions of the 'Social Cure' perspective of group dynamics. *Social and Personality Psychology Compass, 13*(3), e12440. doi:10.1111/spc3.12440

Waller, S. (2010). *Serial Killers – Philosophy for Everyone: Being and Killing*. Hoboken, NJ: John Wiley & Sons.

Walters, B. K., & Hickey, E. W. (2015). Homicide: A national and global perspective. In C. A. Pietz & C. A. Mattson (Eds.), *Violent Offenders: Understanding and Assessment*. Oxford & New York: Oxford University Press.

Warburton, D. (2007). R v Hendy-Freegard [2007] EWCA Crim 1236, Court of Appeal. *Journal of Criminal Law, 71*, 484–486.

Ward, V. (2018). What do we know about suicide bombing? *Politics and the Life Sciences, 37*(1), 88–112. doi:10.1017/pls.2017.31

Warner, S. (2015). Forensic psychology clinical and critical. In I. Parker (Ed.), *Handbook of Critical Psychology*. London: Routledge.

Websdale, N. (2010). *Familicidal Hearts: The Emotional Styles of 211 Killers*. Oxford: Oxford University Press.

Weisburd, D., Waring, E., & Leeper Piquero, N. (2008). Getting beyond the moral drama of crime: What we learn from studying white-collar criminal careers. In J. Minkes & L. Minkes (Eds.), *Corporate and White Collar Crime* (pp. 179–201). Thousand Oaks, CA: Sage.

Westcott, H. (2006). Children and the legal system. In C. Wood, K. Littleton, & K. Sheehy (Eds.), *Developmental Psychology in Action*. Hoboken, NJ: John Wiley & Sons.

Whitaker, R. (2010). Behavioural profiling in Israeli aviation security as a tool for social control. In E. Zureik, D. Lyon, & Y. Abu-Laban (Eds.), *Surveillance and Control in Israel/Palestine: Population, Territory and Power*. London: Routledge.

White, J. K. (2013). *Do the Math!: On Growth, Greed, and Strategic Thinking*. Thousand Oaks, CA: SAGE.

White, J. H., Lester, D., Gentile, M., & Rosenbleeth, J. (2011). The utilization of forensic science and criminal profiling for capturing serial killers. *Forensic Science International, 209*(1–3), 160–165. doi:10.1016/j.forsciint.2011.01.022

Wiersma, E. (2007). Commercial burglars in the Netherlands: Reasoning decision-makers? In R. I. Mawby (Ed.), *Burglary*. Aldershot, UK: Gower.

Wiktorowicz, Q. (2006). *Radical Islam Rising: Muslim Extremism in the West*. Lanham, MD: Rowman & Littlefield.

Wilson, D. (2012). Murder. In B. Winder & P. Banyard (Eds.), *A Psychologist's Casebook of Crime: From Arson to Voyeurism*. Basingstoke: Palgrave Macmillan.

Winder, B., & Banyard, P. (2012). *A Psychologist's Casebook of Crime: From Arson to Voyeurism*. Basingstoke: Palgrave Macmillan.

Wittgenstein, L. J. (1967). *Zettel*. Berkeley, CA: University of California Press.

Wolfe, D. T., & Hermanson, D. R. (2004). The Fraud Diamond: Considering the four elements of fraud. *CPA Journal, 74*(12), 38–42.

World Health Organization. (1992). *The ICD-10 Classification of Mental and Behavioural Disorders: Clinical Descriptions and Diagnostic Guidelines*. Geneva: World Health Organization.

Wright, R., Brookman, F., & Bennett, T. (2006). The foreground dynamics of street robbery in Britain. *The British Journal of Criminology, 46*(1), 1–15. doi:10.1093/bjc/azi055

Yakeley, J. (2018). Psychoanalytic perspectives on paraphilias and perversions. *European Journal of Psychotherapy & Counselling, 20*(2), 164–183. doi:10.1080/13642537.2018.1459768

Yokota, K., & Canter, D. (2004). Burglars' specialisation: Development of a thematic approach in investigative psychology. *Behaviormetrika, 31*(2), 153–167. doi:10.2333/bhmk.31.153

Zannoni, F. (2003). *Kidnapping: Understanding and managing the threat*. Retrieved from: www.homesecuritysa.com/article.aspx?pklarticleid=2443

Zimbardo, P. G. (1971). The power and pathology of imprisonment. *Congressional Record*. (Serial No. 15, October 25, 1971). Hearings before Subcommittee No. 3, of the Committee on the Judiciary, House of Representatives, Ninety-Second Congress, *First Session on Corrections, Part II, Prisons, Prison Reform and Prisoners' Rights: California*. Washington, DC: U.S. Government Printing Office.

Zimbardo, P. (2007). *The Lucifer Effect: Understanding How Good People Turn Evil*. New York: Random House.

Zona, M. A., Palarea, R. E., & Lane, J. C. (1998). Psychiatric diagnosis and the offender-victim typology of stalking. In J. R. Meloy (Ed.), *The Psychology of Stalking: Clinical and Forensic Perspectives* (pp. 69–73). Cambridge, MA: Academic Press.

INDEX